Stories, Stats and Stuff About Iowa State™ Football & Basketball

By Todd Stevens, Editor of Cyclone Illustrated

Printed in the United States of America by
Mennonite Press, Inc.

ISBN 1-880652-64-1

PHOTO CREDITS All photographs were supplied
by Iowa State Media Relations and *Cyclone
Illustrated*.

COLLEGIATE
LICENSED
PRODUCT™

ACKNOWLEDGMENTS

The *Cyclones Handbook* couldn't have come to fruition without the aid of several people equally as dedicated as myself to seeing it through.

First, a heartfelt thanks to Bruce Janssen at Midwest Sports Publications. His steadying hand through the entire process was crucial. There are many others at MSP who played a key role in the editing, marketing, and publishing of this book. To all of you, I tip my hat in humble appreciation.

Special mention must go to Iowa State University's assistant sports information director, Erin Davison. Without her help this book would have been many times harder to complete. Whatever I asked for, Erin got it for me. Such carte blanche is rare these days. Thanks also to Sports Information Director Tom Kroeschell and Assistant Sports Information Director Beth Haag, who also graciously helped me as the need arose.

It would be folly to leave out Steve Waters of *Cyclone Illustrated*, who first proposed the idea for the book to me. Then there's my wife, Angie, who gave up all of April and May to allow me to finish the project. Special thanks also go to my father, Robert, and my mother, Mary. Respectively, they taught me to be diplomatic when possible, and fiery when absolutely necessary.

I also owe a debt of gratitude to my grandmother, Joyce Scheetz, who got me started in the writing business by giving me subscriptions to the Sunday newspaper as a birthday present when I was a teen-ager. She knew nothing moved me like great copy. Thanks, Gram.

But most of all I'd like to give thanks to my Lord and Savior, Jesus Christ, for presenting me with yet another tremendous writing opportunity. I don't know where exactly You're taking me on this earth, but I certainly am enjoying the journey.

—*Todd Stevens*

To Mackenzie and Cameron: Thanks for being angels so Daddy could finish this.

INTRODUCTION

Iowa State Athletic Director Gene Smith told me not too long ago that now is the time for Cyclone fans to get back in touch with their school.

With the basketball team enjoying its first Big Eight Tournament championship in 1996 and Coach Tim Floyd taking the program to perhaps its highest level ever, and Dan McCarney and Troy Davis bringing a spark back to ISU football, I'd have to say I agree.

That is why I've written the Cyclones Handbook. So many memorable, nationally prominent things have happened to Iowa State football and basketball in just the past year that I felt cardinal and gold fans needed something to save the cherished moments so they wouldn't fade.

That's what the *Cyclones Handbook* is, a compilation of stories, stats, and stuff about Iowa State football and basketball from their earliest origins to their present-day status.

The emphasis is on recent history. You'll go back to Minneapolis for a weekend in the Metrodome in 1986 that no Cyclone fan will ever forget. You'll travel to the Downtown Athletic Club for the presentation of the Heisman Trophy. You'll stand at center court in Kemper Arena as Kenny Pratt, Dedric Willoughby, Kelvin Cato, and the rest of the 1995-96 basketball team dances around you in wild celebration after knocking off Kansas for ISU's first conference tourney title. And you'll run down Missouri's Faurot Field sidelines with Davis as he shakes hands with 2,000 yards.

But the past is held in high esteem. Pop Warner. Clyde Williams. The Dirty 30. Louis Menze. Gary Thompson. Johnny Majors. Johnny Orr. The Sun, Liberty, Peach, and Hall of Fame bowls. The numerous other NCAA Tournament basketball trips.

Cyclone fans, you've waited so long for the cheering to return. The sun is rising on your long-dormant programs. Grab 'hold, as Smith said, and ride along with the cardinal and gold for a while. Grab 'hold of the *Cyclones Handbook*. Enjoy.

— T.S.

TABLE OF CONTENTS

1892 to 1959:
A Developing Storm

CYCLONES QUIZ

1. I.C. Brownlie was the official coach of the first Iowa State football team in 1892. Who was the first official team captain in Cyclone history?

More than a century ago, a man by the name of I.C. Brownlie thought the newly invented game of football might catch on at the Iowa Agricultural College in Ames. Brownlie found enough adventure-seekers to form a team, and the first Iowa State football team took the field in 1892.

Only two contests were played that first season — a 6-6 tie against a team from State Center, and a 30-0 victory over a gathering of outclassed hooligans from the Des Moines YMCA. Two years later, with Bert German at the helm, the team won 6 of 7 games, including a hard-fought 16-8 verdict over Iowa.

But it was in 1895 that the team received its time-honored name. Under the leadership of the legendary Glenn "Pop" Warner, the club took on a heavily favored Northwestern team in Evanston, and punished it in every manner possible on the way to a 36-0 triumph.

Earlier that fall there had been a number of tornadoes, which were referred to back then as cyclones, in the state of Iowa. Warner's team had been known as the Cardinals, but the day after the win over the Wildcats the headline in the Chicago Tribune read "Struck By A Cyclone." The article went on to say that "Northwestern might as well have tried to play football with an Iowa cyclone as with the Iowa team it met yesterday."

The "Cyclones" were born.

"STATE FIELD" The first Iowa State football teams played on the athletic fields west of Morrill Hall, where the Parks Library stands today. The field was fenced in and wood bleachers were installed in 1900, and four new seating sections were added in 1904. The November 16,

State Field served as the football team's first home. Today the Parks Library stands where the early cardinal and gold gridders toiled.

"POP" LAYS THE FOUNDATION

Warner, whose name has become synonymous with youth football, was and remains to this day one of college football's greatest coaches and innovators.

Warner was just beginning a career that would span 44 years and 313 victories (currently fourth on the all-time NCAA coaching list behind Eddie Robinson, Paul "Bear" Bryant, and Amos Alonzo Stagg). He came to Ames each summer from 1895 to 1899 to coach the Cyclones before heading

to Georgia where he was the head coach. In five seasons in Ames, Warner went 22-12-1, including an 8-2 mark in 1896 when the Cyclones allowed just 46 points.

Warner, the inventor of the double wingback system of offense, would go on to coach Olympic star Jim Thorpe and the Carlisle Indians, as well as at Pitt, Stanford, and Temple. He was paid the then unheard-of sum of $80 to coach the Cyclones that first season.

Glenn "Pop" Warner, top row left, one of college football's biggest coaching legends, coached the Cyclones in their earliest years.

1901, issue of the ISC Student suggested that a name be given to field. No official name was ever bestowed on the gridiron, though it was often called "State Field."

A HAWK BEATS THE HAWKS A.W. Ristine went 36-10-1 as coach of the team from 1902-1906 and remains to this day ISU's coaching leader in winning percentage (.766). But the man who replaced him, a University of Iowa graduate by the name of Clyde Williams, became an even bigger fixture in the history of Cyclone football. Williams possessed a degree in dentistry, yet wanted to coach college football. Iowa State gave him his chance, and in his first season in 1907, he inherited an almost entirely

Clyde Williams not only had a hand in getting the Cyclone football program running, but he also coached the cardinal and gold basketball team.

new ball club.

The Cyclones played above expectations through six games, winning four of them and losing close contests to powerful Minnesota, 8-0, and Nebraska, 10-9. The heavily-favored Hawkeyes — still stinging from a 2-0 upset loss to Iowa State the year before in Iowa City — were up next.

Captain Ralph McEihinney scored on a 30-yard gallop to get the Cyclones within 8-7, then W.C. Johnson raced 40 yards for the deciding touchdown, bowling over two Iowa defenders at the goal line, to give Iowa State a lead it would not relinquish. The final would be 16-8 in favor of Williams' supposedly overmatched team in front of 5,000 fans at State Field. The Cyclones finished the season 6-2 and state champions of Iowa.

Williams coached the Cyclones until 1912, posting a 33-14-2 mark. He went on to become Iowa State's athletic director in 1914 and oversaw the building of a new football stadium that would wind up bearing his name.

WILLIAMS FIELD In October 1914, Iowa State President Raymond Pearson began pushing to build a concrete bleacher on the west side of a field adjacent to the Pike Street line (now known as Sheldon Street), and halfway between State Gymnasium and Boone Street (now Lincoln Way).

The new facility seated 5,600 fans and was referred to as "New State Field." As Cyclone football improved, so did seating. In 1925 approval was given for construction of concrete bleachers on the east side of the stadium, which brought the capacity up to 14,500.

In 1938, New State Field was renamed Clyde Williams Field before the homecoming game against

Clyde Williams Field served as the home of Iowa State football from 1914 through the 1974 season. It underwent several expansions during that period.

Kansas on October 22. Williams had been one of six men to sign the bank note for the original construction in 1914, and he held out for three years to construct the stadium at its eventual site, which had been coveted by the Horticultural Department. After Williams' death in 1938, the field was renamed in his honor. Another series of additions moved capacity to 36,000, and the Cyclones played at the site until 1974.

CHARLES IN CHARGE Charles Mayser duplicated Williams' feat in 1915, winning another state championship for the Cyclones. But it came with a heavy dose of the unexpected.

After routing Simpson 27-0 to get out to a 2-0 start, Mayser lost starting fullback Ed Uhl to a rib injury. But that was only the beginning. A constant rain combined with the lime used to line the field, which caused a chemical reaction that burned the skin of every player that came into contact with the substance. Many Cyclones sustained burns serious enough to keep them out of action for two weeks.

Mayser couldn't even gather enough bodies to hold a scrimmage prior to the Minnesota game. "I do not expect us to score," he said. "I think Minnesota could score between five and seven touchdowns on us."

Instead, Iowa State fought bitterly against the Gophers and only lost by three, 9-6. Lifted by the performance, the Cyclones went on to lose just one more game the rest of the season and finish 6-2, including a 16-0 whitewashing of Iowa in Iowa City before 11,000 fans.

THE 1920S: GLORY AND TRAGEDY

Polly Wallace was one of Iowa State's first All-Americans, named in 1920 for his work at center.

ALL-AMERICANS The end of the decade saw Iowa State crown its first two All-Americans — guard Dick Barker was honored in 1919, and center Polly Wallace in 1920.

But this period is best remembered for one player: Jack Trice, the first black player at Iowa State. Trice, an interior lineman, was considered all-conference material after his freshman season in 1922. He saw little action in the season-opener in 1923, then traveled with the team to Minnesota the following week.

With the Cyclones trailing 14-10 at halftime, Trice complained of a sore left shoulder but continued playing. Midway through the third quarter the Gophers ran his way, and Trice threw himself into the oncoming blockers and was trampled. He left the game and did not return.

The situation was serious. The Minnesota fans chanted, "We're sorry, Ames, we're sorry." Doctors at a Minneapolis hospital allowed Trice to return to Ames with the team, but upon his arrival back on campus it

Jack Trice is Iowa State football's most enduring legend.

was discovered that he had suffered a broken collarbone. His condition worsened as respiratory problems set in the next afternoon. Surgery was deemed too risky.

Jack Trice died at 3 p.m. Monday, October 8, 1923, of hemorrhaged lungs and internal bleeding throughout the abdomen. Classes were canceled Tuesday, and more than 4,000 students and faculty attended his funeral on central campus. A letter written by Trice to himself on the eve of the Minnesota game was found in his coat pocket the day of the funeral. It read:

"My thoughts just before the first real college game of my life: The honor of my race, family and self is at stake. Everyone is expecting me to do big things. I will. My whole body and soul are to be thrown recklessly about the field. Every time the ball is snapped, I will be trying to do more than my part. Fight low, with your eyes open and toward the play. Watch out for cross bucks and reverse end runs. Be on your toes every minute if you expect to make good. Jack"

A memorial scholarship was created in Trice's memory, and a memorial to him erected just north of Cyclone Stadium. The playing surface at Cyclone Stadium is named after him.

THE 1930S: TOMMY, FRED, ED, AND THE RABBIT

The Sunday sports page said it all after the Cyclones' unforeseen rout of Iowa in 1934. The Hawks would not agree to play the Cyclones again until 1977.

THAT'S ALL, FOLKS The Iowa athletic department decided to end its annual rivalry with Iowa State following the 1934 season, primarily because the Hawkeyes didn't consider the Cyclones a quality opponent. That may not have been the entire truth. Embarrassment also may have been a factor.

With Tommy Neal slicing through the Iowa defense for three touchdowns and punter Fred Poole keeping the Hawkeyes constantly pinned in their own end of the field with stellar coffin-corner kicks, the Cyclones routed the supposedly superior Hawks, 31-6, in Ames October 20, 1934. Legendary *Des Moines Register* sportswriter Sec Taylor saw it this way in Sunday's paper:

"Tommy Neal, a midget of 155 pounds from Sioux City; Fred Poole, a kicking fool from Ames and a troupe of their inspired teammates wrote football history here Saturday when they not only brought victory for Iowa State over Iowa, but humiliated the Hawkeyes by piling up the almost unbelievable score of 31 to 6.

"The victors deserved the spoils. They outplayed the Hawkeyes in every department of the game, ripped Iowa's marshmallow line in shreds at times, wreaked havoc with the rivals throughout most of the sixty minutes, and at times had the leaderless university team on the point of demoralization."

Iowa refused to play the Cyclones again until 1977.

SMILE, JIM Nothing was expected of the 1938 team. It had won just three games the year before under first-year coach "Smilin' Jim" Yeager, and had only won five Big Six games in the previous six seasons.

But behind the talent of guard Ed Bock, who would go on to be an All-American, and quarterback Everett "Rabbit" Kischer, as well as bruising fullback Gordon Ruepke, the Cyclones were about to surprise everyone, including their coach.

"We're figuring on winning a game or two in the Big Six," Yeager said before the season. "We should be stronger this year, but every other team in the league should be better also."

Yeager went on to cement his reputation as a frequent grinner. Iowa State started the season 7-0, including an 8-7 win at Nebraska, the Cyclones' first win over the Big Red in 19 years. "We've waited 19 years for this victory," Yeager said. "I can hardly talk."

He'd have been completely speechless if he'd known his team was going to play powerful Oklahoma in the final week of the season for the conference championship. A record crowd of more than 21,000 packed Williams Field, but the Sooners pulled out a tough 10-0 victory. OU hadn't allowed a league foe to score all season. But the Cyclones' 7-1-1 season was the bright spot of the 1930s, and several players earned all-league recognition.

Ed Bock was an All-America guard for the Cyclones in 1938.

Quarterback Everett Kischer was the guiding force behind ISU's unexpected 7-1-1 season of 1938.

THE 1940S AND 1950S: SUCCESS IS SIDETRACKED

BOGGING DOWN With the nation's attention focused on World War II for half of the decade, Iowa State football had trouble finding an identity. Four coaches held the Cyclone head job during the 1940s, and only once, in 1944, did the team manage more than five wins in a season. Mike Michalske's unit went 6-1-1 that year, including a 19-6 victory at Nebraska.

PITCH AND CATCH

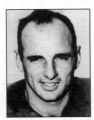

Jim Doran was named an All-American in 1950. He would one day watch two of his sons suit up for the Cyclones.

Bill Weeks had an arm that was born to throw a football, and Jim Doran certainly was given the hands to catch it. And from 1949 to 1951, the Iowa State quarterback and receiver teamed up to wow everyone who paid to watch them on Saturdays.

Doran finished his Cyclone career with 79 receptions for 1,410 yards, and his 203 yards receiving in a game against Bud Wilkinson's Oklahoma Sooners in 1950 remained an ISU record for 34 seasons (Tracy Henderson set a new standard in 1984). After the game, Wilkinson said the Weeks-to-Doran combination was the best he'd ever seen. Doran went on to a 10-year professional football career with the Detroit Lions and Dallas Cowboys. He also sent two sons, Jim Jr. and Lant, on to play at Iowa State. Doran, named an All-American in 1950, died in 1994.

Lant, left, and Jim Doran Jr., right, followed their father's footsteps to Iowa State.

RUST-ING OUT The center on the 1949 Iowa State team was a student named Rod Rust. Intrigued by the game of football, Rust went into coaching after his playing career was finished. After several stints at the high school and college level, Rust reached the National Football League as an assistant coach in the 1970s. He reached the coaching pinnacle in 1988 when he was named the head coach of the New England Patriots.

BROTHER, CAN YOU SPARE A WIN? Neither Abe Stuber, Vince DiFrancesca, or J.A. Myers could post more than a four-win season through 1957, and in Clay Stapleton's first season in 1958 ISU went just 4-6. It had been 20 years since a Cyclone football team had won seven games in a season. The memories of Bock, Kischer, and Ruepke were beginning to fade. It was time for an injection of life into Iowa State football.

THE DIRTY THIRTY In Stapleton's second season, the Cyclones were hit with the injury bug — hard. Player after player was sidelined, until only 30 stalwarts remained. They hung together for a 41-0 win at Drake to

start the season, and it was there that the legend of the 1959 season was born.

The undermanned, undersized Cyclones (the largest player on the squad weighed 195 pounds; the average starter's weight was 179) were coated from head to cleat with mud after pounding the Bulldogs in the opener on a rain-soaked field. As they trudged into the locker room, Iowa State trainer Warren Ariail took one look at them and said, "Here comes the Dirty Thirty." The players thought so much of Ariail's statement that they immediately made it their rallying point of the season, and gave Ariail the game ball in the shutout victory.

After injuries and attrition decimated the 1959 Iowa State football team, the remaining 30 players made a pact to finish the season, no matter what.

FEISTY FIELD LEADER Knoxville is known nationally as the home to the Tennessee Volunteers, but a small town by the same name in Iowa produced one of Iowa State's finest gridiron stars.

Dwight Nichols, who ran for 87 yards and passed for 93 more in the win over Drake, was a supremely talented, supremely confident quarterback who ran the ball with a snarl and threw it with aplomb. He was the driving force behind the Dirty Thirty — a player that conjured up adjectives such as "intimidating" and "ornery."

When 1959's defections and injuries dwindled the ranks down to 30, Nichols called a players-only meeting just before the start of the season to find out who was

All-America quarterback Dwight Nichols was the fuel that made the Dirty Thirty run efficiently.

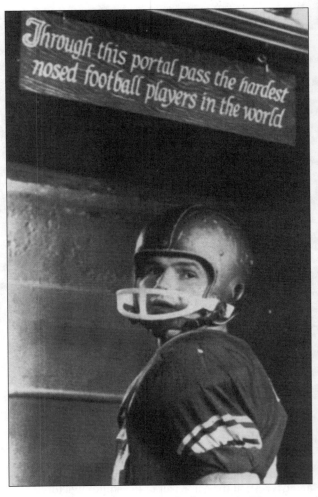

Through this portal pass the hardest nosed football players in the world

going to go to war with him and who wasn't. The meeting served as contact cement for the Cyclones — no one left the team the rest of the way, or allowed an injury to keep them off the field come Saturday.

A MILE HIGH, AND CLIMBING Nichols ran for two touchdowns and passed for two more as the Dirty Thirty posted a 28-12 win at Denver to move to 2-0. A 14-0 loss at home to Missouri temporarily derailed things, but the Cyclones got back into the win column a week later with a 41-6 rout of South Dakota, then got a pair of resounding conference victories with a 27-0 shutout of Colorado and a 26-0 whitewash of Kansas State. At 5-1, the Dirty Thirty was starting to attract national attention.

THE TELEPHONE TROPHY One of the lesser-known prizes in college football is the "Telephone Trophy" that is up for grabs every season when Iowa State and Missouri meet. In the time before the Cyclones' 14-0 home loss to the Tigers, the field phones were tested and found that both teams could hear each other. Not good.

The problem was solved by game time, but not without two coaching staffs worrying themselves into ulcers. The Northwestern Bell Telephone Company of Ames had a trophy made and presented it to Iowa State to be awarded each year to the winning team.

COOPED UP The star of the South Dakota win, and one of Iowa State's defensive leaders the entire 1959 season, was defensive back John Cooper. Like former Cyclone Rod Rust, the game of football coursed through Cooper's veins. He went on to become an assistant coach at ISU and head coach at Tulsa and Arizona State before taking the head coaching job with his current employer, Ohio State.

SABOTAGED? Cyclone fans were starting to entertain Orange Bowl thoughts as the team packed for Lawrence to take on Kansas. But just as the team was set to depart for the game, Iowa State's plane reservations were mysteriously canceled. Buses were hastily chartered, but the Cyclones didn't arrive in Lawrence until after 2 a.m. Their lack of rest showed up on the field hours later,

The Telephone Trophy is up for grabs every year when Iowa State and Missouri meet.

HOW "CY" CAME OF AGE

Back in the 1950s, Ames was host to one of the largest makers of stuffed animals in the nation. The company's president had long lobbied Iowa State to change the school's nickname because, "We cannot make a stuffed Cyclone!"

ISU Sports Information Director Harry Burrell teamed up with the president of the company in 1955 to see about developing a contest to choose a mascot. The winner of the student-run contest was a cardinal. Another contest was held to name the bird, and the entry "Cy" was chosen, which was short for Cyclones.

Coach Clay Stapleton said he'd rather coach the Dirty Thirty than "be president of the United States."

The Dirty Thirty will always be remembered by Cyclone fans as the toughest gang that ever suited up for the cardinal and gold.

when the Jayhawks posted a lackluster 7-0 victory. The loss dropped Iowa State to 5-2 with a home game against mighty Nebraska on the horizon.

Still, Stapleton was fiercely proud of the way his team had battled the Jayhawks despite a major change in travel arrangements and lack of sleep. "How can you help but be proud of this team? I'd rather be coach of the Dirty Thirty than president of the United States."

BIG RED-FACED Never before had the Cornhuskers entered Ames on a bigger roll. Just a week earlier Nebraska had put a stop to Oklahoma's remarkable 75-game win streak in conference play.

But the Dirty Thirty was ready. Running back Tom Watkins took the second-half kickoff and raced 84 yards for a touchdown to give Iowa State a 10-0 lead. The Cyclones upped the ante to 18-0 before Nebraska posted a meaningless late score. The shocking upset was complete, and Stapleton's team had its biggest victory in 15 years. The victory made news coast to coast, and the cardinal and gold were the new darlings of underdog devotees.

WINNER TAKE ALL A 55-0 Nichols-led rout of San Jose State pushed the Iowa State ledger to 7-2 and set up a

Big Six championship meeting with Bud Wilkinson's Sooners in Norman for the right to go to the Orange Bowl.

A crowd of 47,000, many of them wearing Cyclone colors, looked on to see if Iowa State would make its first-ever appearance in the Orange Bowl. But the Dirty Thirty came out with a notable case of the jitters and quickly fell into a 21-0 hole.

But the muddy men of Ames showed their true grit in the third quarter, scoring twice to narrow the gap to 21-12. Wilkinson's Sooners put the game away in the fourth quarter to win the game, 35-12, the Big Six title, and the Orange Bowl trip. The Dirty Thirty, small in numbers, stature, and preseason respect, had finished 7-3 and second in the league. It was an impossible season made possible through mental toughness, and it was one of the most colorful in Iowa State history.

HONORS, HONORS Nichols and Watkins, respectively, finished second and third nationally in rushing. Nichols was named all-conference and All-America. Watkins and split end Don Webb were voted all-conference. Coach Stapleton guided the Cyclones another eight seasons and remains ISU's all-time leader in victories (42-53-4), though he never had another season with the drama of the 1959 Dirty Thirty. He later became the school's athletic director.

SIGN OF THE TIMES Perhaps a fitting tribute to the Dirty Thirty was the sign hanging over the entrance to the Cyclone locker room during the 1959 season. It read: "Through this portal pass the hardest-nosed football players in the world."

2. What former Iowa State assistant coach led another team to a Top 10 Associated Press final ranking in 1995?

The 1960s–80s:
Majors, Bruce Take ISU Bowling

STUCK IN NEUTRAL Clay Stapleton remained the head coach of the Cyclones until 1968. His Iowa State teams started off the '60s well enough, going 7-3, 5-5 and 5-5. But the 1963 campaign brought a losing record of 4-5 and a hint of things to come.

In 1964 the Cyclones won just one game. There was a brief parting of the clouds the next season when ISU went 5-4-1, but Stapleton won just two games in each of the next two seasons.

SUPER DAVE Before Troy Davis, there was Dave Hoppmann. In 1961 and 1962 Hoppmann earned back-to-back All-America awards, one of only two Cyclones to ever earn that distinction. In 1961 Hoppmann led the nation in total offense with 1,638 yards, and his 271-yard effort that season against Kansas State was a single-game record that stood until Davis' 291-yard outing against Ohio in the first game of the 1995 season. Hoppmann went on to play professional football for the Canadian Football League's Montreal Alouettes from 1963-67. Sadly, his life came to an abrupt end in 1975 when he was killed in an automobile accident in Florida.

VAUGHN KEEPS RUNNING BACK ROLL GOING Tom Vaughn took Hoppmann's place in the backfield in 1963, and he kept the All-America spotlight shining on the Iowa State backfield by earning the honor that season. Over his three-year career, Vaughn rushed for nearly 1,900 yards. He went on to play six seasons in the National Football League with the Detroit Lions, later becoming an assistant to Earle Bruce at Iowa State.

Two-time All-American running back Dave Hoppmann, left, held the Cyclone single-game rushing mark of 271 until Troy Davis eclipsed it in 1995. He was an All-American during the 1961 and 1962 seasons.

Running back Tom Vaughn, middle, was honored with All-America accolades following the 1963 campaign.

Johnny Majors, right, was only 32 years old when he accepted the Iowa State coaching job.

READY TO WIN AGAIN ISU President Robert Parks, an ardent follower of his school's athletic programs, wanted an injection of new blood into the Iowa State football program in 1968. With input from Bob Dillon, chairman of the Iowa State Athletic Council, Parks hired a new head coach, a 32-year-old Arkansas assistant coach named Johnny Majors.

Convinced he could make the Cyclones winners again, Majors began by recruiting a staff of assistant coaches who would go on to staggering success. Among Majors' colleagues was Jimmy Johnson, who would win a national championship as head coach at Miami (Fla.) and win two Super Bowls with the NFL's Dallas Cowboys. He is currently the coach of Miami Dolphins.

Another future big-timer was assistant Jackie Sherrill, who would go onto to become the head coach at Pitt, Texas A&M, and Southern Mississippi.

GETTING USED TO AMES One of the first things Majors and his staff did when they arrived in Ames was go ice skating with their wives. None of the coaches had ever laced up skates before, and the following day there were more coaches in the trainer's office than there were players. Majors wound up with a knot on his head, and he was playfully miffed at Johnson, who'd secretly gone out for days prior to the event and practiced on his own.

A SLOW START Majors' first two Iowa State teams each won only three games, were beaten that first season by Nebraska and Oklahoma by identical 42-7 scores, and shut out by Oklahoma State 35-0 to conclude the second campaign. But the players were learning and improving under the new staff's guidance.

Few times before has such football genius been cramped into such a small space. Johnny Majors (center) also had Miami Dolphins Coach Jimmy Johnson (2nd from left) and former Pitt and Texas A&M Coach Jackie Sherrill (4th from left) on staff.

As Johnny Majors was turning the Cyclones into contenders, talented players such as quarterback Dean Carlson, left, running back George Amundson, middle, and linebacker Matt Blair, right, were making names for themselves.

THE 1970S: A DECADE OF CYCLONE DOMINANCE

MAJORS LEAGUE IMPROVEMENT Majors' third season in Ames saw the Cyclones go 5-6, including two much better performances against Oklahoma (a 29-28 loss) and Nebraska (a 54-29 loss). Players such as quarterback Dean Carlson were emerging as elite performers. The next season, 1971, was the breakthrough year that everyone had been waiting for.

PRIDE AND ENTHUSIASM Those were the two things that Majors and his staff constantly pounded into his Cyclones. No matter how well or how badly a game was going, Iowa State was to never lose its pride or enthusiasm for four quarters.

OFF TO A GOOD START Led by the likes of Carlson, Amundson, Blair, wideout Ike Harris, tight end Keith Krepfle, and lineman Lawrence "Big Daddy" Hunt, the Cyclones leapt out to a 3-0 start with a 24-7 win over Idaho, a 44-20 rout of New Mexico on the road, and a 17-14 squeaker at Kent State.

After a 24-14 setback against Colorado to open the Big Eight season, Majors' Cyclones roared back with a 24-0 blanking of Kansas State in Manhattan and a 40-24 shellacking of Kansas at Williams Field. At 5-1, Iowa State couldn't be faulted for looking ahead at what could be the school's first-ever bowl bid. But first came consecutive road games against the Sooners and Cornhuskers.

Oklahoma bounced ISU back to earth with a 43-12 win; then Nebraska posted a 37-0 shutout one week later. At 5-3, the Cyclones still had a winning record but needed a confidence boost. They would get it.

Keith Krepfle ranks fifth in all-time receptions at ISU with 94, and in yardage with 1,368 from 1971-73. He played several seasons of pro football with the Philadelphia Eagles.

TIGERS TAMED Missouri had the misfortune to be the guest the following Saturday at Williams

Johnny Majors was concerned about the Oklahoma State game early on, but the Cyclones soon put his mind at ease.

Field. Carlson, Amundson, and the rest of the Cyclones vented their frustrations on the Tigers with a resounding 45-17 win that moved ISU to 6-3. A few days later, Majors and his staff learned that the next game, against Oklahoma State, was for high stakes: If Iowa State beat the Cowboys, it would be Sun Bowl-bound.

MAJORS' FINEST HOUR Majors was worried about the OSU game. The Cowboys were not a big rival, and he was concerned about how much fire his club would bring out of the locker room. Just two years before, Oklahoma State had shut Iowa State out, 35-0, to end the 1969 season.

The Cyclones won the coin toss, but with a brisk wind howling Majors decided to kick off and make the Cowboys go against the wind. OSU returned the opening boot to midfield, causing immediate concern for the ISU staff.

But on the first play from scrimmage the Cowboys fumbled and the Cyclones recovered. On the next snap Carlson looked deep down the left sideline for Harris and hit him in stride for a 55-yard touchdown and the momentum necessary to corral the Cowboys and the Sun Bowl bid. The final score: 54-0. Majors, who was carried off the field by his players through a teeming throng of Cyclone fans, called it the best performance he ever had a team display. The Cyclones finished off an 8-3 season the next week with a win over San Diego State, and made travel plans for

Ike Harris grabbed a 55-yard pass from Dean Carlson to open the scoring in the Cyclones' Sun Bowl-clinching 54-0 win over Oklahoma State.

El Paso, Texas, to meet the Louisiana State Tigers in the Cyclones' first postseason game in school history.

CHRISTMAS CHEER December 17, 1971 — smack in the middle of the holiday season was Iowa State's first postseason gridiron date. It was a cold, rainy day in El Paso, and the opposing Tigers would showcase rifle-armed quarterback Bert Jones (who would go on to a stellar pro career with the Baltimore Colts).

LSU struck in the first half with a pair of field goals for a 6-0 lead, then watched Cyclone kicker Reggie Shumate halve the margin with a 32-yard field goal of his own.

Jones revved the LSU attack up in the third quarter,

LSU's Bert Jones, right, hands into the line against the Cyclone defense with the El Paso skyline in the background.

George Amundson, below, leaps over the line while the pitch goes to the left in the 1971 Sun Bowl against Louisiana State.

tossing scoring passes of 37 and 21 yards for a 19-3 advantage. But Carlson matched Jones' aerial performance with a 30-yard touchdown throw and a one-yard toss to Krepfle to narrow the lead to 19-15.

Majors' team would get no closer, though. Jones iced the game with two more touchdown passes in the fourth quarter for a 33-15 final, making Iowa State's first bowl trip a losing one. But defeat in El Paso did not drain any excitement from the Cyclones' watershed season.

1972: LIFE, "LIBERTY," AND THE PURSUIT OF FOOTBALL HAPPINESS

HIGH TIMES   With Amundson now doing the quarterbacking, the Cyclones jumped out to another 5-1 start in 1972. Colorado State fell by a 41-0 count. Utah was humbled, 44-22. New Mexico was sacked, 31-0. Kansas State was embarrassed, 55-22. Kansas was pummeled, 34-8. ISU was scoring points with the frequency of the Cyclones' basketball team and gaining national acclaim.

STOLEN, REWARD IF FOUND   Then, in mysterious fashion, the offense disappeared. A 20-6 loss to Oklahoma certainly wasn't anything to be glum about, nor was a 23-23 tie with Nebraska (only a Tom Goedjen missed extra point kept the Cyclones from an upset victory). But a week later in Columbia the Cyclones managed just five points against a Missouri team it had run up 45 on the year before. Then Oklahoma State gained revenge for

With George Amundson under center, the Cyclones jumped out to a 5-1 start in 1972.

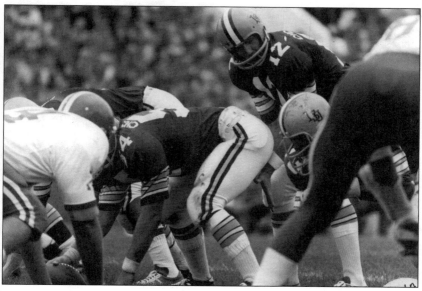

Tom Goedjen's missed extra point cost the Cyclones an upset of mighty Nebraska in 1972. The two teams settled for a 23-23 tie.

Merv Krakau was Iowa State's first All-American on the defensive side of the football.

the previous year's shutout loss, raking ISU, 45-14. Even San Diego State got its licks in, 27-14. A 5-1 start had metamorphosed into a 5-5-1 regular season finish. But the fast start and the tie with the Cornhuskers earned Majors and the Cyclones another bowl berth nonetheless, in the Liberty Bowl against Georgia Tech.

RAMBLIN' AGAINST THE WRECK Perhaps learning a lesson from the Louisiana State contest the year before in the Sun Bowl, Amundson and the Cyclone offense roared to life early against Georgia Tech, scoring on a 30-yard pass from Amundson to Harris and a one-yard Amundson run for a 14-3 lead.

But Amundson had a pass intercepted for a touchdown in the second quarter, and Tech rallied to within 21-17 at halftime. The Yellowjackets tallied again in the third quarter with a touchdown, while the Cyclones answered with a Goedjen field goal to tie the game at 24-24. A fantastic finish seemed to be in order.

JUST OUT OF REACH Tech scored again early in the fourth period to take a 31-24 lead. The margin remained until Amundson rallied his team for one more crack at the Ramblin' Wreck. Smartly moving the Cyclones downfield against the clock, Amundson found Harris again for a touchdown with just 1:30 left.

Trailing 31-30 and not wanting to settle for a tie, Majors opted for a two-point try and a win. But Amundson was rushed hard as he dropped back to pass,

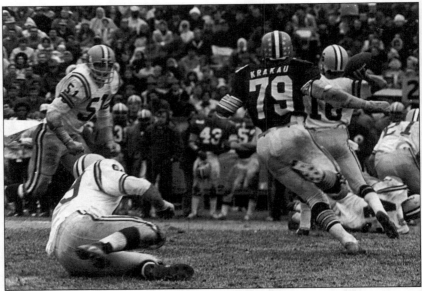

and a desperate heave into the right corner of the end zone was too strong. The Cyclones lost, 31-30.

SURPRISE ANNOUNCEMENT After the loss, Majors told his team that he was resigning to become head coach at the University of Pittsburgh. The guiding force that put the Cyclones in back-to-back bowl games was gone.

INTO THE RECORD BOOKS Cyclone defensive end Merv Krakau was named an All-American after the 1972 season, the first defensive player ever honored in that manner for Iowa State. He was also named All-Big Eight in 1972, and went on to a long NFL career, most notably with the Buffalo Bills.

Amundson was also voted All-America. He remains second on ISU's total-offense chart with 4,798 yards, and he is the only Cyclone player in history to both run and pass for 2,000 yards. Amundson went on to play professionally for the Houston Oilers and Philadelphia Eagles.

Murdock, an offensive guard, was the third ISU All-American from the 1972 team. He was also named all-conference in '72.

Offensive guard Geary Murdock was one of three Cyclones named All-America on the 1972 Liberty Bowl team.

1973: A NEW COACH, A NEW ERA

BRUCE HIRED Athletic Director Lou McCullough said that Iowa State was looking for a coach with "stability and sincerity" to replace Majors. A coach who would "go out and meet the people of Iowa, progress our program, and help us build that great (Cyclone) stadium." McCullough found what he was looking for as he announced Major's successor. "Gentlemen, we have I think the finest football coach in the country in Earle Bruce."

FOUR-PLAY Before Majors resigned, Cyclone fans were sure their team was primed to take its place among the nation's top football powers. But Bruce's first three seasons at ISU produced records of 4-7, 4-7, and 4-7. But Bruce was slowly injecting confidence into his charges, while bringing in more talented players. A breakthrough season was inevitable.

Athletic Director Lou McCullough's 1973 search for a new coach ended with the naming of Earle Bruce to the job.

BLAIR FACTS Matt Blair played a crucial role at linebacker in ISU's 1971 run to the Sun Bowl, making 121 tackles. But it wasn't until 1973 that he was named an All-American. He was picked to play in three postseason all-star games in '73, and went on to an All-Pro career with the Minnesota Vikings.

HELLACIOUS HILL Barry Hill became ISU's only All-American safety after the 1974 season when he

New coach Earle Bruce digs up the first shovel of dirt for the new Cyclone Stadium.

intercepted a school and Big Eight-record nine passes. Four of the pickoffs came in a game against Kansas. Hill also holds ISU and Big Eight records for career interceptions with 21. After college Hill played professionally for the Miami Dolphins.

CYCLONE STADIUM Iowa State's current home was opened in 1975 to replace aging Williams Field, with a capacity of more than 50,000. Bruce's club made the unveiling of the new facility a successful one September 20, 1975, with a 17-12 conquest of Air Force. In that game Air Force kicker Dave Lawson booted a 62-yard field goal, a record that still stands as the longest in Cyclone Stadium history.

1976: MORE THAN A BICENTENNIAL The 1976 Iowa State campaign may go down in Cyclone annals as one of the greatest, and yet most unsatisfactory, on record. It was certainly the greatest team statistically in cardinal and gold history. But it ended without a bowl bid.

Twelve of the 22 starters were seniors in '76, but seven other starters including defensive linemen Mike Stensrud and

Barry Hill is ISU's only All-American safety; he holds the Big Eight record for most interceptions with 21.

Dexter Green was just a sophomore in 1976, yet he played a big role in what wound up being the best statistical year ever for an Iowa State offense.

quarterback Terry Rubley, were only sophomores. The combination of experience and youth proved to be a fiery combination.

Bruce saw his team average better than 48 points a game as the Cyclones leaped out to a 3-0 start. A 24-10 loss to Oklahoma was avenged with a 44-14 win over Utah and a 21-17 verdict over Missouri, a victory that moved ISU into the nation's Top 20 at No. 16. A loss to Orange Bowl-bound Colorado dropped ISU to 5-2, but wins over Kansas State and Kansas moved the Cyclones to 7-2 before an electrifying 37-28 win over Nebraska at Cyclone Stadium. Wideout Luther Blue provided the ·game's enduring memory with a second-half kickoff return for a touchdown. It was ISU's first win over Nebraska since 1960, and it moved the Cyclones to 14th in the nation's rankings.

Mike Stensrud was one of the top defensive linemen in ISU history.

EVERYTHING'S BETTER WITH BLUEBONNET ON IT With an 8-2 record heading into the final weekend of the regular season, ISU could nail down a share of its first Big Eight

Luther Blue endures to this day as one of the biggest highlight film heroes. His second-half kickoff return for a touchdown against Nebraska was the catalyst that allowed ISU to upset the Huskers, 37-28, in 1976.

championship and make plans for the Bluebonnet Bowl. But Tangerine Bowl-bound Oklahoma State needed the game, too, and it pounded the Cyclones, 42-21. Sadly and incredibly, with four other conference teams already slated to appear in the smaller number of bowl games in 1976, Iowa State was on the outside looking in at the postseason.

RECORD-SETTERS For his efforts, Bruce was named Big Eight Coach of the Year, and four Cyclones were named first-team all-Big Eight — safety Tony Hawkins, guard Dave Greenwood, defensive lineman Maynard Stensrud, and Blue (who was also named an All-American).

Green rushed for 1,074 yards on 208 attempts, the first of three times he would break the 1,000-yard mark. Junior Buddy Hardeman and senior Wayne Stanley shared the quarterbacking chores, combining for 1,771 yards and 19 touchdowns. Punter Rick Blabolil averaged 42.8 yards per punt, still an ISU record. Kicker Scott Kollman booted 42 extra points, also a Cyclone record that stands today.

Perhaps the most impressive team statistic was the

Wayne Stanley, above, and Buddy Hardeman shared the quarterbacking duties nicely during the Cyclones' record-breaking 1976 season.

Buddy Hardeman led Iowa State to an eight win season in 1977.

Cyclone offense. Bruce's I-formation attack had averaged 439.6 yards per game, a figure that led the Big Eight and placed Iowa State second nationally. The Cyclones had scored 369 points, or more than 33 a game. They had scored 49 touchdowns (27 of them on the ground), made 262 first downs, rushed for 2,970 total yards, and had 4,836 yards of total offense. One of college football's top-flight teams had been locked out of the bowl process.

1977: ROLLING ANOTHER "8" With Hardeman and Green back offensively and Mike Stensrud, Tom Boskey, and Tom Randall back on the defensive line, the Cyclones set out under Bruce to prove to the experts how wrong they had been to exclude ISU from a bowl the year before.

A 12-10 loss at Iowa (the first meeting between the Cyclones and Hawkeyes since Tommy Neal's big game in 1934) was the only sour note struck during the season's first six weeks. Wichita State, Bowling Green, Dayton, and Missouri all fell by the wayside, as did mighty Nebraska, which was beaten for the second straight time by the Cyclones — this time in Lincoln, 24-21, as Green showed the way to victory over the Big Red.

3. Who holds the Cyclone record for receiving touchdowns?

Mike Stensrud, right, and Tom Randall, above, were a pair of defensive-line stalwarts during the 1977 campaign. Each went on to play in the NFL.

Earle Bruce earned his first postseason trip at Iowa State in 1977 with a berth in the Peach Bowl.

After losing two of the next three, ISU rebounded with wins over Kansas State and Oklahoma State to post another 8-3 season. This time the bowls did not overlook Bruce's club. The Peach Bowl came calling with an invitation to face North Carolina State.

LIFE'S A PEACH Despite Green's rushing for 172 yards, the Cyclones could not overcome the Wolfpack and lost their third bowl game in three tries, 24-14. John Quinn scored from a yard out and passed 10 yards for another, but North Carolina State's 21-0 halftime lead was too much to overcome. Terry Rubley hit on 10 of 12 passes for 133 yards for the Cyclones. Quinn connected on 9 of 20 for 94 yards but threw two costly interceptions.

But Green would be back for another season, and so would ISU.

1978: LET'S DO IT AGAIN Led by cocaptains Green and Boskey, and quarterback Walter

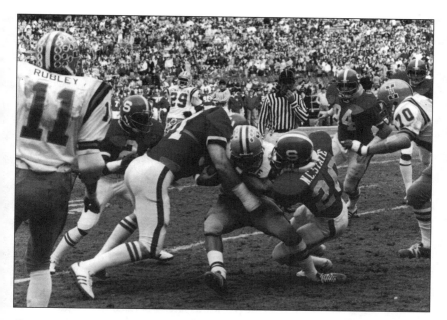

Grant, Iowa State posted yet another 8-3 regular season log. The team got off to a 4-0 start that included a 31-0 pasting of the Hawkeyes, and four consecutive wins to complete the campaign. Bruce and the Cyclones were invited to take part in the Hall of Fame Bowl against Texas A&M. With Green in his senior season and fresh off another 1,000-yard effort, Cyclone fans were hopeful of finally attaining a bowl triumph. It was not to be, however, as A&M's Curtis Dickey was the one who ran wild to the tune of 274 yards in a 28-12 Aggies victory. Green rushed for 148 in his final game as a Cyclone.

Dexter Green ran for 172 yards, but it was not enough against the Wolfpack.

ON TO COLUMBUS Following the 1978 season, Bruce announced he would resign to become head coach at Ohio State. As the 1970s drew to a close, so did the greatest decade of football in Cyclone history.

THE 1980S:
TRYING TO RETRACE THE STEPS

DUNCAN ARRIVES ON THE SCENE Donnie Duncan was named to replace Bruce, and fans were wondering if the right choice had been made after Duncan's first Cyclone unit won only three games in 1979. Even more frightening than ISU's precipitous drop from college football's upper echelon was the fact that the team had scored 10 or fewer points in eight of the 11 games.

Donnie Duncan's Cyclone teams are remembered for their late-season tailspins — and for beating Iowa.

Running back Rocky Gillis (1978-82) remains ISU's career average-per-carry leader at 6.2 yards per attempt.

NO BOWLS IN SIGHT Duncan's next three seasons in Ames went 6-5 (the mark was later amended to 7-4 after Kansas was forced by the NCAA to forfeit a victory over the Cyclones), 5-5-1, and 4-6-1.

BEAT IOWA The one knack that Duncan had was an uncanny ability to beat Hayden Fry's Hawkeyes. After losing his first game to Iowa in 1979, Duncan posted 10-7, 23-12, and 19-7 wins over the black and gold to remain the most successful modern-era Cyclone coach against the Hawks. Interestingly, he is criticized by some to this day for putting too much emphasis on the rivalry, which takes place early in the season. His clubs invariably faded down the stretch.

HOT STARTS Had Duncan's clubs been allowed to play their entire schedule of games in the month of September, Iowa State might have won a national championship. During both the 1980 and 1981 seasons, ISU rose into the nation's Top 25. In '80 the Cyclones roared out of the blocks 5-0 with wins over N.E. Louisiana, San Jose State, Iowa, Colorado State, and Kansas State, a feat that pushed them up to 19th in The Associated Press rankings. In '81 the cardinal and gold did even better, staying ranked for four straight weeks. ISU debuted in the polls on September 28 with a 3-0 record after beating West Texas State, Iowa, and Kent State. A 7-7 tie with mighty Oklahoma leapfrogged the Cyclones to 12th in the subsequent poll. A 52-31 loss at San Diego State dropped ISU out of the poll, but they got back in a week later at No. 14 after a 34-13 clubbing of Missouri. A 17-10 victory over Colorado the next week gave ISU its highest ranking in history, 11th, with a 5-1-1 record. The team would not win another game.

FALL FADE Duncan's October/November fades were profoundly perplexing. His 1979 team lost five of its last six. The 1980 club did the same thing, while the 1981 unit dropped six of its final seven and the 1982 outfit lost its last four games. Duncan went 2-12 in the month of November in his four years at ISU.

USING THE "CRUTCH" One of Duncan's most effective tools was running back Dwayne Crutchfield, who was nothing short of a battering ram out of the Cyclone backfield. Crutchfield lugged the ball 47 times in a single game against Colorado in 1981, and his 1,312 yards rushing in 1980 rank third all-time on the ISU single-season rushing list. He finished his college career with 2,501 yards on the ground. He also ranks second on the single-season rush attempts charts, with 307 in 1981. Crutchfield went on to a lengthy NFL career with the New York Jets, among other teams, as did one of his chief blockers, Karl Nelson, who won a Super Bowl ring with the New York Giants.

Dwayne Crutchfield rushed for 1,312 yards in 1980, and once lugged the ball 47 times in a single game against Colorado.

THE MIGHTY QUINN Today John Quinn works in law enforcement. When he quarterbacked the Cyclones in 1981, he policed his way to the head of the Big Eight Conference in passing, with 1,576 yards.

Alex Giffords' four field goals against Iowa in 1982 propelled the Cyclones to a 19-7 win, ISU's latest in the series.

BIG FOOT When Cyclone football fans bring up the name of former kicker Alex Giffords, they remember fondly when he beat the Iowa Hawkeyes in Iowa City, kicking four field goals in a 19-7 Cyclone victory. The 1982 triumph marks the last time ISU has beaten Iowa in football. Giffords still holds the ISU record for point-after kicks in one game with nine, and shares the record for the longest field goal in ISU history — 58 yards — with Ty Stewart.

"FINER WITH CRINER" That was the rallying cry that ISU used to introduce its new coach when Duncan resigned to enter private business after the 1982 season.

While at Division I-AA Idaho State, Criner had guided the Broncos to a 59-21-1 record, as well as a national championship in 1980. He had never endured a losing season in 20 years as a head coach.

"This is the most thrilling day of my life," Criner said as he was introduced.

ENDORSEMENT "He's a very sound football coach. I think Iowa State is very fortunate to get him," said Idaho's Dennis Erickson of Criner's hiring. Erickson would go on to coach at Washington State, Miami, and with the NFL's Seattle Seahawks.

Chris Washington is No. 1 on Iowa State's all-time tackle chart with 457, 59 better than his closest rival.

THE BUBBLE BURSTS Things didn't quite work out as Cyclone fans had hoped, however. Criner's streak of coaching winning teams came to an abrupt halt in his first season, as the 1983 team won just four games, despite

having future pro stars David Archer at quarterback and Chris Washington at linebacker. There were also the good hands of wideout Tracy Henderson, and the strong hands of offensive lineman Bruce Reimers. Archer, Washington, and Reimers would all go on to careers in the NFL.

CLASS OF '83 Archer had a season to remember in 1983. Although the season didn't bring a superlative record, Archer was on target as he put up 403 passes, completing 234, for 2,639 yards, 18 touchdowns, and a microscopic interception percentage of .029. He went a stretch of 137 attempts without being intercepted, and he threw at least one scoring pass in 10 straight games.

A STATISTICAL ABERRATION The 1984 team won just two games — over Drake and West Texas State — and failed to win a Big Eight game. But despite the poor win-loss

Jim Criner replaced Donnie Duncan in 1983.

David Archer passed for more than 2,600 yards and 18 touchdowns for Iowa State in 1983. His interception percentage that season was a microscopic .029.

HENDU CAN DO

Who knows how good Tracy Henderson could have been had he not foregone his senior season at Iowa State? Henderson was a two-time All-American in 1983 and in 1984. He left ISU as the school record-holder in receptions with 150 and in reception yardage with 2,048. In 1983 alone Henderson caught 81 balls for 1,051 yards, which ranked him third in the nation.

The slick, sure-handed Henderson was the first receiver in the history of the Big Eight Conference to amass 1,000 yards receiving in a single season, and in 1983 he caught 16 passes in a single game against Kansas State, good for 165 yards.

But after his junior season, Henderson left the Cyclones and declared himself eligible for the NFL draft. He was taken by the New York Giants, but was never able to dominate the pro game as he did the college ranks. His professional career was brief, leaving Cyclone fans who remember him to wonder how much better he might have been with one more season of competition.

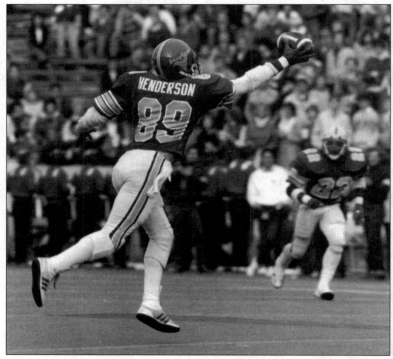

A two-time All-American, Tracy Henderson owns ISU records for receptions (150) and yards (2,048).

mark, ISU finished the season with the nation's No. 17 defense, which allowed just 297 yards per game. The unit was best against the pass, allowing just 136.1 yards a contest, good for seventh nationally.

Even more stunning was the attendance. Cyclone Stadium was filled to 98.6 percent of its capacity during the 1984 season, for an average of 49,374 per game. Three games were sold out.

Henderson was named a Football News first-team All-American with 64 receptions for 941 yards and six scores. Linebacker Jeff Braswell was Sports Illustrated's National Defensive Player of the Week after a 19-tackle outing against Oklahoma in a close 12-10 loss. Quarterback Alex Espinoza passed for more than 1,500 yards in only eight games. And still the Cyclones won just two games.

Jeff Braswell's 19-tackle effort in a nationally televised game against Oklahoma in 1984 earned him Sports Illustrated *Defensive Player of the Week honors.*

SEPARATING THE WHEAT FROM THE CHAFF Criner employed an odd strategy for rewarding his best players: He would give them special red helmets, while the rest of the team

Alex Espinoza (1984-86) is Iowa State's all-time leader in pass attempts (891), completions (454), yards (5,307), and touchdowns (33).

wore yellow. Criner said the red hats went to players who he felt were "all-Big Eight caliber players." Critics said the ploy created division on the team, made the best players more visible on the field for opponents and made the club look like they'd gotten their helmets at a flea market.

A LANDMARK LOSS The 1985 Cyclones improved a bit, winning five games. But the season is best remembered for a horrendous 20-17 loss at home to lowly Drake. The Bulldogs managed just 10 first downs and 150 total yards, yet somehow handed ISU one of its most damaging defeats in history.

When the NCAA pressed in on Jim Criner, Iowa State squeezed him out.

START OF ANOTHER STREAK While his predecessor beat arch-rival Iowa with regularity, Criner couldn't come close. In the four games he coached against the Hawkeyes, Criner's teams went 0-4 and were outscored 210-41, for an average score of 52-10.

ENDING WITH AN INVESTIGATION Criner guided ISU to a 6-5 winning season in 1986, thanks to the passing of Espinoza, who finished his career as the all-time Cyclone leader in pass attempts (891), completions (454), yards (5,307), and touchdowns (33). There was also linebacker Dennis Gibson, who pummeled opposing ball carriers and eventually wound up in the NFL with the Detroit Lions and San Diego Chargers.

But it would wind up being Criner's final season in Ames. An NCAA investigation revealed violations within the program, and an embarrassed ISU fired Criner shortly thereafter.

Walden Promises Clean Program

BLOOD FROM A TURNIP With the program gutted and the scholarship numbers nearing the ridiculous, Jim Walden somehow squeezed three victories out of his first Cyclone team in 1987. He got his first win in a wild 39-38 game against Northern Iowa in the fifth week of the season, then won a pair of Big Eight games over Kansas (42-28) and Kansas State (16-14). Quarterback Brett Sadek was the team's biggest offensive weapon, completing 117 of 229 passes for 1,443 yards and seven touchdowns, four of them going to wideout Dennis Ross. A freshman kicker, Jeff Shudak, led the Cyclones in scoring with 77 points.

TWO MORE THAN BEFORE Walden's second ISU team continued to amaze the naysayers, as it won five games and came within a half-game of a winning season.

A 30-13 rout of Tulane in a special night game at Cyclone Stadium got the Cyclones rolling. In the third week ISU sent shock waves through the state when it nearly pulled off an upset of Iowa. Quarterback Bret

Taking over a program ravaged by NCAA sanctions, Jim Walden still managed to post three victories in his first season in Ames.

Bret Oberg's fiery leadership helped pave the way to a 6-5 season for Iowa State in Jim Walden's third season in 1989.

Joe Henderson rushed for a pair of 1,000-yard seasons in 1987 and 1988.

Oberg hooked up with Eddie Brown on a late desperation heave down the right sideline that set up shop inside the Hawkeyes' 10 with time running out. But Oberg was intercepted soon after that, allowing Iowa to hold on for the win. Still, Cyclone fans were loving their football again.

Jeff Shudak kicked a late field goal to beat UNI, 20-17. The Cyclones routed Missouri in Columbia, 21-3. Joe Henderson scored five touchdowns in a 42-14 bombing of Kansas on the way to a 1,000-yard season. A 16-7 win over Kansas State put ISU at 5-5, with Barry Sanders and powerful Oklahoma State coming to Cyclone Stadium for the season finale.

ISU hung tough with the Cowboys for the first half, but Sanders ran wild in the final 30 minutes, finishing with 293 yards rushing, as OSU ran away, 49-28, to leave ISU at 5-6. Fans were seeing a turnaround, however, and with Oberg and defensive demons Mike Shane and Jeff Dole back in '89, anything was possible.

Mike Shane was an all-Big Eight linebacker for Jim Walden in 1989.

Keith Sims opened the holes for backs like Joe Henderson and Blaise Bryant from 1985-89. He became an All-Pro for the Miami Dolphins.

1989: A BREAK IN THE CLOUDS Walden's 1989 team might have been the most talented of any since Bruce's 1978 Hall of Fame Bowl squad. Oberg, the cocky, strong-armed slinger, was back under center. Future NFL All-Pro Keith Sims anchored the line with another future pro, Gene Williams. Tight end Mike Busch would go on to be named first-team All-America and then play Major League Baseball for the Los Angeles Dodgers. Mike Shane would be named all-Big Eight. Shudak would go on to become ISU's all-time leading scorer. Defensive back Marcus Robertson would enjoy a lengthy pro career with the Houston Oilers. And then there was Blaise Bryant.

Mike Busch, left, was a first-team All-American at tight end in 1989 but gave it all up to play baseball. He is a third-baseman for the Los Angeles Dodgers. Jeff Shudak, middle, remains the Cyclones' all-time leading scorer with 266 points. Blaise Bryant, right, got early attention in Ames for his unique hairstyle.

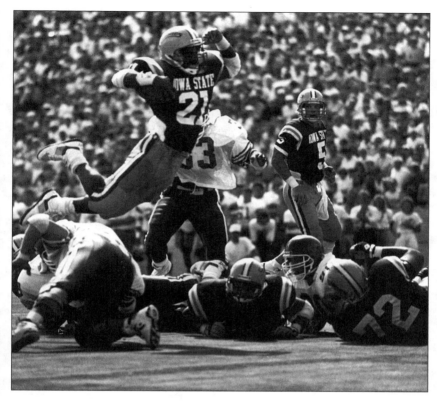

BIG HAIR, BIG GAME The 6-0, 200-pound Bryant arrived on the ISU campus with next to nothing in fanfare — except his hairdo, which was an afro with a flat-top. The surfer from Huntington Beach, Calif., arrived from Golden West Junior College in California as a first-team All-American after rushing for 1,691 yards on 334 carries as a sophomore. But how would he fare as he made the quantum leap to NCAA Division I football?

Blaise Bryant's 1989 season ended with 1,516 yards and 20 touchdowns.

Just fine, thank you. Bryant got the nation's attention by leading the Cyclones to a 6-5 record with 1,516 yards rushing, a Cyclone record for a single season. He scored 20 touchdowns, an ISU single-season record that still stands. He was a consensus first-team all-Big Eight selection, Big Eight Newcomer of the Year, and a third-team All-America pick.

FLYING HIGH UNDER THE NIGHT SKY Bryant captured ISU fans' imaginations on opening night by rushing for 213 yards and scoring twice under the portable lights in a 28-3 rout of Ohio. He followed that a week later with 98 yards and two more scores. But eight ISU fumbles and two interceptions against Minnesota hurt the Cyclones

A LIFELINE TO THE NFL

Anyone spending time as an assistant coach at Iowa State seems destined to get a shot at the big time: the National Football League. Among former ISU employees who have moved up

Joe Avezzano, left, works today with the Super Bowl champion Dallas Cowboys; Joe Bugel, middle, toils for the Oakland Raiders, and at right, Jimmy Johnson, who won a pair of Super Bowls in Dallas, had taken over for Don Shula as the head coach of the Miami Dolphins.

to the top floor are Joe Avezzano (ISU 1969-72), currently with the Dallas Cowboys; Craig Boller (1987-94), also with the Cowboys; Joe Bugel (1973), who was the head coach of the Phoenix Cardinals and is currently on the Oakland Raiders staff; Dave Campo (1983), currently with the Dallas Cowboys; Larry Coyer (1979-82, 95-present), with the New York Jets; Pete Carroll (1978), with the New York Jets; and of course, Jimmy Johnson (1968-69), who coached the Dallas Cowboys to two Super Bowl championships and is currently head coach of the Miami Dolphins.

---

dearly in a 30-20 defeat.

Bryant scored two more times at home the next week against Iowa, as the Cyclones took a 21-14 lead into the locker room. But ISU fumbled the ball in its own end zone and Iowa recovered to tie the game. The Hawks went on to win, 31-21, dropping ISU to 1-2.

Marcus Robertson, nicknamed "The General," went on to star in the NFL with the Houston Oilers.

GETTING EVEN ISU evened its mark the next week with a 25-24 win over Tulane in the Superdome. Bryant raced 72 yards to paydirt to open the scoring, and later added a 39-yard TD on the way to 181 yards on the ground. It was Oberg who iced the game for the Cyclones, however, with a nine-yard touchdown run for the winning points.

BIG EIGHT VICTORY Walden saw his team win its conference opener and move to 3-2 overall with a 24-20 win at Kansas. The two offenses combined for more than 1,000 yards, with Bryant rushing for 126 and Oberg passing for 275. KU's Kelly Donohoe passed for 411.

The biggest play of the day was a defensive one, ironically. With ISU leading by 10 late in the third, Donohoe hit Jim New, who streaked toward the end zone.

But Marcus Robertson grabbed New and stripped him of the ball at the one-yard-line. The ball rolled through the end zone, and ISU was awarded possession. KU did not muster another score until very late in the game.

THE MEAT GRINDER TAKES ITS TOLL Iowa State had to take some hard lumps the next three weeks, as No. 1 Colorado hammered the Cyclones at home 52-17, and No. 4 Nebraska handled ISU 49-17 two weeks later. In between those two games, however, was one of the most entertaining games in recent cardinal and gold history.

SO, SO CLOSE Oklahoma entered Cyclone Stadium with the nation's third-best defensive unit. Bret Oberg took one look at it and smiled.

The senior from Tehachapi, Calif., passed for 411 yards, four touchdowns, and ran for 38 yards and two more scores to set an ISU single-game total offense record of 449. He also guided the Cyclone offense to 609 total yards, the most ever surrendered by a Sooner defense.

Even with Oberg putting the ball in the air 48 times, Bryant rushed for 151 more yards on 35 carries.

LESTER SHINES Before the OU game, Steve Lester hadn't been much of a newsmaker. Then he caught 13 passes for 203 yards against the Sooners, the first of which went for 71 yards and the game's opening touchdown.

One-year sensation Steve Lester weaved through the OU defense for 203 yards on 13 receptions, including a 71-yard score.

TIED IN THE FOURTH, BUT WITHOUT A KICKER The teams entered the final 15 minutes knotted at 26-26. But Oklahoma quickly ripped off 10 straight points to move to a 36-26 lead. Oberg answered with a five-yard toss to John Glotfelty and a Bryant two-point conversion run to make it 36-34. The Cyclones went for two because Shudak had been suspended earlier in the week for arguing with a member of the coaching staff. Without him to kick field goals and extra points, ISU was forced to go for two points on nearly every score.

NEVER SEEN ANYTHING LIKE IT Walden could never have imagined that an on-side kick would have been when he'd need Shudak the most. After the Bryant run, the Cyclones lined up for an on-side attempt, but the ball bounced crazily into the arms of the Sooners' Eric Bross, who ran it back untouched from 42 yards out to make it 43-34. Glotfelty caught another score from Oberg for the game's final margin. ISU had outgained OU 609 to 313, held the ball for more than 38 minutes, and lost the game, 43-40. It would be an important defeat.

Jeff Shudak was suspended for the Oklahoma game in 1989. Had he played, ISU might well have beaten the Sooners and wound up in a bowl game.

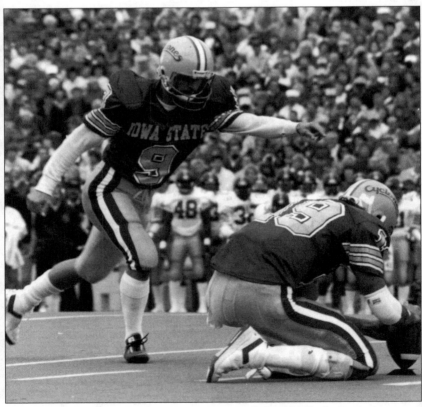

ON THE MEND The Cyclones got well again with wins over Kansas State, 36-11, and Missouri, 35-21, to even their mark at 5-5. Bryant gained 142 and 172 yards, respectively, in the two games and scored six touchdowns. Against K-State, Bryant bolted 62 yards to paydirt on the game's first snap, which also put him over the 1,000-yard mark for the season.

ENDING WITH A FLOURISH, THEN A FLUSH With a winning season on the line against Oklahoma State in Stillwater, Bryant capped his watershed season with 208 yards on the ground and his 19th and 20th scores of the season as the Cyclones beat the Cowboys, 31-21, to finish the season 6-5, and 4-3 in Big Eight Conference play.

It was ISU's first winning season since 1986, and it should have been enough to put the Cyclones in a bowl game.

Measured by today's usual benchmarks of six Division I wins and a winning conference record, the Cyclones should have been shoo-ins. But despite having one of the nation's most lethal offenses, and All-Americans on the line (Williams, 3rd team), at tight end (Busch, 1st team), and in the backfield (Bryant, 3rd team), no one called to invite the cardinal and gold out for the holidays. It was an unseemly end to one of Iowa State's best modern-era teams.

A DOWNWARD SPIRAL Walden openly talked about a postseason bid in 1990 with Bryant, Robertson, and Shudak returning. But Bryant was injured in the second game of the season and hobbled from that point on. Starting quarterback Chris Pedersen was also maimed in that contest and watched several games from the sidelines. The end was a 4-6-1 season. But included in

Athletic Director Max Urick met Jim Walden as the team arrived back in Ames after upsetting Oklahoma, 33-31, in 1990 in Norman.

Mark DouBrava finished his career in 1992 in seventh-place on the ISU all-time tackle list with 334.

the campaign was a 33-31 upset of Oklahoma in Norman, ISU's first win against the Sooners since 1961. Pedersen scored the game-winner from a yard out late in the fourth quarter, as he smartly moved the offense 80 yards for the victory.

OFFENSE STALLS OUT The next season, 1991, brought more disappointment and a stagnant offense. Eight times in 11 games the Cyclones scored 14 points or fewer. Pedersen was knocked out for the season in the sixth game. The quarterback position was physically battered to the point that the scout team quarterback, Ty Yohe, actually had to finish up in a loss to Kansas. The Cyclones finished 3-7-1.

FOUR WINS, ONE A HISTORY-MAKER In 1992 Walden's team finished a half-game better, at 4-7, but Cyclone fans were getting itchy for a return to the season of '89. But one of the victories in that season gave them hope — a mammoth 19-10 upset of seventh-ranked Nebraska at Cyclone Stadium.

MARVIN'S MIRACLE Career backup Marvin Seiler, a fifth-year senior, was handed the starting duties at quarterback in his home finale. He'd rushed for all of 31 yards in his career. Against the Huskers he would rush for 144.

Chris Ulrich rushed for 100 yards and scored the clinching touchdown in the Cyclones' slaying of the goliath Huskers.

DEVANEY'S PROPHECY Earlier in the week, Nebraska Athletic Director (and legendary former coach) Bob Devaney boasted that this Nebraska team, led by freshman quarterback Tommie Frazier and I-backs Derek Brown and Calvin Jones, was better than his 1971 national championship team. It wouldn't matter.

BALL-CONTROL With Seiler running a ground-oriented attack like a master, ISU held the ball for more than 37 minutes on the way to the nationwide shocker. His 144 yards came on 24 carries. He also completed three of four passes. Fullback Chris Ulrich added 105 yards and a touchdown on 17 carries. Artis Garris rushed for 66 yards. And all the while the vaunted attack of Jones and Brown combined for only 92 yards on 23 carries.

BREAKING THE LAW OF AVERAGES The fired-up ISU defense held the Big Red to 223 total yards under its average, just 246 for the game. Nebraska had been rushing for 351 yards every Saturday. This time it managed just 192.

RUN TO THE RECORD BOOKS It was Seiler's 78-yard run down the east sideline in the fourth quarter than nailed down the upset. Somehow, despite being timed at nearly 5.0 in the 40, no Husker defender was able to haul down Seiler until he was inside the NU 5. Ulrich bulled his way in from two yards out, and moments later the cardinal and gold inhabitants of Cyclone Stadium spilled onto the turf in wild celebration. The thousands of Big Red fans

Nebraska's Steve Carmer and Trev Alberts pursue Marvelous Marvin Seiler on his historic 78-yard run that put Tom Osborne's team on the ropes.

THE EEL WAS FOR REAL

James McMillion won't show up on Cyclone all-time rushing, passing, receiving, tackling, or

"The Eel" holds nearly every Iowa State punt return mark.

even kicking charts. Yet he was a crucial weapon for Jim Walden in the 1991-93 seasons.

The bespectacled McMillion, nicknamed "The Eel" by his teammates, was one of the nation's best punt-return men. "The Eel" owns nearly every Cyclone punt return mark.

McMillion is No. 1 in return yards per game (137), for a season (435), and for a career (843). He also returned three punts for touchdowns in the 1992 season.

Against Tulane in 1992, McMillion slithered his way to a record 27.4 yards per return on five punts. He also holds school marks in season return average (18.9 in 1992) and for a career (15.9). James McMillion did one thing well during his tenure as a Cyclone, and he did it better than anyone in history.

who had bought tickets to the game stood in stunned silence.

THE ASTERISK In his unparalleled Nebraska career, Tommie Frazier won two national championships and lost just one regular season game. This was it.

"They shut us down on all circuits," Frazier said after the game. "They took our option away, they took our inside running away, and they took our passing game away."

NO REVERSAL OF FORTUNE Folks looking for the Cyclones to use the Nebraska win as a foundation to build upon were to be disappointed. The 1993 Iowa State team won just three games again, and the pressure was building on Walden, who spent an uncertain Thanksgiving weekend wondering if he would remain as Cyclones coach. After meeting with new Athletic Director Gene Smith, he found that he would be back in 1994 but under the gun to win consistently.

Jim Walden needed victories in 1994 to strengthen his job status. Unfortunately, there were none to be had.

1994: REACHING THE GROUND FLOOR
Walden was a coach on a hot seat when practice opened for the 1994 season. But things didn't work out the way Walden wanted, beginning with the season-opener against Northern Iowa. Just two years earlier the Panthers had walked out of Cyclone Stadium with an upset win. Everyone expected ISU to be in a nasty frame of mind for the rematch. But to the shock of all in attendance, UNI dominated the Cyclones even more thoroughly than in 1992, winning 28-14 and traumatizing the players.

CAN'T BOUNCE BACK
The non-conference schedule got no better. Iowa routed ISU in Iowa City, 37-9. Then Western Michigan, from the Mid-American Conference,

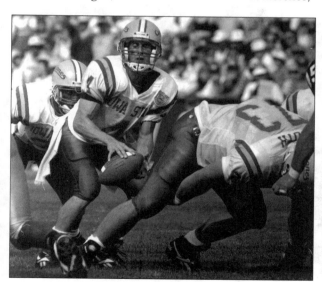

Four turnovers in the third quarter doomed Iowa State to another loss to Iowa, 37-9.

topped the Cyclones by four. Finally, Rice ground out a 28-18 win in the rain and gloom in Ames. At 0-4 and heading to Oklahoma to start Big Eight play, fans were starting to wonder if the cardinal and gold would ever have their day.

THE DROUGHT CONTINUES The Sooners dropped Walden's team to 0-5 with a 34-6 verdict. Kansas bounced the Cyclones a week later, 41-23. Now 0-6, Walden and his players were reaching the breaking point emotionally. Press conferences and interviews became testy, touchy exchanges. Each microphone and video camera seemed more and more intrusive.

FINALLY, A DRAW But in Stillwater the next week, the Cyclones didn't lose. Instead the teams battled to a 31-31 standoff, and Walden led the club in the singing of the ISU fight song in the locker room. Artis Garris scored two touchdowns, and OSU kicker Lawson Vaughn missed a 53-yard field goal at the final gun by less than a foot. Todd Doxzon passed for 209 yards and two scores.

"We didn't lose," said Walden. "We're going to find every way we can to sing the fight song."

Artis Garris scored two touchdowns, but ISU would have to settle for a 31-31 draw with Oklahoma State.

VICTORY CONTINUES A STRANGER Missouri held off the Cyclones a week later 34-20, and mighty Kansas State rolled out to a 38-0 lead the following Saturday in Manhattan before settling for a 38-20 win. At 0-8-1, with national powers Nebraska and Colorado looming, Walden knew his time was growing short.

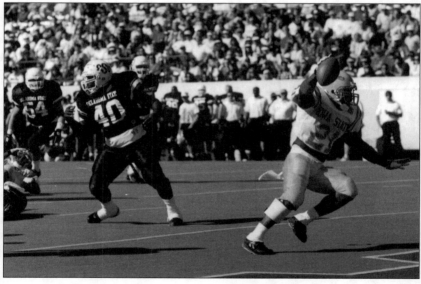

THE RESIGNATION Walden announced in a news release on Thursday, November 4, that he would resign at the end of the season. He told his team of his plans after practice that afternoon.

"Let me assure everyone that no one wanted to win more than myself and my staff," Walden said in the release. "No one is more disappointed that the win-loss record is no better. We did the very best we could."

At a news conference later that day, Athletic Director Gene Smith and President Martin Jischke talked about where the program should go and what kind of coach they wanted to take them there.

"We have agreed that it is time for a change; a change in leadership," said Jischke. "Our vision of being the nation's best land-grant university includes having a strong football program. I am personally committed to making this vision a reality. It can be done at Iowa State. It will be done at Iowa State."

Said Smith of the coaching search, "I will do everything I can to find a coach who operates with integrity, who is an outstanding recruiter, an outstanding teacher."

THE BIG TWO Nebraska held off a stubborn Cyclone squad 28-12 in Ames, and Colorado bopped the cardinal and gold in Boulder, 41-20, to complete the first winless season at Iowa State in 64 years. The last two weeks were an afterthought, however, as all eyes were focused on the future and who would be the man to lead the Cyclones.

THE SEARCH BEGINS Possible replacements for Walden began popping up in the news almost immediately. There was Kansas State assistant Del Miller, Nebraska assistants Ron Brown and Frank Solich, and an assistant to Barry Alvarez at Wisconsin by the name of Dan McCarney.

THEY SAID IT As the process of elimination proceeded, the field narrowed to Miller and McCarney. The Badgers defensive coordinator had played and coached at Iowa, and despite his black-and-gold ties he was coming on strong.

Former Wisconsin defensive lineman Don Davey and ex-Iowa lineman Mark Bortz, both of whom went on to careers in the National Football League, praised McCarney's rapport with players and his ability to motivate. Alvarez and Fry also touted his abilities. When Iowa State announced a press conference the day before Thanksgiving 1994, everyone knew who had gotten the Cyclone head position.

4. Everett Kischer quarterbacked the 1938 Cyclones to an unexpected 7-1-1 season. What else did he do over his ISU career that went largely unnoticed?

5. Who did Troy Davis pass in 1995 on the way to becoming ISU's 8th all-time leading rusher?

The McCarney Era Begins

MAC'S THE MAN "Dan McCarney has played key roles in taking two losing Big Ten programs and turning them into nationally recognized football powers," said Athletic Director Gene Smith. "He is extremely well-liked by his players and his coaching peers, and he was highly recommended by everyone I talked to. In short, he was the right man for the job."

McCarney's resume included a 13-year stint at Iowa under Fry, and a five-year tour with Alvarez in Madison. He also had a Big Ten Championship ring and a Rose Bowl ring on his fingers. Iowa State was asking him to take it places it had never been before. He promised he would do his utmost to make it happen.

Dan McCarney took the podium less than a week after a winless football season and promised to "bring back respect" to Cyclone football.

TAKING COMMAND McCarney took the podium in front of a swarm of state media and ISU boosters and launched into a fire-and-brimstone oration on reforming Iowa State football that left him dripping with sweat and Cyclone fans dripping with anticipation for the 1995 season.

"We will bring back respect," he said. "We're going to bring back winning. We're going to bring back fun. We are going to turn Cyclone Stadium into one of the most exciting places to play in college football."

REALITY CHECK But how would it be done? Sure, McCarney had worked minor miracles in getting quarterback Todd Doxzon and running back Troy Davis to reconsider leaving school, which each player was pondering prior to his hiring. But ISU had failed to win a game in 1994, the first time in 64 years the cardinal and gold hadn't sniffed victory in a season. The defense was among the nation's worst, and the run defense was the worst, 108th in all of college football.

One of the first things McCarney did was immediately ditch the Jurassic triple-option offense that had been used, installing in its place a pro-style attack, one that fans would pay to see. Then he promised Davis that his immense talents would no longer be so mistreated as when he was a freshman. If he would stay, McCarney promised, the offense would be built around his talents. Davis agreed to remain at ISU, a decision that was nothing short of momentous.

One of Dan McCarney's first orders of business was to tell Troy Davis that he would be the focal point of the offense, not an afterthought.

CATCHING THEIR LIMIT Mac's first recruiting class proved to be an impressive one, as he was able to snare two state players of the year, including Colorado running back Damian Brown.

SPRING FORWARD The spring scrimmage was a story in itself. The game was a ho-hummer, with the Red bringing down the White late on a 13-yard pass from Doxzon to Calvin Branch. The big news was the attendance, which was announced at 6,200 but felt more like 8,000. Jim Walden's final two scrimmages in 1993 and 1994 combined might have approached 800 fans. Cyclone football faithful who had been lulled to sleep by several years of bad football had hope, and they rubbed their sleepy eyes to take a wary look at McCarney's first team.

"It seemed like we had this many fans at some games last year," said backup quarterback Jeff St. Clair. "You know the people here want a good football team. They want to see something good happen."

Davis rushed for 119 yards on 17 carries in his first public work in the new offense.

Dan McCarney immediately made the Cyclones part of the community by having them clean up recreation areas and visit sick children.

Cocaptains Tim Sanders, Matt Straight, Byron Heitz, and Mike Horacek don the new Cyclone colors.

TAKING A HARD LINE Immediately after McCarney had been hired, he installed a choke-chain on the team as far as off-field conduct was concerned. Unfortunately, several players disregarded the rules and found themselves off the team before the season began. Six Cyclones were dismissed from the team before August practice began. He also got the team involved in the community, doing clean-up projects and visiting schools and hospitals.

THE EMPEROR HAS NEW CLOTHES Media Day brought new uniforms for the cardinal and gold: gone were the corn-fed yellow pants, in were all-white pants with deep red jerseys and a touch of navy blue. From a distance ISU looked like the Kansas City Chiefs.

SOUND BITES Mac told fans what they wanted to hear on Media Day, especially when it concerned Troy Davis.

"The plan is to get him the ball 20 to 25 times a game," he said. "He's going to be an outstanding running back."

For his part, Davis was ready to roll. "I'm the man that, if they get the ball to me, they can count on me. I'll just show off. It'll be a big turnaround for Iowa State."

Davis also informed reporters than his brother Darren, one of the nation's most sought-after prep running backs, had spent three weeks with him at ISU over the summer and enjoyed himself. The prospect of dueling Davises in the Cyclone backfield was nearly too much to stand.

LIGHTS UNTO THEIR PATH Iowa State moved its season-opener against Ohio up to Thursday, August 31, and brought in portable lighting for the contest. The hope was to catch fans before they made Labor Day plans, and to kick off the McCarney era in style. Todd Doxzon, unfortunately, would miss the game with an injury.

OHIO

291! That was the headline on the cover of *Cyclone Illustrated* after the Ohio game, and that said it all. Davis lived up to his billing and backed up all of his talk with a

A star is born: Troy Davis splits the night with 291 yards in a 36-21 victory over Ohio.

In 1995, Dan McCarney became the first Cyclone coach to win his opener since Donnie Duncan.

36-carry, 291-yard effort that shattered Dave Hoppmann's 271-yard single-game rushing mark and led Iowa State to a 36-21 conquest of the Bobcats. McCarney's coaching debut was a smash, and ISU's 13-game winless streak was also smashed as the students rushed the field after the game, celebrated with the joyous players at midfield, and proceeded to tear down the north goal posts.

"Troy Davis was sensational," Mac said. "You could sense on the sidelines that Troy Davis was going to take the game over. He was hot, and we knew it."

BUSTING OUT Davis broke off gallops of 12, 14, 15, 18, 37, 42, and 50 yards against Ohio, and scored from two, seven, and nine yards out. He was the nation's leading rusher after one week of play. "Just give me the ball, and I'll take it to another level," Davis said afterward as he rested in a folding chair. "I told the line, 'Just block, and I'll take it the distance.' "

TEXAS CHRISTIAN

ROAD TRIP Texas Christian had gone to the Independence Bowl in 1994 and returned the gridders who had shared the offensive-player-of-the-year award in the Southwest Conference: quarterback Max Knake and running back Andre Davis. On the other side of the ball, Iowa State hadn't won a road game since October 1991.

On ISU's first offensive snap, Jeff St. Clair, again subbing for the injured Doxzon, was picked off by linebacker Lenoy Jones, who sprinted into the end zone untouched from 28 yards out. The Horned Frogs used that early momentum to jump out to a 13-0 lead, and never looked back in a 27-10 win that left McCarney ticked off.

Dan McCarney was miffed that his team didn't come out on fire for Texas Christian.

"I just can't say enough about how disappointed I am," he said. "I thought we'd play better football tonight. We made too many mistakes and did not improve as much as I thought we would."

STILL NO. 1 Troy Davis stunned the nation again with 180 yards rushing against the Horned Frogs, giving him 471 in just two games and leaving him firmly at the top of the country's rushing chart. Some thought that Davis' Ohio outing the week before might have been a freak occurrence. Not anymore.

PRIDE Players who had seen losing become commonplace the previous few seasons were angry with themselves after their first defeat. "Any time you lose a game, there had better be frustration and disappointment or you're not competitors," said safety Matt Straight, a senior. "You can't take positives out of losses. That's the thing that Coach McCarney's taught us. We can't be proud of our effort. If we are, then we're losers."

TURNAROUND The Cyclones recovered three fumbles against the Horned Frogs, while turning the ball over just once themselves. That left ISU at +5 in turnover ratio through two games.

IOWA

STUDENT MEETS MASTER At 1-1, McCarney looked forward to his next opponent. He'd played at Iowa under Bob Commings. He'd coached for 13 years with Hayden Fry. Now he would do his best to beat his former team and ex-employer and bring some much-needed balance to the Iowa State-Iowa rivalry.

CHANGING PLACES As the third week of the season kicked off at a sold-out Cyclone Stadium, the Hawkeyes held a stranglehold on the series: 12 straight victories, many by knockout. At no time since 1989 had the Cyclones held the lead.

But in the first quarter with the Cyclones trailing 6-0, Davis grabbed a handoff on 3rd and 7 from the ISU 37 and broke to the right.

He was held up momentarily by a would-be tackler but brushed him aside, regained his stride, and was gone down the sideline for a 63-yard touchdown that caused a near meltdown for cardinal and gold fans, who watched kicker Jamie Kohl kick the extra point for a 7-6 lead.

A FATEFUL MISTAKE Trailing 12-10, ISU took the second-half kickoff and moved to the Iowa 24 under the direction of Doxzon, who was seeing his first action of the year (he would complete 11 of 23 passes for 172 yards).

On the next snap Davis again ran right with the ball, reaching the 20 when he was hit and stripped of the football. Iowa's Ed Gibson recovered and ran the ball back 67 yards to the ISU 13. The Cyclones never recovered, losing, 27-10.

"They didn't take it away from me. I was juggling it in the pile and somebody hit me. It just fell out," said a discouraged Davis afterward.

NOTABLES Ed Williams burst onto the offensive scene, as he clicked with Doxzon eight times on aerials for 131 yards. Davis rushed for 139 more to up his nation-leading total to 610. His closest competitor, Wisconsin's Carl McCullough, had just 355. Straight led the defense

6. What ISU runner once ran 98 yards but failed to score a touchdown?

7. What defensive lineman is tops on the all-time tackle chart with 352 stops?

Chapter 4: The McCarney Era Begins **59**

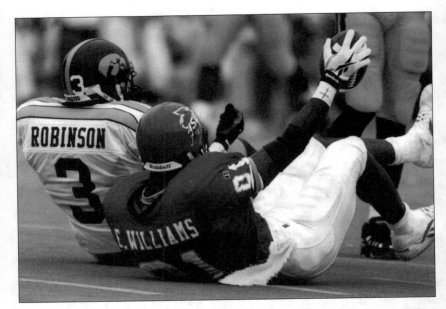

Ed Williams stunned the Hawks with eight catches for 131 yards.

The Hawkeyes were able to "hold" Rudy Ruffolo and the Cyclones off for the 13th straight time.

with 15 tackles in his final game against the Hawks, and the defense recorded its fifth and sixth sacks of the season. Iowa kickers impressed no one, missing three extra points.

GAMBLING ON .500 With just one week left in the non-conference season, the Cyclones badly wanted to taste victory again before the rigors of the Big Eight conference schedule began. Nevada-Las Vegas, which had participated in the Las Vegas Bowl the year before, was next.

UNLV

AN EARLY EXIT With 19 minutes remaining against the Runnin' Rebels, McCarney yanked Davis from the game. Not that he'd been underachieving, mind you, just the opposite. He'd already rushed for a school-record 302 yards (breaking his own record of 291 set three weeks prior) and scored a school-record-tying five touchdowns. After four games he'd gained 912 yards, and surely would have topped the 1,000-yard mark if he'd played out the clock. He was averaging 61 more yards rushing per game than his closest rival, Darnell Autry of Northwestern.

"Three hundred two yards; that's a lot of yards," Davis said after the game.

"302 yards; that's a lot of yards," said Troy Davis after raking the Rebels.

Graston Norris ran roughshod over UNLV, with 128 yards and a 91-yard touchdown.

RUSH TO EXCELLENCE The Cyclones also got a 128-yard day from Graston Norris (including a 91-yard scoring run) and a 90-yard effort from Jahi Arnold en route to a school-record 586 yards and eight scores in a 57-30 Cyclone runaway. ISU led 38-7 at halftime. Davis scored from 5, 8, 20, 66, and 80 yards out.

THE 'H' WORD For the first time, there was chatter of a possible Heisman Trophy candidate in the postgame interview room.

"It's good for Iowa State," said McCarney. "I'll answer every call and talk to every person I can about this program."

Davis didn't seem as interested.

"I'm not thinking about the Heisman. I'm thinking about winning games. I just want to keep on winning," he said.

INJURY DEJA VU On the down side, Doxzon injured his ankle again and had to be replaced by true freshman Todd Bandhauer, a 6-4, 215-pounder with a strong arm. Bandhauer completed both of his passes for 19 yards.

RECORD LIST Numerous school marks were bettered against the Rebels:

Most yards rushing, one game (individual): Troy Davis, 302. (Old mark: 291, Davis vs. Ohio, 1995)

Total rushing yards, team: 586 (Old mark: 445 vs. Colorado State, 1980)

Rushing touchdowns, one game: 8 (Old mark: 6, vs. Kansas State, 1976)

Most rushing first downs, game: 21 (Ties old mark against Drake and Kansas State, 1976)

Most yardage by an Iowa State back in four games: 912, Troy Davis.

Most rushing touchdowns, individual: 5, Davis (Ties old mark by Joe Henderson vs. Kansas, 1988)

Most 200-yard games, season: 2, Davis (Ties mark set by Blaise Bryant, 1989)

Average gain per rush, game: 8.4 (Old mark: 7.3 vs. Dubuque, 1949).

Also: Davis' 302 yards rushing marked the 8th-best effort in Big Eight history. ... Norris' 91-yard score was the second-longest in Cyclone lore (Meredith Warner went 98 yards in 1943). ... McCarney became the first coach since Earle Bruce in 1973 to go 2-2 in his first season. ... ISU's total offensive output of 648 yards was just 20 shy of the all-time single-game mark of 668 set against Dubuque in 1949.

A CHANCE FOR HISTORY Davis found out just hours later

QUIZ

8. Who did Iowa State beat in 1968 for win No. 300 in school history?

than only five running backs in NCAA history had rushed for 1,000 yards in the first five games of the season: Marcus Allen of USC in 1981, Ed Marino at Cornell in 1971, Ricky Bell for USC in 1976, Barry Sanders of Oklahoma State in 1988, and Earnest Anderson of Oklahoma State in 1982. Davis needed just 88 yards against the Oklahoma Sooners to become the sixth to turn the trick.

OKLAHOMA

A DAY OF UPS AND DOWNS
The highs were celestial, the lows were hellish. Despite leading 14th-ranked Oklahoma into the fourth quarter, McCarney's Cyclones couldn't quite finish off the Sooners, losing 39-26.

But it was a game that displayed to the 45,000 fans in attendance at Cyclone Stadium a heart that had been missing from recent ISU clubs, the kind of resilience that will win out down the road.

"We grew up as a football team today. We matured," said McCarney, who watched defensive back Kevin Hudson scoop up a blocked OU punt and return it 22 yards for a touchdown that gave ISU a 26-23 lead with 11:40 remaining. "But now we've got to make the difference. When the game's out there and there's an opportunity for either team to take it late, we've got to make the plays. We didn't today."

BIG PLAYS ABOUND
Besides Hudson's heroics, Doxzon threw a 90-yard scoring pass to Williams down the left sideline. For OU, offensive lineman Harry Stamps recovered a loose ball in the end zone for a score, and the Sooners also had a 90-yard TD pass, from Eric Moore to P.J. Mills. That tally came 18 seconds after ISU's blocked punt, and it sapped the Cyclones' momentum.

Defensive back Kevin Hudson gave the Cyclones a fourth-quarter lead over Oklahoma by returning a blocked punt 22 yards for a score.

BIG RED D
Oklahoma's one-year wonder of a coach, Howard Schnellenberger, entered the game with the nation's No. 1 run defense. The Sooners' D did the job on Davis, holding him to a season-low of 89 yards on 21 carries. The attempts were also a season-low. Yet Davis topped the 1,000-yard plateau on his final rush of the game, a two-yard plunge, to give him 1,001 yards through five games.

KEEPING UP WITH JONES
Oklahoma's stellar defensive end, Cedric Jones, had five sacks the previous week against Colorado. But he met his match in ISU tackle Tim Kohn, who limited him to just three tackles and no sacks. "I think Tim Kohn did an excellent job," said McCarney. "He did some excellent things, and it's got to do wonders

QUIZ

9. How many Cyclone receivers, including tight ends, have earned All-American status?

for Tim from a confidence standpoint because he won't find a better pass rusher in college football than that kid."

Jones went on to become an All-American and was a first-round selection by the New York Giants in the National Football League draft.

POWER SANDERS Linebacker Tim Sanders recorded a career-high 26 tackles against Oklahoma, and also recovered a fumble, one of four turnovers forced by the Cyclone defense.

KANSAS

KANSAS CAN At 2-3, the Cyclones packed for Lawrence and the 10th-rated Jayhawks. Glen Mason's team had been impressive, but there were many who wondered just how good the 5-0 Hawks really were.

Iowa State was to find out. After marching the offense smartly downfield on the first possession of the game, Doxzon threw a pass in the flat where blue jerseys abounded. Linebacker Dick Holt grabbed it at the KU 30 and ran it back 52 yards to the ISU 18. Five plays later Kansas was on the board, and off and running to a 34-7 victory. The Cyclones' lone score came on a 3-yard pass from Doxzon to Williams.

RUNNING MAN Davis kept up his marvelous season on the ground by shredding the Jayhawks' defense for 120 yards on 30 carries. Experts who were waiting for Davis to fade from sight after "inflating" his yardage against "outclassed opponents" would have to wait for another day. And another. And another. Davis now had 1,121 rushing yards on the season, which put him within 395 yards of Blaise Bryant's all-time ISU single season rushing record of 1,516.

RUNNING MEN Kansas rushed for nearly 300 yards against what McCarney said was an ISU defense that lacked the size to compete with the big boys of the Big Eight.

"It's the same thing it's going to be every week of the Big Eight season. We just physically can't go toe-to-toe with people right now. We get physical mismatches too many times late in the game."

THIRD-DOWN BLUES Stopping the opposition in third-down situations had been the Cyclone defense's Achilles' heel through five games, allowing a 52 percent conversion rate. That statistic worsened against Kansas, which succeeded on 11-of-15 third-down opportunities.

COLORADO

UPSET BID SLIPS AWAY, AGAIN For the second time in three weeks Iowa State had a Top 15 foe in a near-fall position in the fourth quarter. Agonizingly, the favored team wriggled free again.

Rick Neuheisel's Buffaloes won the game, 50-28, but had to fight mightily to get the job done. In 40-degree temperatures at Cyclone Stadium, nearly 35,000 watched as Davis raced through Colorado for 203 yards and three touchdowns, the last of which was a 45-yard burst through the middle of the defense to give ISU a 28-27 lead with 14 minutes to go.

"This is not the Iowa State of old," McCarney said. "These kids won't quit, and if they do they won't take the field for me. We've got four huge games left and I do not want to fade into the sunset of college football. I don't want to wait until 1996 for people to say great things about Iowa State. I want to get it done this year."

Said safety Matt Straight, "It reminded you of the Oklahoma game. We got on top, and the next drive they go right down and score on us."

INJURY STRIKES UP THE 'BAND' Doxzon's tender ankle took yet another blow against Colorado, which put true freshman Bandhauer on the field. He responded well given the situation, as he completed 13-of-28 passes for 130 yards. But a fateful interception was returned 30 yards for a touchdown by linebacker Matt Russell during the Buffaloes' big fourth quarter, and it hurt. Instead of being down 34-28 with the football, the Cyclones suddenly trailed 41-28.

"I was nervous, then I got excited, then I got real angry at the end," Bandhauer said. "Now I'm not feeling so good."

CLASSLESS BUFFS As the Buffaloes began to pull away from ISU, CU players on the sidelines began to taunt Cyclones fans on the west side of the stadium, laughing, pointing fingers, even raising the middle one in a sort of mock salute. Neuheisel added to the tension by going for a two-point conversion leading 50-28 with less than five minutes remaining. Asked about it afterward, Neuheisel said he wanted to be absolutely certain that ISU could not come back and beat him.

REMEMBERING No. 35 Linebacker Angelo Provenza played the game with the number 35 on his taped-up wrists in memory of ISU running back Jeff Soucie, who had died the night before the 1994 Colorado game in a car accident.

"I remember being at Colorado, and the sadness that overwhelmed us in the locker room," he said. "I

Cyclone running back Jeff Soucie died in an auto accident the night before ISU's 1994 finale against Colorado.

remember not being able to believe it, and not being able to understand it. As small as it was, I wanted to make some sort of tribute to him."

NO MORE DETRACTORS Davis' pillage of the Colorado defense got big-time play on ESPN and CNN, where his 45-yard score was shown until the tape wore out. His 203 yards put him at 1,324 for the season, more than 300 yards ahead of his closest rival. The previous three games had produced 412 yards against teams ranked 14th, 10th and 9th in the country.

"The offensive line was giving me the holes I was looking for, and I was taking it the distance," Davis said. "There were holes everywhere for me."

A "MESS"? *The Sporting News*, one of America's most highly-thought of sports publications, had it all wrong when it came to Iowa State's offensive line in its preseason college football annual.

"The offensive line is a mess," said TSN. "No one can pass-block, and with the line switching to the pro-set, Todd Doxzon will be hit plenty."

Football Action '95 was no better in assessing the abilities of Tim Kohn, Pat Augafa, Mark Konopka, Byron Heitz, Paul Skartvedt, Matt Rahfaldt, and Doug Easley. "The offensive line is a big question mark," said FA. "The new line is going to have to learn to play together and will experience the usual growing pains along the way."

Tim Kohn: Warmed to the idea that ISU O-line was "a mess" according to The Sporting News.

"I love it when people underestimate us," said the 6-5, 300-pound Kohn, "because I think if we lay low and people do that we have the size to play with anybody."

OKLAHOMA STATE

HEISMAN HYSTERIA GROWS This time he was taken out of the game with eight minutes left. Oklahoma State was a much better football team that UNLV, but Davis was still allowed to punch out early after rumbling for 202 yards (the fourth time he'd crossed the 200-yard mark in the season) on the way to Iowa State's first Big Eight Conference victory in nearly two years, 38-14.

"Excellent, excellent, excellent," were the first three words from the mouth of McCarney after he tasted victory for the first time in league play, and the third time in eight tries. "Hopefully there will be many more in years to come. It's a great feeling, and it was very important for this team to get it."

THE DEFENSE DIDN'T REST The much-maligned ISU defense vindicated itself against OSU, holding the Cowboys without a first down for 27 of 30 minutes in the second half. With three minutes left and the game out of reach, Oklahoma State finally moved the chains. The visitors finished with just 262 total yards. Dawan Anderson and Kip King intercepted passes for ISU, and Mike Lincavage recovered a fumble.

THE FUTURE IS NOW (POSSIBLY) With Doxzon still nursing a bad ankle, Bandhauer got the call against Bob Simmons' Cowboys. And he delivered the mail.

Hitting on 11-of-18 passes for 137 yards and touchdowns of 3 and 19 yards to Williams and 9 yards to tight end Dennis DiBiase, Bandhauer enjoyed an afternoon that had Cyclone fans heading home in gleeful anticipation.

"He carried himself like a veteran, not like a guy who'd played only three games of college football," McCarney said. "He's got a tremendous maturity level."

Said Bandhauer, "I was nervous about starting early in the week, it was all happening so fast. But I had a couple of good practices, and I felt more confident in my game."

MAC STUMPS FOR DAVIS Davis' 202 yards pushed his season total to 1,517, or one more than Bryant's school record. With three games to go, T.D. needed to average 127.6 yards per game to break the 2,000-yard mark. Talk of the Heisman Trophy was turning deadly serious. And McCarney said his sophomore deserved it.

"Unfortunately, we don't have a few more wins, but to

Troy Davis smoked the Cowboys for 202 yards.

me the Heisman Trophy is synonymous with the most outstanding player in college football, and I will put Troy Davis up against any player in America."

IT'S NOT THE TURF With the antiquated Cyclone Stadium turf slated to be replaced after the season, Davis slipped several times on the surface over the course of the game. Was it the slick turf? No way, said Davis.

"It's just my quickness," he said. "I just cut so quick."

NEBRASKA

NOT READY FOR THE NATIONAL CHAMPS No. 1 Nebraska was on course for a second consecutive national championship. Iowa State took its turn at bat in a sold-out Memorial Stadium a week after pummeling Oklahoma State and was routed by the Big Red's ground forces, 73-14.

The lone bright spot was Davis' 121 yards on 28 carries, which moved him to 1,647 with two games to go.

"I've been around college football for 25 years as a coach and a player, and that's as fine a team as I've ever seen," said McCarney. "They're a totally, totally dominating football team. I didn't think it would be as

ISU's game at top-ranked Nebraska featured the return of Lawrence Phillips. Here Tim Sanders applies the hit.

bad as it was, but it was the men and the boys."

PHILLIPS RETURNS The game marked the return of Husker I-back Lawrence Phillips who had been suspended for six games after pleading no contest to assaulting his former girlfriend. But when he entered the game, Phillips did so to resounding cheers from Memorial Stadium fans. Phillips rushed for 68 yards on 12 carries against the Cyclones, and scored a touchdown. Nebraska finished with 624 yards rushing, 776 yards total.

KANSAS STATE

170 TO IMMORTALITY With the Iowa State defense beaten down and worn out, Kansas State's 49-7 victory at Cyclone Stadium in the final home contest of the season wasn't surprising. Troy Davis' 183-yard effort against the nation's toughest defense was.

Taking the ball up the middle on nearly every rush, Davis raised his season total to 1,830 yards, or just 170 short of the 2,000 mark with a game remaining.

He also smashed the Big Eight sophomore single-season rushing record of 1,722 yards, held by Nebraska's Phillips. He moved up to fifth on the Big Eight's all-time single-season rushing list, 14th on the NCAA all-time single-season list, and was within 79 yards of the all-time single-season sophomore record, held by Michigan State's Lorenzo White with 1,908 in 1985.

MORE HYPE-MAN TROY-PHY TALK Heisman Trophy experts around the nation gave Davis little chance of getting to the Downtown Athletic Club for the Heisman ceremonies, and no chance of winning the prize, all because of the Cyclones' season record.

The more sober among the nation's sporting media debated the criteria that would be used to select the winner: Should the Heisman go to the best player in college football, or the best player on the best team? Everyone had an opinion. Notre Dame great Paul Hornung, who had won the award in the 1960s with an Irish team that won just two games, talked with Davis and told him to keep his chin up.

"The people on the outside think he's a long shot, but I don't think he's a long shot," said McCarney. "When you look at what this man has done against outstanding defenses every week, and he's dominated every week, I think it would be a shame (if he gets 2,000 and doesn't win)."

Said Davis, "I would vote for myself. I ran against the No. 1 defense in the country, and I got 183 yards."

Dan McCarney said Davis should win the Heisman because he "dominated" the nation's top defenses.

12. Who is the all-time losingest football coach?

COMPARING NOTES Davis had taken his game against three of the nation's toughest defenses (Oklahoma and Kansas State had been ranked No. 1 when they played ISU; Nebraska had been in the top five). He had the most yards. He had the most 200-yard games. Yet in the *USA Today* Monday edition after the K-State game, oddsmaker Danny Sheridan listed Davis as a 25-to-1 shot to win the Heisman. The odds on Ohio State's Eddie George and fellow sophomore Darnell Autry of Northwestern were even money.

MORE T.D. Davis had 285 all-purpose yards against the Wildcats, giving him 2,243 for the season, putting him third on the all-time Big Eight list behind Barry Sanders (3,250 for Oklahoma State in 1988) and Mike Rozier (2,486 for Nebraska in 1983). He remained the nation's leader in all-purpose yardage per game at 224.3, the 10th-best all-time, all-purpose total in NCAA history.

MISSOURI

A NEW STANDARD IS SET With six minutes remaining in the season finale against Missouri at Faurot Field, Davis was 38 yards shy of the 170 needed to break the 2,000-yard mark. Iowa State trailed the Tigers big, so McCarney asked offensive coordinator Steve Loney what the T.D. O-Meter, which a quartet of ISU students had loaded up and brought down to Columbia, read.

"I didn't ask all day until the last possession," McCarney said of Davis' yardage totals. "Loney said he needed 38 yards, so I said, 'Let's get a draw to him. And he broke the draw for a big run.'"

13. What was special about ISU's 1926 football campaign?

Forty-one yards, to be exact. As the play unfolded, Davis cut to his right, found a huge hole in the middle of the Missouri defense, cut back to his left, then hit the turbocharger, leaping over a tackler on the way to the Tigers' 1-yard-line. That gave Davis 2,003 yards, making him the first sophomore ever to break that magical rushing plane. He finished with 180 yards for the game, and 2,010 yards for the year.

Furthermore, it meant that the Cyclones would have a player making the trip to the Downtown Athletic Club for the Heisman Trophy announcement.

"I never had any doubt," Davis said afterward. "It was up to my linemen, and they did a great job in the second half. I just took over the game."

Davis also felt good about his Heisman chances.

"I'm going to win it," he beamed as he held the game ball. "This is the ball right here. I'm going to take it home and give it to my family."

Troy Davis cuts right against Missouri during the draw play that pushed him over the 2,000-yard mark.

Troy Davis was mobbed by the media after his record-breaking run.

AS FOR THE GAME It wasn't what Davis, McCarney, and the Cyclones had hoped for. Missouri attacked ISU from the outset and zipped out to a 21-0 first quarter lead, with a 51-yard interception return for a touchdown putting the exclamation point on the blitzkrieg.

ISU got back into the game with touchdown passes of 10 yards to Williams and 11 yards to DiBiase from Doxzon, and a 17-yard tally by Davis. But the cardinal and gold defense simply didn't have the strength or the depth to slow down Missouri's revved-up offense.

McCarney's first season in Ames had ended at 3-8 — a three-game improvement from the previous year.

O-LINE IS PLEASED Mark Konopka, a senior, and Tim Kohn, a junior, were ecstatic over paving a path for Davis throughout the campaign. "A lot of us are thinking about road-tripping out there," said Kohn. Konopka said, "There's a lot of linemen who have been blocking over the last 100 years, but only about 25 of us who have blocked for 2,000-yard rushers. All of us fat guys are real happy about it."

FANS JOIN IN THE HEISMAN CHORUS Cyclone fans hung over the walk ramps above the ISU locker room, clamoring for a look at Davis. While they waited, they

Ed Williams celebrates after hauling in a 10-yard scoring pass against Missouri.

baited the gaggle of media by the door. Some chanted "Heisman! Heisman!" Another yelled to reporters, "Are you aware that every running back who has ever rushed for 2,000 yards in a season has won the Heisman? Are there any Heisman voters down there?"

There were, but they didn't need additional persuading.

A throng of admirers and media met Troy Davis in Ames upon his return from Columbia.

THE HEISMAN CHASE

JOINING AN ELITE CLASS By breaking the 2,000-yard mark, Davis had joined Nebraska quarterback Tommie Frazier, Florida quarterback Danny Wuerffel, Northwestern running back Darnell Autry and Ohio State running back Eddie George as finalists in the Heisman voting.

"It's a great day for Iowa State," McCarney said after hearing the news. "Four of the five representatives are from the top five teams in the country, and Troy's a member of a team that's in the process of a turnaround.

"It's staggering what it can do for our program to help jump-start it for the future. To get this kind of publicity, recognition, and exposure, it's all positive. We're proud of Troy, and it's an honor that's very deserved."

DAVIS SPEAKS "I'm not nervous about it at all," Davis said prior to departing for the Big Apple. "I don't have any idea about my chances. I have a chance to get it, but I can't pick for it. I've just got to wait for the votes to come in."

Davis flew to New York on December 8, where he met his parents, William and Eular Webster. Mom and

Dad had not been able to see their son in person all season long, but they were flown to New York, all expenses paid, to see their son take his place as one of the top five players in the nation.

Davis said he'd taken numerous calls earlier in the week from well-wishers.

"They say they want to come over and shake the hand of a Heisman candidate," he said. "They say they just want to come over and touch me."

THE RACE NARROWS A few days before the December 9 ceremony, experts around the nation were hailing either George or Frazier as the winner of college football's top prize. Many discounted Davis' efforts because he played for a 3-8 team. McCarney defended his back, saying Davis did the most with the least.

"I know the others have had so much more success as a team than Iowa State did, yet I believe there's a lot of support out there for somebody that's done what he's been able to do with a much less supporting cast.

"You start thinking, what if we'd had a good defense? What if we'd had the talent that some of these other players had to get him the ball, to get the turnovers. The sky's the limit on what he might have been able to accomplish."

Troy Davis and Dan McCarney struck a pose at the December 9, 1995, Heisman Trophy ceremony at the Downtown Athletic Club in New York.

HEISMAN TIME ARRIVES ESPN carried the Downtown Athletic Club ceremonies live December 9, showing Davis sitting in a row with Frazier, George, Autry, and Wuerffel. It was heady stuff, but Cyclone fans were to be disappointed: Davis wound up fifth in the Heisman voting, with George taking home the bronze bust.

"It's over now. The best man won," Davis said minutes after the announcement. "I have a lot of respect for him. Eddie George is the real deal.

"I don't feel bad about not winning it because I'm a sophomore, and a sophomore has never won it. I've just got to work harder on and off the field. I'm not going to be big-headed, and I don't think I'll feel the pressure of being a favorite next year. The 2,000 yards helped put me and Iowa State on the map. Next year I plan on taking a step to a bowl game."

Sporting a Heisman hat, Troy Davis vowed to return in 1996 to claim the prize that was so close in 1995.

THE NEXT STEP: RECRUITING

LITTLE BROTHER IS WATCHING Darren Davis had to stay home in Miami and baby-sit while Mom and Dad went to New York City to watch older brother Troy take part in the Heisman ceremonies. He saw him occasionally on ESPN and CNN making long scoring runs. He talked with him every Saturday night after Iowa State's game, win or lose. And by the time signing day arrived in February, Davis knew where he wanted to play his college football: alongside his brother at Iowa State.

"He's a sensational football player," said McCarney as he unveiled his class. "Outstanding. Big-Time. I have no reservations that he'll make a major impact here at Iowa State."

The younger Davis had rushed for 747 yards in just four games his senior year at Southridge before a broken leg ended his season. He was expected to make a full recovery. Doctors said that with the proper rehabilitation, Davis' leg could become even stronger than before the break.

Like Troy, Darren had also experienced a 2,000-yard season, in his junior year at Southridge. He was rated one of the top three halfbacks in the nation by SuperPrep magazine.

Dan McCarney promised Cyclone fans that the ISU defense would never again finish last in the nation against the run.

DEFENSE ALSO STOCKS UP McCarney also inked four defensive linemen, four linebackers, and five defensive backs in an effort to change the Cyclones' defense. The average weight of the incoming linemen was 272 pounds, the average 'backer went 239. Junior college transfer Derrik Clark enrolled at ISU in January and had cracked the starting lineup by the end of spring practice.

PACIFIC IMPORT When Pacific decided after the end of the 1995 season to discontinue its football program, McCarney asked assistant Paul Rhodes, a former assistant to Chuck Shelton at the school, if there was anyone on the Tigers team that could help the Cyclones immediately. Rhodes brought up the name of wide receiver Tyrone Watley.

The senior-to-be caught 37 passes for 388 yards in '95, and like Clark, he joined the Cyclone program in January. He, too, was a starter by the end of spring practice.

Watley missed his sophomore season with what was determined to be a heart virus. Cleared to play after sitting out that year, Watley will petition the NCAA for another year of competition after the 1996 season. McCarney thinks he'll get it.

"He's got one year left for sure and hopefully two," McCarney said. "We feel very confident that he will be here for two years."

SPRING BRINGS BIG CHANGES McCarney used spring practice to emphasize the Cyclone passing game and to continue to plug in the holes in the defense.

"Not one area of the defense was I satisfied with last year," McCarney said. "We've got to get stronger, we've got to get tougher, and we've got to get more consistent.

"We were ridiculous against the run. We were soft consistently. We were too slow and too small."

Cyclone Stadium has been home to the Cyclones since 1975.

The big rub for the former Wisconsin defensive coordinator was that ISU finished last in the nation in rushing defense, allowing 296.6 yards per game on the

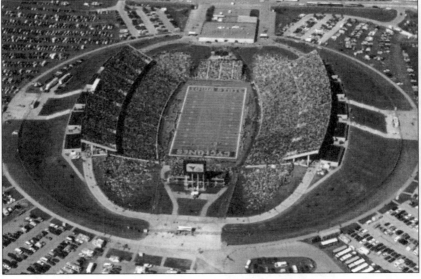

ground, and 458.4 yards per game overall in 1995.

"It'll be the last time, I promise you this, that we'll ever finish last in defense against the rush," he said. "That'll never happen again. Ever. As long as I'm the head coach here.

"It was embarrassing to me, the coaches, and the players. If you're going to be in the mix for bowl games, national championships and first-division finishes, you better play defense. And that's the challenge that lies ahead."

SPRING GAME PLAYED AT WILLIAMS FIELD No, not old Clyde Williams Field. That venerable old coliseum is long gone. Cyclone Stadium was out of commission due to the installation of grass to the Jack Trice Field turf. So the Cyclones agreed to hold the annual spring scrimmage at Williams Field in Des Moines, located at East High School.

CARDINAL DOMINATES, AS EXPECTED After watching the starters come within four yards of losing to the reserves in McCarney's first spring game, he told the media he expected, and hoped, that this Cardinal (starters)-White (reserves) game would be a little more one-sided. It was.

Led by Doxzon and Davis, the Cardinal team scored 28 points in the second quarter and cruised to an easy 42-7 win before more than 6,000 Cyclone fans at Williams Field. Davis rushed for 111 yards in the first half and took the rest of the game off, while Doxzon completed 13-of-24 passes for 179 yards and three touchdowns without an interception. The Cardinal also got a defensive score late in the first half when Clark made his first big play at Iowa State by intercepting Bandhauer and racing 73 yards up the right sideline to paydirt.

14. When is the last time the Cyclones were able to put together a five-game winning streak?

15. When is the last time the Cyclones shut out an opponent on the football field?

Clyde Williams Takes Up Hoops

Clyde Williams had a hand in the emergence of both the football and basketball programs at Iowa State.

After getting the Iowa State football program on its feet, Clyde Williams took up the sport of basketball at the school in 1908. He coached a total of four seasons, posting a record of 20-29. Some of the early Cyclone stars included H.S. Luberger, Joe D. Brown, H.M. Herbert and Clark Mosher.

The team's first victory came in Williams' first season. ISU played only two games that first season, losing to Phog Allen and Kansas in its first-ever contest, 53-35, and beating Drake 36-16.

THE TEENS AND TWENTIES: GROWING PAINS Homer Hubbard took over for Williams in 1911, and his first club posted a record of 8-7 against the likes of Missouri, Drake, Grinnell, and Nebraska. Hubbard's next three years were downers. His squads went 3-13, 4-14, and 6-7. Included in the 1912-13 season results was an 18-3 loss to Grinnell, which set the record for the fewest number of points put up by an Iowa State team.

H.H. Walters, R.N. Berryman, and Maury Kent followed as Cyclone coaches, but none of the three lasted very long. In Kent's case, the tenure was only one season. Bill Chandler took over in time for the 1921-22 season and stayed for seven years, but his cardinal and gold teams were usually black and blue from beatings administered by opponents. Chandler went 40-85 as coach at ISU, and suffered through 2-16, 2-15, 4-14, and 3-15 seasons before calling it quits in 1928.

Louis Menze coached at ISU for 19 seasons, the longest tenure in history.

THE THIRTIES AND FORTIES: LOUIE, LOUIE For 19 consecutive seasons, the same name was on the door of the Iowa State men's basketball coach's office. Louis Menze had staying power, to be certain. Until Johnny Orr came along, he was also the winningest Cyclone coach in history.

Menze guided ISU from 1929 to 1947, compiling a 166-153 overall record. The seasons then were much shorter than they are today; many times Menze had fewer than 17 games on the schedule. Some years were better than others. He was down on his luck in 1937, when the Cyclones lost 15 of 18 games. But in 1941 he piloted ISU to a 15-4 mark behind captains Gordon Nicholas and Al Budolfson. That club won the Big Six championship and went to the NCAA Tournament. His 1944 team went 14-4 and won another Big Six title and an NCAA bid.

The 1944 Iowa State Cyclones.

GOING WEST, TO KANSAS CITY The 1944 team landed in the NCAA Tournament Western Sectional, which was played at the Municipal Auditorium in Kansas City, Mo. The Cyclones' opponent was Pepperdine, which led at halftime, 19-15. But the Cyclones came storming back in the second half, despite losing two starters, Gene Oulman and Ray Wehde, to fouls. The Wave came back to tie the game with six minutes remaining, but baskets by Roy Wehde and Jim Meyers iced the game for the Cyclones. The final was 44-39, setting up a West Sectional final with Utah.

But a Final Four was not to be. Utah won the game, 40-31, leaving the Cyclones one step short.

WHERE'S WALDO? Waldo Wegner was the first basketball All-American at ISU, having earned that distinction after the 1934 season.

As a senior for the 1935 team, Wegner led the Cyclones to their first-ever Big Six championship with a 13-3 record. The team also played dogged defense, limiting foes to an average of just 28.4 points per game.

Wegner was a two-time all-Big Six center for Menze. His jersey was retired in 1992. Because he and Jeff Hornacek had shared the same jersey number (14), the retirement occurred during a joint ceremony. (Other retired ISU numbers belong to Jeff Grayer (44) and Gary Thompson (20).)

KEEPING GOOD COMPANY Wegner wasn't the only leader on that 1935 Big Six championship squad. Jack Flemming was a sophomore that year. After Wegner moved on, Flemming took over, averaging 10 points a

Waldo Wegner was Iowa State's first basketball All-American, having received the award after the 1935 season.

game as a junior and 12 a night as a senior. He was named an All-American after the 1937 season.

THE FIFTIES: BETTER LATER THAN SOONER The early 1950s were mostly uneventful. Coach Clay Sutherland did not win more than 10 games in any season. In 1955, Bill Strannigan took over. And when he did, things

THE ROLAND ROCKET

Gary Thompson has always been an Iowa boy. Raised in the tiny town of Roland, Iowa, just 15 minutes northeast of Ames, Thompson's college choice was easy. He would take his dead-eye shooting accuracy to Iowa State.

Gary Thompson was also an All-American at shortstop for the Iowa State baseball team.

Thompson, who was the first Cyclone player ever to score 40 points in a single game, was also ISU's first 1,000-point scorer and was selected as an All-American after his senior season in 1957.

The "Roland Rocket" as he was known, finished with 1,253 points and was an integral part of the 1956-57 team that racked up 18 victories, which was a school record at the time. He was also a factor in the Cyclones' mammoth 39-37 upset of Wilt Chamberlain and Kansas at the Armory. Crazed ISU fans stormed the court following the game and cut down the nets in celebration.

Thompson's talents stretched beyond the hardwood. He also earned All-America honors as a shortstop for the Cyclone baseball team in 1957, helping the club to a berth in the College World Series. He was drafted professionally by the NBA's Minneapolis Lakers. In recent years, he has worked as a color commentator with both Iowa State and Big Eight basketball games. To this day he remains one of the best analysts in college basketball.

The "Roland Rocket" was ISU's first 1,000-point scorer and was named an All-American after the 1957 season.

improved quickly.

Led by players such as Chuck Duncan, Gary Thompson, and John Crawford, Iowa State surged forward. Duncan and Thompson got things started in 1955 by helping the Cyclones to an 11-10 mark, the best of the decade at that point. Duncan averaged 21 points and 12 rebounds, while Thompson, a sophomore, clicked for 16 points and five boards a contest.

BUSTING OUT Thompson, Crawford, Don Medsker, and Chuck Vogt all averaged in double figures the next season as Strannigan's bunch exploded to an 18-5 record. ISU went 8-4 in Big Seven play, good for a second place tie in 1956-57. The Cyclones lost back-to-back games just once during the season and captured the Big Seven Holiday Tournament by beating Kansas State, Colorado, and Kansas.

MORE OF THE SAME Now a senior, Thompson showed why he was one of the nation's finest by breaking the magic 20-point barrier. He finished the season with a 20.7 average, and ISU finished with a 16-7 record in 1957-58. Crawford averaged double digits in both scoring and rebounding.

With Crawford leading the way in 1958-59, Strannigan coached ISU to a 16-7 mark. The Cyclones opened the season with five straight wins and closed the campaign in the same fashion.

Bill Strannigan, above, took over for Clay Sutherland, below, in 1955, and led Iowa State to some of its finest seasons in the latter half of the decade.

The Armory, where Iowa State topped Wilt Chamberlain and Kansas in 1957.

Chapter 5: Clyde Williams Takes Up Hoops **81**

John Crawford scored and boarded with equal aggressiveness for the Iowa State teams of the late 1950s.

Al Koch, right, and Vince Brewer, above, each cracked the 1,000-point club at ISU in the early 1960s.

THE SIXTIES: PLAYING .500 Glen Anderson held the reins of the Iowa State program through the turbulent '60s. ISU finished the decade with a record of 125-125. The best ledger was a 15-9 mark in 1960, the worst campaign a 9-16 outing in 1965. Anderson coached 12 years at ISU, finishing in 1971 with a 142-161 record.

RAISING CAIN If the Cyclones had had another Bill Cain on their roster from 1968-70, Iowa State would have been a different basketball team.

Cain, a monstrous scorer and rebounder, rolled up nearly 1,500 points and 1,000 rebounds in his three-year stint at ISU, leaving him in the top 10 in both categories on the Cyclone all-time charts. Cain saved the best for

last, averaging 19 points and 15 rebounds a game in 1970.

DON'T MESS WITH 'THE DON' For three straight years Don Smith was a first-team all-Big Eight selection. A tremendous scorer and a punishing rebounder, Smith ranks eighth on ISU's all-time scoring charts with 1,672 points, or 22.3 per game from 1965-67. He is second to Dean Uthoff in career rebounds with 1,025, or better than 13 caroms per contest.

The forward/center is one of only two Cyclones to score 1,000 points and pull down 1,000 rebounds in a career. Smith was named the Big Eight's top sophomore in 1965, and was the league's Most Valuable Player in 1966.

Smith was named an All-American following the 1967 season, when he scored 24.2 points and hauled down 14.6 rebounds per game. He was a first-round draft choice of the NBA's Cincinnati Royals in 1968, and also played with the Houston Rockets.

LIKE DISCO, THE SEVENTIES WEREN'T SUPER Iowa State went through four coaches in the 1970s — Glen Anderson, Maury John, Ken Trickey, and Lynn Nance. Yet only three winning seasons were posted in the decade that did "The Hustle," and the best mark of the three was a 16-10 record in 1973 by John.

Some great individuals did pass through the program, however. Hercle Ivy and Andrew Parker still rank in Iowa State's top 10 on the all-time scoring list, as Ivy averaged 22.2 points a game on the way to 1,729 points from 1973-76, good for sixth place; and Parker, who played from 1976-79, finished with 1,531 career points, which currently ranks him ninth.

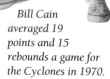

Bill Cain averaged 19 points and 15 rebounds a game for the Cyclones in 1970.

1980 to 1994:
The Johnny Orr Era

Johnny Orr stunned his college basketball coaching colleagues when he left Michigan in 1980 for Iowa State.

With the energetic Johnny Orr pacing the sidelines, attendance jumped at Hilton by an average of 3,000 fans per game in his first season.

SHOCKER Johnny Orr surprised the college basketball world, and the University of Michigan in particular, when he resigned in 1980 to take over a long-dormant Iowa State program. When he arrived in March of that year, the Cyclones hadn't appeared in a postseason tournament in more than 40 years and were averaging just more than 6,400 fans a game in 14,000-seat Hilton Coliseum, which opened in 1971.

INSTANT RESULTS While Orr's first ISU team won just nine games, attendance at Hilton leaped by more than 3,000 fans per game. His first Cyclone victory came in a 74-72 decision over a Drake team that included All-American Lewis "Black Magic" Lloyd. More than 13,000 fans packed Hilton that night to watch Ron Harris pump in 28 points to lead the Cyclones to victory. ISU won just two league games during the 1980-81 season, but the program was on the move.

NEARING .500 Just two seasons later, Orr guided Iowa State to within a game of .500 at 13-15, and the squad finished in a tie for fifth in the Big Eight. Included in the campaign were wins over two Top 20 teams: Minnesota (80-78) and Missouri (73-72). The Cyclones overcame the Gophers' inside tandem of future NBA stars Kevin McHale and Randy Breuer for Orr's first big ISU upset.

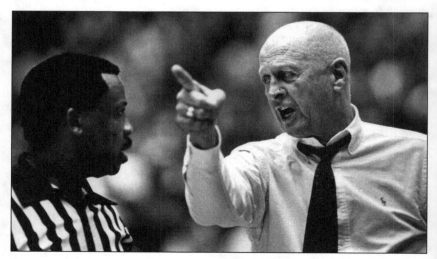

Barry Stevens' play against Missouri is one of the best-loved memories of Iowa State fans.

The win over the 10th-ranked Tigers is especially memorable for ISU fans, as Barry Stevens squared up and hit a long-distance bomb at the buzzer for the winning points as a regional ESPN audience looked on.

TOURNAMENT TIME The next season Stevens, seniors Terrance Allen and Ron Harris, and sophomores Jeff Hornacek and David Moss helped propel the Cyclones to a 16-13 season, and most importantly, to the National Invitation Tournament (where ISU was ousted in the first round by Marquette). It was ISU's first postseason trip since 1944. High points of the season included a 76-72 double overtime victory over Iowa and a 61-56 triumph over Kansas.

TOPPING 20 FOR THE FIRST TIME Orr was an excited coach as the 1984-85 season arrived. Stevens was a polished senior. Hornacek a steely junior. And there were some new faces to go with the old: Jeff Grayer, a highly-regarded freshman from Flint, Mich.; lanky sophomore Sam Hill, a center with potential; and freshman Gary

Terrance Allen helped get Johnny Orr to his first postseason tournament in 1983-84, the NIT.

Jeff Hornacek and Barry Stevens helped the Cyclones to their first-ever 20-win season in 1984-85.

Thompkins, who bolstered the backcourt.

Stevens, Hornacek, Grayer, and Hill all would average in double figures in scoring, and the Cyclones would post a 21-13 record, the first time in ISU history that a club reached the 20-win plateau.

BIG EIGHT TOURNAMENT Eight appearances in the Big Eight Tournament had left Iowa State with an 0-8 record. That streak changed during the first round of the

Jeff Grayer made mush of Danny Manning and Kansas in a 75-59 Big Eight Tournament semifinal victory at Kemper Arena.

1985 tourney, however. ISU pounded Colorado 76-52 in Ames as Stevens scorched the nets for 25. Hill added 14 points and Grayer 13.

The semifinal opponent at Kemper Arena in Kansas City was the home favorite, Kansas, and Coach Larry Brown. The Jayhawks came out with Danny Manning and Ron Kellogg, but they couldn't make a game of it.

Stevens added 25 more points, 16 of them in the second half, Hornacek had 16 and Grayer 15 in a 75-59 Cyclone rout. It was on to the championship game for the team that prior to the weekend had never even won a tournament game.

Orr's club fell just short of victory in the title game against Oklahoma, 73-71. Despite being saddled with four fouls, Wayman Tisdale pumped in 20 for the Sooners and Tim McCalister added 18.

ISU had earned its first bid to the NCAA Tournament since 1944. The season would end with a first-round loss to Ohio State, but this was a program on its way up.

1985-86: SWEETEST OF SEASONS

THE CUPBOARD WAS FULL Orr's 1985-86 Cyclones had every intangible necessary for a record-breaking season. There was the outside presence and assist capabilities of Hornacek. There was the still-evolving Hill in the middle of the paint. There was the slashing Thompkins, the do-everything well Ron Virgil. And, of course, there was Grayer, the leader, heart, soul, and will of the team.

The team got off to a 7-1 start, including a 74-61 rout of Iowa and an 82-80 overtime win against Michigan State at Hilton. The Cyclones slumped a bit over the holidays, losing at Indiana, at Illinois, and at Detroit but rebounded during conference play, finishing with a 9-5 mark and an 18-9 overall record. Again came the Big Eight Tournament. Again ISU was ready.

BUFFED AND POLISHED For the first time, all tournament games were held in Kemper Arena. The change of venue didn't help Colorado, which was no match for ISU in a 78-60 first-round assault. Hill and Virgil scored 16 and 14, respectively, as Grayer and Hornacek endured off nights. The semifinal game was another rout, as Nebraska fell by the wayside 75-58. Hornacek showed the way with 17, while Elmer Robinson added 13. For the second straight year Iowa State would play in the championship game. This time the foe would be Kansas.

WOODY'S REVENGE Woody Mayfield might have begun the championship game against Kansas as just another anonymous referee. But before the contest ended, his

16. What Cyclone was drafted in the 10th round of the 1982 NBA draft by the Kansas City Kings?

Elmer Robinson's 13 points knocked Nebraska out of the conference tournament and set up a title tilt with Kansas.

Did Sam Hill travel or didn't he?

name was forever etched in the minds of Cyclone basketball fans.

With the Jayhawks leading 73-71, Hornacek intercepted a pass from the Jayhawks' Cedric Hunter. Driving the length of the floor, he dished to Hill near the top of the key. Precious seconds remained in the game as Hill drove toward the basket. There was contact, and the official under the basketball whistled a foul on a Kansas player, which would have sent Hill to the line with a chance to force overtime.

But Mayfield, standing away from the action on the other side of the court, raced in and whistled Hill for traveling. While Orr, the players, and ISU fans in Kemper seethed with rage, Mayfield made sure his call stood. Final score: Kansas 73, Iowa State 71. As the final seconds ticked off, an enraged Orr chased Mayfield off the court.

NCAAs BECKON AGAIN The controversy in Kansas City was soon forgotten when the Cyclones found out they would be staying in the Midwest Regional of the NCAA Tournament, and playing in the Hubert Humphrey Metrodome in Minneapolis, Minn. It was a short drive for

Jeff Hornacek's never-say-die persona pushed the Cyclones past Miami of Ohio in the first round of the 1986 NCAA Tournament.

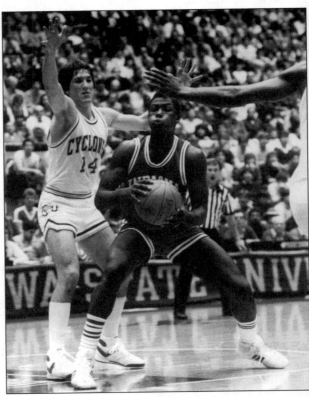

ISU's loyal fans, and when the ball went up against Miami of Ohio and future NBA star Ron Harper in the first round, the crowd noise for the Cyclones was deafening.

BUZZER-BEATER Harper and the Redskins were a game bunch, taking the Cyclones into overtime. Hornacek's 18-footer with 27 seconds left in regulation forced the extra session. The game was still knotted at 79-79 as ISU held the ball for the final shot of overtime. Hornacek rolled off a pick, took the inbounds pass, and tossed up a 25-foot shot as the clock swung toward zero. As the ball nestled in the cords, he was immortalized in Cyclone basketball lore and ISU's ticket to the second round had been punched with the 81-79 victory.

"As soon as it left his hands, I knew we were done," said Miami Coach Jerry Pierson. "Hornacek's a leader. He makes things happen."

BEATING THE BOSS Orr wanted nothing more than to beat the Cyclones' next foe. Michigan, after all, was his former employer. But the 28-4 and fifth-ranked Wolverines had an intimidating lineup with center Roy Tarpley, guards

An Elmer Robinson slam dunk helped put the Wolverines on ice for good.

Antoine Joubert and Gary Grant, and forwards Butch Wade and Richard Rellford. Early in the game CBS announcer Dick Stockton said, "It looks like the JV against the varsity." ISU made Stockton look foolish as it took a 40-31 halftime lead.

Michigan clawed its way back to within 64-63 with 1:19 to go. But Hornacek found a cutting Robinson on an inbounds pass for a rim-rattling dunk and a three-point lead. Clutch free throw shooting the rest of the way jolted the Wolverines out of the tournament, and put ISU basketball at its highest point in history: the Sweet 16.

A CANDLELIGHT 'VIRGIL' Virgil held his own against Tarpley, who had the Cyclone by seven inches. Tarpley finished with 25 points, but he couldn't stop Virgil on offense as he clicked on 7 of 8 shots. As the buzzer sounded, Tarpley raced off the court, tearing at his jersey. As he reached the tunnel he had ripped it from his chest, sobbing.

"Ron Virgil is the skinniest kid in the United States" Orr said later. "He kept telling us he didn't think he could go in there against the big guys, but he did."

Though he was taller, wider, and a better athlete, Michigan's Roy Tarpley couldn't handle Ron Virgil in the second round NCAA Tournament matchup. ISU won 72-69.

Ron Virgil takes a swipe at a North Carolina State field goal attempt in the Elite Eight NCAA Tournament game of 1986.

KEMPER PROVES CRUEL ONCE MORE The matchup against North Carolina State pitted Orr against Wolfpack legend Jim Valvano. ISU had Grayer and Hornacek; N.C. State had Charles Shackleford and Chris Washburn.

The Wolfpack came out aggressively, shooting 65 percent on the way to a 40-29 halftime lead. Hornacek, who finished with only 6 points, hit a jumper to tie the game at 47-47 with 13:47 to go. But Valvano's club held off the Cyclones down the stretch for a 70-66 victory. Grayer and Hill each scored 21 for ISU. The Cyclones' season ended one step shy of the Midwest Regional Final.

PAINFUL TESTIMONY How much did Hornacek's floor leadership mean to the Cyclones? With the savvy point guard off to the NBA, Orr's team was to find out in 1986-87. Grayer, Hill, Thompkins, and Robinson were still wearing the cardinal and gold, as was Illinois transfer Tom Schafer, who averaged 18 points and 8 rebounds in his first season in Ames. Yet without Hornacek the team struggled.

Illinois transfer Tom Schafer averaged 18 points and 8 rebounds in his first campaign with the Cyclones.

THE KID NOBODY WANTED

Jeff Hornacek arrived at Iowa State in 1983 as a walk-on. Nothing about his appearance made fans think of him in terms of basketball wizardry, yet he finished his Iowa State career as the all-time leader in assists with 665, a mark that still stands. The LaGrange, Illinois, guard didn't get a single offer out of high school, so he went to work driving a forklift for a paper cup company. ISU Assistant Coach Gary Cook found him, however, and got him to come to Ames without a scholarship.

That scenario didn't last long. Along with his 665 assists came 1,313 points and 412 rebounds. By the time he was a senior Hornacek was an all-Big Eight selection, and he has gone on to become Iowa State's most successful pro player, with a lengthy NBA career with the Phoenix Suns, Philadelphia 76ers, and Utah Jazz.

Jeff Hornacek came to ISU without a scholarship. He left as a member of the Phoenix Suns.

A 15-point loss at Creighton in the second game of the season raised the red flags. Then came a two-point loss at home to Illinois State, a stunning defeat that snapped the Cyclones' 22-game home court win streak. Things didn't improve in Big Eight play, where ISU placed 6th with a 5-9 log. The 13-15 season ended with an opening-round loss to Oklahoma at the Big Eight Tournament.

"HILTON MAGIC" Perhaps Orr's crowning achievement was his ability to turn Hilton Coliseum from a mausoleum in the late 1970s to one of the nation's noisiest dens of din. Teams entered Hilton, teams quickly became intimidated at Hilton, and teams then lost at Hilton.

Nowhere was this more apparent than two 22-game home winning streaks. The first ran from February 16, 1985, to December 22, 1986. The foes that fell, in chronological order, were Kansas, Oklahoma State, Colorado, Colorado, South Dakota State, San Francisco

State, Northern Iowa, Iowa, Michigan State, South Dakota, Missouri, Colorado, Kansas, Oklahoma, Kansas State, Nebraska, Oklahoma State, Detroit, Wisconsin-Green Bay, Drake, Northern Iowa, and Florida International.

The second 22-game unbeaten string began on March 4, 1992, and lasted through December 21, 1993. Teams that received failing grades were Kansas, Indiana State, SUNY-Buffalo, Mercer, Texas Southern, Minnesota, Bethune-Cookman, Oklahoma State, Southern Utah, Oklahoma, Drake, Nebraska, Colorado, Missouri,

THE BEST EVER

Jeff Grayer was the total package. When the Flint, Mich., schoolboy star first stepped onto the Hilton Coliseum floor, Cyclone fans knew they were watching greatness. From his first game in the 1984-85 season to his final game in 1987-88, Grayer put on a display of athleticism and court smarts that had not been seen in the annals of Iowa State.

After averaging 12.2 points a game as a true freshman, Grayer heated up for his final three campaigns, scoring 20.7 points per game as a sophomore, 22.4 as a junior, and 25.3 as a senior. For his career Grayer averaged an even 20.0 points in 125 games and finished with 2,502 points, a record that is approached only by Barry Stevens, who ranks second with 2,190.

But Grayer could also go after the basketball, as his 910 career rebounds (7.3 average per game) attest. He hit 52 percent from the floor, nearly 69 percent from the line, and finished as an All-American. He also played salty defense, a part of his game that was rarely spotlighted.

Grayer went on to play for the 1988 Olympic team, which earned a bronze medal. He was a first-

Jeff Grayer, who played on the bronze medal-winning 1988 Olympic team, is regarded as the best player ever to come through Iowa State.

round NBA draft choice of the Milwaukee Bucks, and has gone on to a solid pro career with the Bucks, Philadelphia 76ers, and Golden State Warriors. When Iowa State fans ponder the question, "Who was the best ever?" the conversation stops at Jeff Grayer.

Twice in the last 11 years Iowa State has gone on a 22-game home court unbeaten streak.

Kansas, Florida-Atlantic, Kansas State, Creighton, Northern Iowa, Iowa, Texas-Arlington, and Charleston Southern. Oddly enough, the Kansas Jayhawks were the unlucky team to start each streak.

Former Iowa coach and current CBS color commentator George Raveling once said of Hilton and its fans, "They made the crowds at Michigan State and Michigan look like Mary Poppins. It was the best road crowd I've observed in 10 years."

CYCLONES QUIZ

18. What was memorable about the Cyclones' 1985 meeting at Hilton with Morgan State?

CHOMPING AT THE BIT Angry over the way the 1986-87 season soured, a determined gang of Cyclones worked to recapture the magic as practice began for the 1987-88 year.

Grayer was a seasoned senior, as was Thompkins. Robinson, stepping into his junior season, was on the verge of claiming a major role. Sophomore Terry Woods looked like the heir apparent to Hornacek at the point, and junior transfer Mike Born could provide some extra perimeter punch.

No one was counting on senior Lafester Rhodes for much, however.

CYCLONE WARNING Teams that got in the way of this determined ISU club early on were simply pushed aside. Texas was pounded, 100-83. Second-ranked Purdue got whipped in its own house, 104-96, as the Cyclones placed third in the preseason NIT. Creighton was ripped, 115-73. Rhodes' 54-point night did in the Hawkeyes, 102-100. After bumping off Kansas, 88-78, and

Lafester Rhodes' instant offense pushed Iowa State over the 100-point mark several times in the 1986-87 season as the Cyclones leaped to a 16-2 start and a No. 10 national ranking.

Nebraska, 114-76, Orr's club had a sparkling 16-2 record and a No. 10 ranking.

Then, inexplicably, the bottom fell out.

Missouri laid a 119-93 whipping on ISU to start a seven-game slide that wasn't stopped until the Cyclones beat the Tigers in Ames, 102-89. A loss to Kansas State dropped once-lofty ISU to just 17-10, and worse, just 3-8 in Big Eight play. Orr circled the wagons and prevailed in the final three league games, two of which came on the road. But a first-round loss to Missouri in Kansas City left the Cyclones with a 20-11 mark.

NCAA DOOR OPENS, BUT TECH SLAMS IT The three-game win streak to end the regular season proved vital, as the Cyclones were just able to reach the NCAA Tournament. ISU was sent to the East Regional, where tough Georgia Tech awaited in the first round at Hartford, Conn.

The Yellowjackets sported future NBA players in Tom Hammonds and Duane Ferrell, and they proved to be more than the Cyclones could handle. Grayer, Thompkins (who would finish his career with 600 assists, second to Hornacek), and Rhodes played their

RHODES SCHOLAR

For three seasons, Lafester Rhodes had a prime seat on the Iowa State bench. He got the mop-up minutes at the end of games and was a practice body for the first team to bang against. Then, for whatever reason, Rhodes became something special.

It was as if a part had been missing in Rhodes' machinery for

After three years on the bench, Lafester Rhodes averaged 22.5 points a game as a senior.

three years and suddenly it was repaired. The guy whose biggest contributions had come as a spectator became a leader during the 1987-88 season. He began driving the lane, slamming the ball home with his left hand. He would square up and drill the three-pointer as if he had done it his entire career. By the end of the year he was one of the nation's best, finishing his super senior season with a 22.5 scoring average. The nation's media told Iowa State fans what they already knew, voting him the country's most improved player.

Never were his out-of-the-blue skills more in evidence than on December 19, 1987, at Hilton. The arch-rival Iowa Hawkeyes were in town, but Rhodes owned the night. He hit from deep. He hit from close in. He hit whatever he wanted on the way to a record 54-point scoring night in a 102-100 Cyclone victory. Rhodes played a big part in ISU's return to the NCAA Tournament, and his accomplishments did not go unnoticed by the Continental Basketball Association's Topeka Sizzlers, which made him the first overall choice of that league's draft in 1988.

Gary Thompkins' career came to an end with a first-round NCAA loss to Georgia Tech, but he finished with 600 assists, second to Jeff Hornacek on the all-time list.

final games for ISU in a 90-78 defeat to close out a season that started in a blaze but ended with a smolder.

1988-89: DANCE CARD IS FULL AGAIN A 7-7 Big Eight Conference record got the 17-11 Cyclones back to the NCAAs again in 1988-89. Three fresh faces held great promise for the future. Center Victor Alexander averaged 19.9 points in the paint and had baby soft hands that aided his shooting touch. Forwards Sam Mack and Mark Baugh also averaged in double figures at 11.8 and 13.3, respectively, and they showed the slash, flash, and dash that could raise the Hilton roof. Woods, now a junior, directed the floor attack, and Born was the gunner's mate from outside.

After a last-second three-pointer by Oklahoma smashed the hearts and hopes of ISU fans in the Big Eight Tournament semifinals, 76-74, Orr got his club

Mark Baugh averaged 13.3 points a game in 1988-89.

ready for Atlanta and the Southeast Regional. The opponent: the UCLA Bruins.

Despite being the lower seed, UCLA led nearly the entire way in an 84-74 victory behind guard Pooh Richardson. The young Cyclones were out of the tournament, but that did nothing to dash ISU hopes for the future, as Born was the only senior to depart.

ALL THE JOY TURNS TO SORROW In the wee hours of March 31, 1989, Orr was jolted from sleep in a Seattle hotel room by a phone call. In Seattle for the Final Four, Orr was rocked by the news that Sam Mack had been shot by Ames police after an apparent robbery attempt at a local Burger King restaurant.

The team had barely been back two weeks from Atlanta, and now Mack was in the hospital with gunshot wounds to the hip and thigh, and was neck-deep in trouble.

According to police, Mack, a freshman who had started 14 games, entered the restaurant with Cyclone football player Levin White. Mack had a knife, White an automatic rifle. Mack, who was charged with first-degree robbery and other charges, said White forced him into the crime.

After a week-long trial and four hours of jury deliberation, Mack was found not guilty. For his own interest and the interests of Orr and ISU, however, Mack left school and transferred to Arizona State. Not long after that, it was disclosed that Baugh was academically ineligible for the next season and had dropped out of school.

Just like that, the foundation for the future of Cyclone basketball had crumbled.

Already reeling from the loss of Sam Mack, the program took another hit when Mark Baugh left school.

THE OUTCOME IS PREDICTABLE Without Mack and Baugh, life became that much harder for Victor Alexander in the paint. Although the big center, nicknamed "Pasta," averaged 21.6 points and 8.8 rebounds over the next two seasons, the Cyclones staggered to 10-18 and 12-19 seasons. The 1990-91 team played the nation's roughest schedule that year, with Syracuse, North Carolina, Minnesota, Iowa, Michigan, Indiana, Temple, and Arizona on the menu in addition to the usual Big Eight opponents.

Point guard Terry Woods guided ISU back to the NCAA tournament in 1988-89.

Victor Alexander averaged 21 points and 9 rebounds a game for two sub-par Cyclone squads in 1989-90 and 1990-91.

Justus Thigpen played the game of his life in the famous "earthquake" game of 1992 against Oklahoma State.

RUNNING AND STUNNING With his team reloaded for the 1991-92 season, Orr turned Fred Hoiberg, Loren Meyer, Justus Thigpen, Hurl Beechum, and Julius Michalik loose. Included in Iowa State's 8-1 start was a 98-84 upset of nationally-ranked Iowa at Hilton Coliseum, a game which is best remembered by ISU fans for freshman Hoiberg jamming the ball over the Hawkeyes' best player, Acie Earl.

"I'm proud of 'em," Orr said. "That was a good win for a young team. Like I told you, down the line, boy, they're gonna be pretty good."

During January the club had a 13-2 mark. A Thigpen put-back with just seconds remaining gave the Cyclones a confidence-building 76-73 win at Minnesota.

And the upsets just kept coming. Michalik took the ball into the lane as time ran down against Oklahoma and stuck a running jumper for a 73-71 win. Thigpen had the game of his life in the second half against Oklahoma State, hitting everything in sight as ISU rallied from an 18-point halftime deficit to win, 84-83, in overtime in the famous "earthquake" game.

I CAN'T HEAR YOU! The Cyclones hit 24 of 30 shots after halftime to come back from a 38-20 deficit against the Cowboys. Thigpen dished to Hoiberg for a bucket and foul to put the Cyclones on top with time running down,

THE CLASS OF CLASSES

With back-to-back losing seasons hanging over Hilton Coliseum and Victor Alexander off to the NBA's Golden State Warriors at the end of the '90-'91 season, Coach Johnny Orr needed an injection of new blood. He had

Fred Hoiberg, the crown jewel of the Class of '91, turned down Arizona and Stanford to play for Orr at ISU.

sweet-shooting junior Justus Thigpen, who had averaged 12 points a game as a sophomore, back in the fold. But Orr knew that his club needed a complete renovation. So he went out and put together the best recruiting class in ISU basketball history.

Orr started in Ames with the signing of favorite son Fred Hoiberg, a prep star oozing with natural ability. He'd led Ames High School to the Class 3A state title his senior season and was named Mr. Basketball in Iowa. Orr persuaded Hoiberg to come to ISU instead of joining Lute Olson at Arizona.

Orr followed that by inking the Ruthven Rumbler, 6-11 center Loren Meyer, a first-team all-stater who was regarded as the third-best center in the nation and the 21st-best player overall. Another Iowan, sharpshooter Hurl Beechum, signed on with the Cyclones.

Then Orr and assistants Jim Hallihan, Ric Wesley, and Steve Krafcisin went to the junior-college ranks to come up with point guard Ron Bayless and small forward Howard Eaton. Wesley helped Orr round out the class with 19-year-old Julius Michalik of Prievidza, Slovakia, who was regarded as one of the best young players in Europe. Michalik chose ISU instead of UCLA because of the Iowa weather, which was more like his native land's.

Meshed with Thigpen, this class of classes would win 41 games over the next two seasons, and 78 games over the next four years. The team would go to three NCAA Tournaments, and two players — Hoiberg and Meyer — would become NBA draft picks and go on to pro careers.

A glimmer of hope returned to Orr's eye after signing day in 1991, when he imported Fred Hoiberg, Loren Meyer, Hurl Beechum, Ron Bayless, Howard Eaton, and Julius Michalik.

driving the decibel level in Hilton to unprecedented heights. After the game, the players said they could feel the floor vibrating from the crowd noise.

"My legs were shaking because the floor was rocking," said Hoiberg.

"If you were there, you got to see the greatest comeback I've ever seen," said Orr, who had been coaching for 42 years. "I've never seen a greater comeback in my career. Down the stretch I've never seen a greater performance than what Justus Thigpen put on. He was absolutely fantastic."

ON TO THE PROMISED LAND The Cyclones returned to the NCAA Tournament with a 20-12 record. Their first foe in the East Regional would be North Carolina-Charlotte and super scorer Henry Williams.

Thanks to Bayless' superb defense on Williams and a late breakaway dunk by Hoiberg, the Cyclones held off UNCC, 76-74, for their first NCAA win since Michigan in 1986. Thigpen scored a game-high 20 to give ISU its 21st victory.

Freshman Loren Meyer goes up for a jumper against North Carolina-Charlotte in the first round of the East Regional in 1991-92. ISU won the game, 76-74.

SECOND ROUND BRINGS 'CATS

Rick Pitino's Kentucky Wildcats were the second-round opponent, a high-flying, high-scoring outfit that loved to race and shoot the three-pointer.

Thigpen, Bayless, and Hoiberg were ready from the outside to match the 'Cats, as they helped the Cyclones blister the nets with 68 percent shooting in the first half. Eight Kentucky three-pointers, however, left ISU in a 57-49 hole.

Thigpen would finish with 32 and Bayless with 30, but Kentucky sophomore Jamal Mashburn was overwhelming: He hit 9 of 14 shots on the way to a 27-point, 9-rebound night. The Cyclones gave the Wildcats all they wanted, but were excused from the tournament, 106-98.

"Me and J had the shots, so we took them," said Bayless, who was 7 of 14 from the field and 15 of 16 from the free throw line. "We wanted an up-and-down-the-court game, but we wanted to contain them a little more on the defensive end."

"It was an exciting game," Orr said. "We couldn't stop them. But we'll be bigger and better next year, and we'll give it another go."

1992-93: START IT UP

With all five starters returning, Orr had high hopes that the '92-'93 season would approach the greatness and magic of the '85-'86 team. Things didn't start off well, however.

A 27-point loss to Iowa in Iowa City made national

Justus Thigpen and Ron Bayless tried to make a game of it against the Bruins, but a vacant inside game doomed the Cyclones in the West Regional game in 1993.

Rugged, intimidating Howard Eaton helped snap the much-ballyhooed Cyclones out of an early-season slump in 1992-93.

news. A blowout loss at Michigan a week later didn't help. But seniors Thigpen, Bayless, and Eaton helped pick the team up from that point and bring the Cyclones another 20-win season, including an 8-6 Big Eight mark, good for a second place tie.

But the second-seeded Cyclones were upset in the Big Eight Tournament semifinals by Missouri and unheard-of center Chris Heller.

Worse, ISU was bounced from the West Regional of the NCAA Tournament by a pumped-up UCLA team, 81-70. Ed O'Bannon led the way for the Bruins. It was a somber end to the careers of Thigpen, Bayless, and Eaton, who sobbed in the locker room for nearly a half an hour after the game at the McKale Center in Tucson, Ariz.

"It's over. It's over," Orr repeated to himself in the post-game press conference as he sat stunned by the loss. "We could never get the loose balls or the rebounds."

A BRUSH WITH DEATH, A BRUSH WITH MEDIOCRITY The 1993-94 Cyclones got off to a 9-3 start behind Hoiberg, Michalik, and Meyer. But in the early morning hours of January 17, 1994, Meyer was nearly killed in a car-train accident in Des Moines. He sustained a broken collarbone and other injuries and was lost for the season. Without him in the middle, ISU was done for the season, finishing just a game over .500 at 14-13, and 4-10 in conference play. As the season ended with a first-round loss to Oklahoma State in the conference tournament, Orr began to openly ponder retirement.

ORR RESIGNS The day of decision came April 14, 1994. Orr called a news conference at Hilton Coliseum for that afternoon, inviting everyone to attend.

The stage for his announcement was grandiose, and appropriate. Singer Barry Manilow had given a concert days earlier, and the large platform and ceiling-length curtain provided a big-time backdrop. At 2 p.m., it was time for the coach to take center stage.

With his players at his side, Orr read from a prepared statement. "Having fulfilled my contract as basketball coach for 14 years to the best of my ability ... it is my decision to resign this responsibility as of May 1, 1994.

"This decision has been extremely difficult, but it is in my estimation the only professional action available to benefit the long-range reputation of our basketball program."

Orr continued, often pausing to control his emotions, which were getting the best of him.

"To all you wonderful fans and friends who wrote encouraging letters, I thank you very much," he said as his voice wavered and his eyes grew moist. "And I thank

19. Who holds the Iowa State record for free throw percentage in a season, having made 87 of 99?

my team and my staff, who gave their very best. Please remember, I'll never stop cheering. Go Cyclones."

And with that, a 14-year love affair was over.

REFLECTIONS Later, under the Hilton stands, Orr looked back on what he'd been able to accomplish at ISU.

"Everybody knows about Iowa State now in basketball," he said. "We made basketball the biggest thing at Iowa State. I'm disappointed I never won the Big Eight, but when I came here they'd never been to the NCAAs in 44 years. We've been there six times. Now we play in all the major tournaments. We get invited everywhere."

Orr stepped down as the winningest coach in ISU history at 218-200. He led Iowa State to five 20-win seasons and more than doubled attendance at Hilton Coliseum for men's basketball.

Orr would eventually decide to summer in Ames and winter at his home in Georgia. But he said his heart will forever be linked with the state of Iowa.

"I'm not going away," he said. "I'm going to live here in Iowa. I'm going to stay here until I die. You'll get a chance to come to my funeral."

STAR SEARCH BEGINS Possible replacements for Orr began surfacing almost immediately. Jim Hallihan, Orr's longtime assistant; Saint Louis coach Charlie Spoonhour; Wisconsin's Stu Jackson; George Washington's Mike Jarvis; Tulsa's Tubby Smith; and Utah's Rick Majerus were all mentioned. Even Purdue's Gene Keady reportedly was approached. After Jackson, Spoonhour, and Majerus had said thanks but no thanks, another name came to the fore.

20. Who is the all-time Cyclone leader in fouling out, with 28 games under his belt?

No matter how high Cyclone basketball soars, fans know it was Johnny Orr who started it all.

Up From The Bayou

New Orleans coach Tim Floyd had a record of 126-59 in six seasons with the Privateers, and a 62-22 Sun Belt Conference mark. During eight years of coaching, Floyd had a ledger of 161-84, and a league mark of 78-36. He'd never had a losing record and his low-water mark for wins in a season was 16. A former assistant to UTEP legend Don Haskins, Floyd had a penchant for pressure man-to-man defense and possession-conscious offense. He was an Iba man, to be sure, and Athletic Director Gene Smith felt Floyd was the right fit for ISU.

Initially, Floyd rejected ISU's offer, saying that he "liked bass fishing more than ice fishing." But after a passionate plea from former Cyclone great Gary Thompson to reconsider, Floyd did just that — and packed his bags for Ames.

After reconsidering the Iowa State job, Tim Floyd met the media and told Iowa State fans he was thrilled to be their new coach.

ANOTHER NEWS CONFERENCE Three weeks after the coaching search began, it was over, and again there was a news conference at Hilton. This one carried a much happier message, however.

"Iowa State University fits everything that I set out to do as a coach and what our family has set out to do long-term," Floyd said to the media. "I am thrilled to be here."

DEE-FENSE ISU's new coach talked freely about his desire to improve the Cyclones defensively.

"If you look at the NFL, the old Bears and Giants teams had the great defense," he said. "In Major League Baseball you've got to have the great pitching and be great up the middle and in center field. It's no different in college basketball. Our teams will be very, very competitive on the defensive end.

"I've always felt like championships are won with great man-to-man defense. That doesn't mean you can't play some zone now and then, but it really is a four-letter word with me."

TIPPING THINGS OFF As practice began for the 1994-95 season, the attitude of ISU fans turned from wistful reflection on Orr's loss to unbridled enthusiasm. Three 20-point scorers (Hoiberg, Michalik, Meyer) returned — the first time in NCAA history that had happened. All five starters — all of them seniors — were back. The talented Cyclones were drawing high praise from the nation's media.

College Preview magazine picked ISU as Big Eight champs and No. 14 in the country, as did Lindy's. No one picked the Cyclones lower than 4th in the league. Before he coached his first game in Ames, Floyd was picked as Big Eight Coach of the Year by *Athlon's* and *College Basketball Scene*. The expectations were enormous, and early on Floyd and his club handled the strain well.

FIRST WINS COME IN HAWAII Floyd got his first win as a Cyclone in an 88-71 victory over Illinois State in the first round of the Big Island Invitational in Hilo, Hawaii. After beating Virginia Commonwealth to advance to the title game, a controversial last-second basket and foul by Purdue's Cuonzo Martin handed Floyd his first Cyclone loss, 88-87. But better things were still to come.

IOWA CITY ISU entered Carver-Hawkeye Arena with a 5-1 record. But Iowa had lost at home only five times to non-Big Ten foes since the building opened in 1982, and the Cyclones had been pasted there just two years earlier, 78-51. None of that would matter this time.

Julius Michalik ignited the Cyclones with 20 points, and the other three seniors from the Class of '91 also came up big in a 76-63 win at Carver-Hawkeye Arena.

Hoiberg, held to a career-low 1 point two years before, hit for 15 this time. Michalik added a game-high 20. Hurl Beechum went a perfect 4 of 4 from the field and 5 of 5

THE MAYOR

He was a town legend before he ever set foot on campus at Iowa State.

Fred Hoiberg was Mr. Everything at Ames High School — star quarterback, star basketball player, pitcher on the baseball team. He had All-American boy good looks.

If he was Ames' favorite son, it was because everyone in town wanted a son like him, someone who was unfailingly gracious and unflinchingly competitive, a dependable teammate and an unmatchable ambassador for his school and community.

Toss in the fact that he went on to rival Jeff Grayer as the greatest all-around player in Cyclone history and you can see why it wasn't hard for the locals to start referring to him as "The Mayor."

Hoiberg, a four-year starter, is the only player in ISU history to record at least 1,400 points, 600 rebounds, 300 assists, and 175 steals. He was the first Cyclone to rank among the top 10 in 10 different statistical categories. Today he ranks in the top five in six all-time charts and the top three in five others.

A third-team All-America selection following the 1994-95 season, Hoiberg finished his ISU career with 1,993 points, placing him third all-time. His senior season was loaded with accolades: He was the leading scorer for a Cyclone squad that won a school-record 23 games and was in the AP Top 25 for 11 straight weeks.

He was a unanimous all-Big Eight selection and was named Co-Big Eight Male Athlete of the Year, and was picked the Star of Stars at the NABC All-Star game in Seattle the weekend of the Final Four.

Everywhere he went in Ames he was immediately recognized — even hounded — by well-wishers, autograph-seekers, and general hangers-on.

What separated The Mayor from politicians, and too many athletes, was that he always sported a smile and a wave, and never turned away from a conversation or a child with a pen and paper in hand.

"The Mayor" did it all in his four years at Iowa State, and he did it with a smile and handshake for everyone.

from the line for 16 points, and Meyer enjoyed a huge night with 14 points, 13 rebounds, and five blocked shots as ISU ruled the Hawkeyes' roost, 76-63. It was the third undisputed state title in four years for the Cyclones, and winning in Iowa City made it all the sweeter.

A reporter approached Hoiberg at his locker after the game and said, "You've been quoted as saying you hate the Hawkeyes." Hoiberg replied, "I was quoted as saying that? I don't remember saying that." Then he grinned. "At least, not to the media."

BIGGER AND BETTER WINS Iowa State stayed hot over Christmas break. A loss at Colorado to open the Big Eight season was the only setback as the Cyclones moved out to a 12-2 mark and awaited No. 3 Kansas at Hilton.

HIS FINEST HOUR By his own admission, Hoiberg had his finest game against the Jayhawks, scoring 32 points, six three-pointers, grabbing 9 rebounds, and not turning the

It became obvious against the third-rated Jayhawks that Fred Hoiberg's will to win was greater than Kansas'.

CYCLONES QUIZ

21. What NBA legend once scored 45 points in a single game against Iowa State in 1967?

ball over a single time. But it was the manner in which he worked his magic that resulted in a 69-65 upset for ISU.

Kansas led 56-50 with 10:18 remaining. Hoiberg hit a layup, two free throws, and a three-pointer at the 8:48 mark to make it a one point KU lead, 58-57. Then came two more charity shots to put ISU up by one. The ebb and flow of the game continued with the Jayhawks hitting six in a row to lead 65-59 with only 3:48 remaining.

But the Mayor had one more run left in him.

Two more free throws made it 65-51. Then came a rainbow three-pointer from the left side at the 2:09 mark to make it a one-point affair. Finally, after a superb pick from Michalik, Hoiberg freed himself for one more trifecta, this one from the right side with 1:11 left, to put ISU up by two and finish the Jayhawks. Seventeen points in a row, all by Hoiberg, all against the No. 3 team in the nation.

"I've never been around a guy like him," said Floyd. "I feel fortunate to have inherited him."

His will to win was simply stronger. And ISU would gain more confidence and momentum from the victory.

SWEET SEVENTEEN An 87-79 home win over Kansas State put ISU's overall mark at a sparkling 17-2. The Cyclones were the nation's 11th-ranked team. Things couldn't have been going any better for the senior-laden team and its new coach.

But a 79-71 home loss to Missouri snapped the utopian feeling. Then came successive losses on the road to Oklahoma, Kansas, and Missouri, dropping the team to 17-6, and more importantly, just 3-5 in league play.

HOME STAND HELPS Overtime was needed to dispatch Nebraska at Hilton, 72-69, as Hoiberg again stood tall in the final moments and finished with 20 points. Two losses to Oklahoma State were sandwiched around a 40-point pummeling of Colorado. But then came an agonizing 71-68 loss at home to Oklahoma on Senior Night. With one conference game left, ISU was 5-8 in the Big Eight. To reach the NCAA Tournament without winning the Big Eight Tournament, the Cyclones had to win the regular season finale at Nebraska or the dream season would slip away.

JULO COMES UP BIG One might have said that the Cyclones simply postponed Senior Night until the Nebraska game at the Devaney Center. It certainly seemed like it.

Meyer had his best game as a Cyclone with 31 points and 15 rebounds. Hoiberg hit for 26, including 12 straight at one point. And with 4.4 seconds left and the game tied at 77-77, Michalik stroked a baseline jumper

CYCLONES QUIZ

22. What is Iowa State's single-largest margin of victory in games played at Hilton Coliseum?

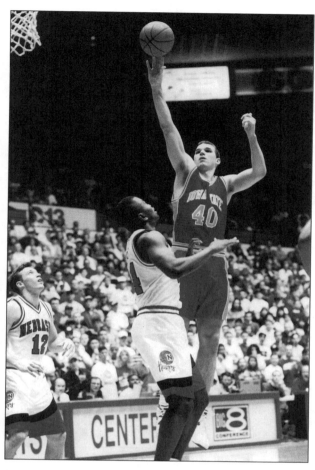

With ISU's back firmly against the wall, Loren Meyer began an assault on opponents that would eventually make him a millionaire with a 31-point, 15-rebound outing in a 79-77 win at Nebraska.

for the game-winner.

"That should put us in the NCAA Tournament." said Floyd after the game. "But we're not going to fall back now. We're going to take this win down to Kansas City and see how far we can go there."

They would go a long way.

FIFTH SEED The fourth-seeded and 17th-ranked Missouri Tigers were ISU's opening foe in the Big Eight Tournament, and the game was one for the statistical oddities file. The Cyclones saw Hoiberg shoot 1 for 16 from the field, shoot 18 percent in the first half, and score just 15 points. Floyd was ejected. The final score? ISU 68, Missouri 50. Go figure.

Meyer led the way with another monster line of 25 points and 15 boards, while Beechum added 15 with 5 three-pointers.

*Beechum hurled in
five three-pointers in
a first-round win
over Missouri.*

For the semifinal meeting with ISU, the top-seeded
Kansas Jayhawks had just as many fans, if not more,
packed into Kemper Arena. They had more talented
players, more size, more everything.

But the Cyclones had Meyer and Beechum, and with a
sprinkling of help from the bench, ISU had an 80-72
overtime win and a trip to Sunday's championship game.

Meyer ruled inside once more with 20 points and 12
rebounds. NBA scouting director Marty Blake was on
hand for the tournament and said that the 6-11 senior
had changed his entire future over the course of the
weekend (he would end up being drafted in the first
round of the NBA draft by the Dallas Mavericks).
Beechum led the team with 25 and drilled six more
threes to give him 11 in two days, a tourney record. The
Cyclones were better from the field, from three-point
land, from the free throw line and held a commanding
42-29 edge on the glass against a Jayhawk front line of

Loren Meyer,
Derrick Hayes, and
Hurl Beechum
whoop it up after
upsetting top-seeded
Kansas in the
semifinals of the
1995 Big Eight
Tournament.

Greg Ostertag, Raef LaFrentz, and Scot Pollard.

"Today was about yesterday," Floyd said, harkening back to the Missouri win. "I've never been prouder of my team, and I mean that."

The win cemented an NCAA Tournament bid for ISU. Now it was only a matter of how high it would be seeded.

THE BEST OF TIMES Having the fan favorite out of the running meant that the tournament ticket prices had bottomed out on the street. So several thousand Iowans packed up after the win over Kansas and drove to K.C. in search of ducats for the title tilt against Oklahoma State. When tip-off arrived, it was safe to say that 75 percent of the Kemper crowd was cardinal and golden.

But the Cowboys, led by tourney MVP Bryant Reeves, were too strong for the upstart Cyclones. OSU won the championship game 62-53 thanks to the great inside-outside combination of Reeves (21 points) and Randy Rutherford (17). Meyer held his own with 9 points and a game-high 13 rebounds, and Beechum hit three more threes to finish the weekend with 14, but the eventual Final Four participants snuffed out every run that ISU made. The Cyclones, now 22-10, would await the NCAA selection show to find out where they were headed and who they would play.

SEVENTH IN THE SOUTHEAST Tallahassee, Fla., was the site for seventh-seeded ISU in the Southeast Regional, where it would face No. 10 seed Florida. Cyclone fans were not

23. What ranks as
ISU's all-time worst
road loss?

pleased. Their team had won 22 games, taken two of three from Kansas, and been 'rewarded' with a seven seed — in the home state of the opponent!

The home cooking seemed to be the perfect elixir for Florida, a Final Four team the year before but a disappointment in 1994. The Gators led 56-48 with 6:40 to go. But Michalik loaded the Cyclones on his back, scoring 12 of ISU's final 16 to rally the team for a 64-61 win.

"Julo, where the hell have you been?" Hoiberg jokingly asked to his teammate after Michalik snapped out of an offensive slump with a game-high 17. Jacy Holloway hit a pair of crucial free throws with 17 seconds left for the final margin. The Cyclones shot a blistering 55 percent in the second half to post their school-record 23rd victory of the season.

"That's going to be something to be remembered by," said Hoiberg. "We've had a great four years. Even though we haven't won a championship, there's still going to be a lot to remember about the senior class."

Second-seeded North Carolina was next in line, a

Jacy Holloway, the 10th option to score on his talent-laden team, hit two critical free throws to make alligator boots out of the Florida Gators.

Loren Meyer had All-American Rasheed Wallace right where he wanted him, and the Cyclones had an early 23-9 lead over the vaunted Tar Heels.

daunting task indeed.

"We're going in against an unbelievable program, and we know we'll be the underdogs," said Hoiberg as he pondered what might be his last game at ISU. "We'll just go out, have some fun, and see what happens."

CAROLINA IS BLUE EARLY With 6:22 to go in the first half, Iowa State held a commanding 23-9 lead over Dean Smith's Tar Heels. All-American Rasheed Wallace had been shut out. So had guard Jeff McInnis. Cyclone fans were letting themselves feel a little bit giddy over the possibility of an upset and a trip to the Sweet 16.

After the season, Fred Hoiberg became a second-round draft pick of the Indiana Pacers, where he edged out Indiana homeboy Damon Bailey for the final roster spot. Loren Meyer would see plenty of action with the Dallas Mavericks in his rookie season. Julius Michalik signed a contract to play professionally in Europe.

ISU IS BLUE LATE But the Tar Heels went on a 14-0 run to tie the game at 23, and finished the half with a 27-25 lead. The Cyclones were shaken and never recovered as the 'Heels ran away to a 73-52 victory that closed the book on the careers of Hoiberg, Meyer, Michalik, Beechum, James Hamilton, and Saun Jackson. Meyer had 15 points in his final game, Hoiberg 12, Beechum 11, and Michalik 9. Jerry Stackhouse and Donald Williams each notched 15 for Carolina.

"I think I speak for all the seniors when I say that this has been the greatest four or five years of our lives," said Hoiberg as he sat in a somber locker room. "There are too many good things to look back on than to sit around and think about this loss for the rest of our lives."

North Carolina guard Dante Calabria was taken with ISU and its new coach.

"ISU has a well thought-out offense," he said. "I think Tim Floyd is a tremendous coach, and I think Iowa State's program is great for the future."

1995-96: "CINDERELLA" FINALLY GETS A SEQUEL

Coming off the best season in school history and with the Cyclone pantry nearly empty due to graduation and transfers, Iowa State fans lowered their expectations for the 1995-96 season. Folks joked that there would be so many new faces on the team that ticket buyers should be given a free media guide to match the names with the mugs. A few hundred folks failed to renew their season tickets. Every preseason magazine picked the Cyclones for the same spot in the Big Eight: eighth.

DID HE KNOW SOMETHING? Floyd held the team's media day in early October, and he seemed to dismiss, or at least fail to acknowledge, his club's supposed mediocrity.

"I'm not looking at this as an Armageddon year for Iowa State basketball," he said. "Realistically, this could be the most challenging year of my career. But I do think we have some ability.

"All the preseason magazines are on the shelf now. I've read four or five of them and all of them have us picked dead last. Those guys are right about one of every 10 times. Hopefully they're not right this year."

Floyd concluded by saying: "I'm not going to tell you how many games we're going to win or how we'll finish in the Big Eight. I do know we're going to put five competitors on the floor night in and night out. How many baskets are in them? I don't know yet, but I think it would be a huge mistake for us to look at this year and say that we're just going to write it off."

QUIZ

24. Name the Cyclones who have worn No. 40 in honor of the late Chris Street of Iowa.

Tim Floyd was hopeful that preseason predictions of a last-place finish would be tossed out the window.

THE LINEUP How would Floyd, who had won 67 percent of his games and never endured a losing season in his nine-year career, come up with a winner with nine new players on the roster? The deck of cards he had to shuffle was full of wild cards:

■ Shawn Bankhead, a 6-6 junior forward from the College of Southern Idaho.

■ Kenny Pratt, a 6-4 forward from Eastern Utah.

■ Dedric Willoughby, a 6-3 guard who had played for Floyd at New Orleans and had spent the previous year at Indian Hills Community College getting his academics in line.

■ Kelvin Cato, a 6-11 junior center transfer from South Alabama who would be eligible for the second semester.

■ Carlo Walton, a 6-0 junior point guard from Seward County (Kans.) Community College.

■ Shelby Walton, a 5-9 junior guard from Seward and Carlo's brother.

■ Tony Rampton, a 6-11 freshman center from Waseca, Minn.

■ Tyler Peterson, a 6-11 freshman center from Washington, Iowa.

■ Jason Justus, a 6-8 junior forward from Mineral Area (Mo.) Community College.

Only junior point guard Jacy Holloway and junior swingman Joe Modderman returned with ISU experience. Redshirt freshman Klay Edwards and reserves Sol Harris and Ha-Keem Abdel-Khaliq rounded out an extremely green roster. Ninety-five percent of the scoring was gone from the previous year's 23-11 team, along with 94 percent of the rebounding.

The team got a double-dose of bad news before the team had even played an exhibition. Pratt was arrested and dismissed from the team, and Modderman was sidelined indefinitely with a stress fracture in his foot.

OPENING ACT DRAWS RAVES A crowd of 9,623 turned out to get its first look at the new-look Cyclones against the Republic of Georgia select team at Hilton Coliseum. The fans' apprehension was tamed a bit, as ISU romped to a 93-49 exhibition victory. Willoughby scored 33 points, and Bankhead chipped in with 14 and eight rebounds. Willoughby, who hit 9 of 17 shots and all 12 of his charity shots, was asked after the scrimmage if he was

BLIND MICE

Coach Tim Floyd proved to be right. The reporters who regularly cover the Big Eight Conference managed to get just about everything wrong.

As always, the sportswriters were asked to predict the order of finish in the league race. Kansas received 72 of 74 first-place votes from the reporters, but that was easy. Picking two through eight was a stickier chore.

Missouri got the other two first-place votes (it finished 6th in the conference). Oklahoma was third (it finished 3rd), then came Nebraska in fourth (finished 7th, a half-game out of last). The pundits then saw Oklahoma State in 5th (OSU wound up 5th), then they chose Colorado in 6th (it finished 8th), followed by Kansas State in 7th (it placed 4th), and in last place, Iowa State (which finished in 2nd place and won the Big Eight Tournament championship).

How Big Eight media saw it	How it actually went
1. Kansas	1. Kansas
2. Missouri	2. Iowa State
3. Oklahoma	3. Oklahoma
4. Nebraska	4. Kansas State
5. Oklahoma State	5. Oklahoma State
6. Colorado	6. Missouri
7. Kansas State	7. Nebraska
8. Iowa State	8. Colorado

Shawn Bankhead pumped in 14 points in his debut as the Cyclones opened the season with an exhibition win before a sparse Hilton crowd.

the heir apparent to the departed Hoiberg.

"That's some big shoes to fill," he said. "I don't know if I want to fill Hoiberg's shoes. Maybe a part of them. There's only one Mayor. I'm from New Orleans, and I'll stay from New Orleans."

VINDICATION FOR PRATT The charges against Pratt proved to be groundless, and the junior was reinstated. Pratt's attorney, Jerry Crawford, said the investigation by campus police that resulted in the original charge "was the worst I have seen in my 22 years as a lawyer. It was incompetent and incomplete."

CHAMPIONS ISU routed Central Connecticut State by 25 points to start the real season, then dispatched Wisconsin-Milwaukee 62-53. Still, not much was thought of the team's 2-0 start due to the level of its

Shawn Bankhead grabbed the basketball and ISU grabbed a tournament title with an 82-64 win over Richmond.

competition. Then came the Cyclone Challenge.

Tennessee State, ISU's first-round opponent, led by eight points in the second half before the home team rallied for a 75-67 triumph.

In the title contest the Cyclones met Richmond, which only a week earlier had pressed mighty North Carolina to the limit at Chapel Hill before losing by a single basket. But with Willoughby scorching the nets from outside and Pratt netting 15 inside, ISU ran away from the Spiders 82-64 to take the title.

Willoughby was named to the all-tournament team and was voted the weekend's Most Valuable Player. "I enjoy it, but it's a team effort. It feels great to be 4-0. Nobody expects us to win any ball games. But listen to this locker room," he said as his teammates whooped it up. "There's a lot of spirit in here."

PRATT PROVES HIS WORTH The Cyclones next took their 4-0 act to Drake's Knapp Center in Des Moines to take on the Bulldogs. The home team played with fire, and the game was deadlocked at 62-62 with time running out. As both the shot clock and game clock wound down, Pratt let fly with a desperation three-point try. Swish. A last-second try by the Bulldogs clanged off the iron, and ISU was suddenly 5-0. Still, no one outside of Ames was giving the cardinal and gold much credit for its early accomplishments.

BETTER THAN EXPECTED? An upset of No. 12 Iowa would turn heads for certain. Tom Davis' talented club had the edge at every position, but from the opening tip the Hawks had their hands full at Hilton in the lowest scoring ISU-Iowa game in 50 years.

A 19-14 halftime lead for the visitors wound up being only a 56-50 victory. The Cyclones could have won the game had they shot the ball more effectively. From the field ISU shot just 35 percent, while hitting a depressing 13 of 23 from the free throw line. Still, the Hawks had to use all the tools in the toolbox to fend off the upstart Cyclones, who had a chance to take the lead with less

Rugged Iowa State defense left Chris Kingsbury without a three-point field goal.

Kenny Pratt's 18 points and 11 rebounds against the Hawks gave Cyclone fans reason to be optimistic for the rest of the season.

When Kelvin Cato arrived as a player, with 18 rebounds in his first game, ISU began to arrive as a team.

than two minutes left but failed on a pair of free throws. Pratt had 18 points and 11 rebounds to lead the way for ISU, and in defeat Floyd saw a silver lining.

"I've got a different belief system in this basketball team," he told the media. "Maybe we're going to be a little better than what people think. At least I want my guys believing that this time of year."

PRAISING PRATT After the win at Drake and the close loss to Iowa, it had become obvious: Kenny Pratt was a player, and his head-faking, tail-bumping, body-contorting schoolyard style of drawing fouls and getting to the line was making the Cyclones better.

"He's doing more and more for us every game," said Floyd. "He's a winner. He had the courage to step up and take a three (at Drake) when he knows ·that's not necessarily his role with our team late in the shot clock. He's got great courage. I like to have him in there late."

THE BALL KEEPS ROLLING Kelvin Cato became eligible just before the next contest, against Wyoming in Laramie, and the 6-11, 245-pound shot swatter came up huge in his first game, recording 18 rebounds in a big 70-66 double overtime win to move ISU to 6-1. Pratt added several twisting, double-pumping hoops, including five straight points in the second overtime, to keep the Cyclones on the upswing.

Three more wins followed — a 76-63 win over Missouri-St. Louis, a 50-47 thriller over Pete Carril's Princeton Tigers, and a 71-57 conquest of Samford, which gave the team the ISU Holiday Classic championship. Willoughby was again named tourney MVP.

DEFYING THE ODDS Legendary basketball writer George Vescey once covered a Princeton game when he saw the Tigers leap in front of their opponent by eight. At that point Vescey got up and prepared to leave. "Where are you going?" a fellow sportswriter asked. "Don't you know anything?" Vescey retorted. "When Pete Carril gets up by eight, the game's over." Princeton attained that magic eight-point lead against the Cyclones, only to see Willoughby and company rally late in the game for the victory against the deliberate Tigers.

Two Willoughby free throws tied the game at 47-47, then a free throw from Carlo Walton and two more points from Pratt put the Cyclones up by three. Princeton went scoreless the final 4:48 of the game.

Kelvin Cato's relentless pursuit of the rebound helped the Cyclones overcome nearly insurmountable odds and beat NCAA Tournament qualifier Princeton.

Chapter 7: Up From The Bayou **123**

OUT OF BOUNDS Floyd packed up his 8-1 Cyclones and flew them to Puerto Rico for the Puerto Rico Invitational to face two-time Big Ten champion Purdue and Conference USA member North Carolina-Charlotte. The get-together with the Boilermakers, which took place three days after Christmas, didn't provide ISU with much holiday cheer.

Four Purdue players scored in double figures as the Cyclones were routed, 79-60. Despite the inside presence of the newly-arrived Cato, ISU was outboarded 47-29.

Floyd got his players to refocus quickly, however, as the Cyclones topped UNCC the next day, 69-61. Willoughby hit six straight free throws over the final 4:30 to ice the verdict.

On January 2, the Cyclones pounded Coppin State 77-59 for win No. 11. Jason Justus had 13 points in his first extended action for ISU.

WERE THEY RIGHT AFTER ALL? The glitter of the 11-2 record lost a lot of its luster in the Big Eight season opener at Kansas State. The contest was televised nationally on ESPN, and the Cyclones played badly. ISU shot just 27 percent, and just 20 percent in the second half, to lose, 72-55. The Cyclones missed 14 of their first 19 shots in the first half, and 16 of their first 17 in the second half. Willoughby scored 19, and Cato had 13 rebounds. But the Wildcats and Cyclones looked very much like the predicted seventh- and eighth-place finishers in the league.

LAST-SECOND HEARTBURN Marquette hosted ISU in the final non-conference game of the year for the Cyclones, and both eventual NCAA Tournament entries battled like heavyweights for the full 15 rounds. Marquette's Aaron Hutchins hit a 15-foot jumper to give the formerly-named Warriors a 58-56 lead. After a time-out, ISU wanted to get the ball inside and did so, getting off three shots from close range in the final eight seconds. None of the three found net, however, leaving ISU with a gut-wrenching loss. It was the first time during the season that ISU had lost successive games. Pratt scored 27 points to lead the Cyclones.

With a two-game losing streak behind them and Oklahoma State, a participant in the previous year's Final Four, on the horizon, Cyclone fans were about to find out whether Iowa State was really a better team than anyone had imagined, or whether its 11-4 record was a combination of luck, smoke, and mirrors.

ANSWERING THE QUESTION With 23 points from Willoughby and 21 from Pratt, the Cyclones held off

QUIZ

25. Who was the last person to wear No. 15 for the ISU basketball team?

Klay Edwards boxed out, and the Cyclones were able to rope the Cowboys in the conference season-opener.

Eddie Sutton's team, 79-71, before 13,707 at Hilton. It was ISU's first conference win and the first notable victory of the season.

ISU led 39-30 at halftime and 44-33 with 16 minutes to go, but OSU countered with the inside game of Jerome Lambert (22 points) to rally for a 52-50 lead.

With the game tied at 54, Floyd called for a rarity on

MONUMENTAL IOWA STATE VICTORIES

First victory: Iowa State 36, Drake 17, February 29, 1908
Victory No. 50: Iowa State 18, Grinnell 8, February 6, 1917
Victory No. 100: Iowa State 24, Oklahoma 19, February 12, 1923
Victory No. 200: Iowa State 38, Missouri 35, February 5, 1938
Victory No. 300: Iowa State 39, Colorado 38, January 31, 1948
Victory No. 400: Iowa State 66, Minnesota 57, December 5, 1957
Victory No. 500: Iowa State 102, Augustana 76, December 11, 1965
Victory No. 600: Iowa State 61, Kansas State 55, December 28, 1973
Victory No. 700: Iowa State 81, Texas 57, December 3, 1983
Victory No. 800: Iowa State 88, Nebraska 76, January 31, 1989
Victory No. 900: Iowa State 87, Kansas State 79, January 28, 1995

defense — a zone. The Cyclones promptly went on a 12-0 run to salt the game away. Cato added 15 points and Bankhead 11 to the cause.

Iowa State converted 26 of 33 free throw shots, while limiting Oklahoma State to just 7 of 10.

SHARP-DRESSED MAN Point guard Carlo Walton sat out the Oklahoma State game in his street clothes. After ISU's victory it was announced that Walton had failed to make his grades and would be academically ineligible. Guards Willoughby and Holloway would soon see their time on the bench dwindle down to next to nothing.

THE NATION LOOKS IN Missouri entered Hilton with a five-game win streak. The Sunday game was broadcast on a nationwide basis by CBS, which sent analyst Bill Raftery along for the trip. CBS was on hand to capture Norm Stewart's mature group of Tigers, not Floyd's young overachievers. But it was Floyd's gang that stole the spotlight.

Stewart, who roamed the Hilton floor and played to the CBS cameras like a politician, had his perfect day ruined in a 73-62 loss to the defensive-minded Cyclones, who held his team to a season-low in points and held his big gun, guard Jason Sutherland, to four points. The

When ISU and Missouri met, it was a sure bet that Jacy Holloway would shackle Tiger guard Jason Sutherland.

Tigers turned the ball over on their first four possessions en route to falling behind by nine points at halftime.

HE KNOWS OF WHAT HE SPEAKS At halftime, CBS returned viewers to its New York studio, where Massachusetts Coach John Calipari was sitting in with sportscaster Pat O'Brien. O'Brien asked the former Kansas assistant what he thought of the halftime score, and the fact that Missouri had been seen as a heavy favorite.

"It doesn't matter," Calipari said. "That's at Hilton Coliseum. That's the toughest place that I've ever been to as a coach. I was at the University of Kansas with Larry Brown, and we never won there. It's a tough place to play."

APPLYING THE FINISHING COAT Willoughby scored 27, including five three-point goals. ISU made nine treys in the contest, and a late scoring flurry by the Tigers made the final closer than the game actually was.

"We've got two more victories than anybody said we'd get in the conference," said Willoughby. "You can't just rate us eighth. You haven't seen us play before."

Stewart, for the record, had seen enough.

"It was a terrible game," he said. "They face-guarded us and we didn't respond. We would get a good shot and miss it, then come down and lose a guy and they would hit a three-pointer. There isn't much to say."

JUST KEEP RAISING THE BAR, FELLAS After the Missouri win, Iowa State could no longer be ignored. They had already won more games (13) than the experts thought they would win all season. Still, the bubble had to burst sometime.

Perhaps, the skeptics said, it would happen at Colorado. After all, the Buffs had wiped out the Cyclones the year before in Boulder.

But Bankhead ripped the Buffaloes for a career-high 23 in a 75-63 victory to put ISU a full 10 games over .500 at 14-4. It was the Cyclones' third straight Big Eight win.

BY THE NUMBERS Oklahoma had to battle a blizzard to reach Hilton for a crucial showdown with Iowa State. No less than 14 inches of snow had fallen overnight. When the Sooners arrived, however, they had to stare right into the teeth of an even more dangerous winter storm — a Cyclone, to be exact. And they weren't properly prepared.

Cato's rebound slam with 37 seconds remaining proved to be the winning points in a 67-61 ISU win that put the cardinal and gold at 4-1 in Big Eight play. It marked the first time in 19 seasons that the Cyclones had gotten off to such an auspicious league start.

26. Against what team did Iowa State play the only five-overtime game in school history?

27. What ISU coach finished with a winning percentage of just .245?

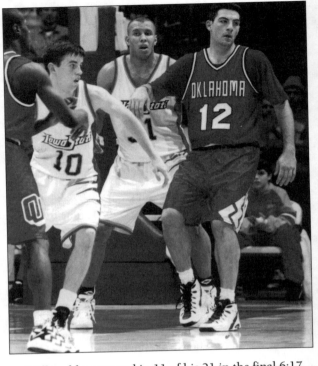

Willoughby pumped in 11 of his 21 in the final 6:17 of the game and earned Big Eight Player of the Week honors for the second time. Bankhead muffled Oklahoma All-American Ryan Minor all game long and limited him to 16 points, five fewer than his league-leading average.

Joe Modderman made his first significant strides in coming back from his stress fracture, hitting all three of his three-point attempts and finishing with 10 points in just 17 minutes.

SAME SONG, NEXT VERSE A trip to Nebraska was next on the agenda, and the seemingly unstoppable Cyclones rolled to a 75-65 win at the Devaney Center to move to 16-4 and 5-1 in Big Eight play. ISU spurted out to a 12-0 lead and never allowed the Huskers to get closer than three points. Pratt and Willoughby scored 23 and 20, respectively, as Nebraska played without guard Jaron Boone, who had been suspended by Husker Coach Danny Nee.

THE NATION FINALLY TAKES NOTICE The media could ignore Floyd's miracle no longer. The road win over the Huskers propelled the Cyclones into The Associated Press poll, at the 21st spot. Next up for ISU would be a fellow member of the Top 25, Kansas. At stake would be first place in the conference.

And while it was fun for a half, the third-rated Jayhawks used the magic of Allen Fieldhouse and the talent on their deep roster to go on a 15-0 second-half run and pull away for an 89-70 victory. Willoughby scored 24 to lead ISU, which had trailed only 40-36 after 20 minutes.

BIG RED SATURDAY, AGAIN One week after playing Nebraska in Lincoln, the Huskers showed up at Hilton for a rematch. Boone was back in uniform, the Big Red needed a win, and the Cyclones needed to show everyone they could bounce back.

After going six minutes without a field goal and missing its first 11 shots, ISU simply pulled together as a team and rolled away to a 74-59 win. The Huskers, conversely, were suffering a mid-season meltdown.

"There was a lot of bickering among them," said

Kenny Pratt said the Cyclones were winning because of togetherness.

Willoughby, who scored a career-high 29 points. "They have a couple of problems with some of their players, and that's probably why they played the way they did. We played together, and I think that's why we got the win."

Pratt, on the other hand, said everything about the Cyclones' 17-5 record was the result of the players' affection for each other and the bonding that had occurred as a result of it.

"We love each other," he said. "I think we're the closest team in the nation right now. We couldn't have done what we've done this year without that closeness. Never. You see teams in this conference and across the nation that don't have any closeness, and they're not winning."

WHAT WAS THAT, COACH? As Floyd addressed the media after the Nebraska win, he touched for the first time upon a subject that had once seemed light-years away: the NCAA Tournament.

"The NCAA Tournament is at least in sight if we can win out at home," said Floyd as he looked at ISU's 17 wins, 6 of them coming in league play. "But hopefully we can steal some games on the road, too."

HILTON MAGIC, PART TWO

According to research done by *The News and Observer* in Raleigh, North Carolina, Hilton Coliseum is one of the toughest places to play in America. Here's a look at the home versus road point differential for league games from 1991 to 1995.

	Home	Road	Pts Better At Home
Iowa State	5.8	-9.14	14.94
Indiana	16.21	2.43	13.78
Vanderbilt	8.21	-5.45	13.66
Mississippi	-2.48	-15.72	13.24
Colorado	-2.46	-15.57	13.11
Mississippi St.	6.38	-6.31	12.69
Oklahoma State	13.31	0.69	12.62
Minnesota	6.90	-5.50	12.40
North Carolina St.	-1.97	-14.31	12.34
Clemson	-1.46	-13.77	12.31
North Carolina	14.08	1.82	12.26
Kansas	15.23	3.14	12.09
Southern Cal	3.89	-7.78	11.67
Stanford	5.07	-6.58	11.65
Wisconsin	2.81	-8.74	11.55
Oregon State	0.04	-11.40	11.44
Louisiana State	8.76	-2.34	11.10
Kentucky	15.34	4.76	10.58

Iowa State is a different basketball team when playing within the magical confines of Hilton Coliseum.

STAYING CLOSE TO KANSAS With preseason contenders Missouri and Nebraska faltering badly, Iowa State had a solid grip on second place with a 6-2 mark. The only club realistically within striking distance of the Cyclones was Kelvin Sampson's Sooners, and they hosted ISU at Lloyd Noble Arena in a crucial Valentine's Day matchup.

But ISU didn't give any love notes to the Sooners, winning their third Big Eight road game, 70-58, behind a career-high 11 from Jacy Holloway, who did all his scoring in the second half. The Cyclones shot 22 of 25 from the free throw line, and Bankhead again choked Minor into a 16-point night.

PLAYING FOR FIRST, AGAIN A sold-out Hilton Coliseum played host to perhaps the biggest Big Eight Conference game in ISU's history. With a 7-2 record, the 22nd-ranked Cyclones had never been this close to first place

In what may have been the biggest Big Eight game ever played in Hilton, Jacy Holloway and the Cyclones came up 11 short against the mighty Jayhawks.

28. What Cyclone once pulled down a school-record 26 rebounds in a single game against the Minnesota Gophers?

so late in the season. Fifth-rated Kansas would be no easier this time around.

After missing its first 10 shots, Floyd's team rallied to tie the game at 28 at intermission. But Roy Williams' team had too much down the stretch again for the new kids on the block, souring the mood at Hilton by a 61-50 count.

Still the cardinal and gold was firmly in second, and fans pinched themselves to make sure that their once-maligned team was really among the nation's elite.

A CHANGED TEAM Oklahoma State had become a different ball club compared with the teams' first meeting in Ames. After getting out of the Big Eight gate 0-5, OSU would go on to finish conference play with a 7-7 mark, and the Cyclones would be one of their victims.

Playing with intensity in front of a national ESPN audience, the Cowboys held ISU to its lowest point total of the season, 58-46. The Cyclones saw their second straight defeat with 32.7 percent shooting from the field.

BREAKING THE JINX The next game, a road trip to Missouri, looked intimidating. ISU was coming off one of its worst games of the year, and the Tigers, though struggling overall, were 13-0 at the Hearnes Center.

But heart and discipline overcame all the odds facing Floyd's Cyclones, as ISU won in Columbia for the first time in 11 years, 78-74. Modderman made a baseline jumper with less than a minute to go for a two-point lead, then Missouri's Julian Winfield blew a layup with time ticking down and Edwards grabbed the rebound. Willoughby made a pair of charity shots to ice the game. It was the first season sweep of the Tigers since 1978, and it moved the Cyclones ever closer to the NCAAs with a 19-7 record, 8-4 in loop action.

29. Who scored 30 or more points in a game 18 times during his ISU career?

WHAT'S A SWARTZENDRUBER? It ended up being a little-known Kansas State sophomore from Kalona, Iowa, who scorched the Cyclones with five three-pointers in a 92-87 Wildcat overtime win at Hilton. K-State hit 13 threes as a team to overcome a career-high 31 from Pratt, who also hit 13 of 16 free throws. Not since an exhibition game during Floyd's first year as ISU coach had his defense allowed so many points.

FINISHING STRONG To cement second place and permanently make the preseason magazines worth nothing more than fireplace kindling, ISU had to beat cellar-dwelling Colorado in the season finale. The 23rd-ranked Cyclones did it, 74-65, to win their 20th game of the season against eight losses. The 9-5 Big Eight mark

Dedric Willoughby led ISU over Colorado for win No. 20 and second place in the conference.

was the best since the 1985-86 team also won 9 of 14 games. After the game, the team and Floyd were honored at halfcourt in a special presentation. The Hilton crowd stayed long afterward, cheering for a team and coach that had brought them so much unexpected joy.

"You knew we weren't going to lose this game," said Pratt.

SAVING THE BEST FOR LAST It was a sentimental journey the following Wednesday as the eight league teams and their fans made their way to Kansas City. This would be the final Big Eight Tournament. The next season would see the first Big 12 Tournament with Baylor, Texas Tech, Texas, and Texas A&M thrown in the mix. Of the Big Eight teams heading to Kansas City, only Iowa State had never won a tournament championship.

ROUND ONE: HUSKING NEE Despite jumping out to a 7-0 lead and hounding Willoughby and Pratt into a

Kelvin Cato rejected Nebraska's Erick Strickland with less than a minute to go to help seal ISU's first-round tourney win.

combined 10-for-31 shooting night, seventh-seeded Nebraska was bounced from the tournament by second-seeded Iowa State because it could do nothing with Cato.

The one-man SWAT team recorded a Big Eight Tournament tying-five blocked shots to go along with 16 points and 10 rebounds in ISU's narrow 62-60 victory.

"I don't know what to say about Cato," said Willoughby. "That was a different guy. I've never seen that Kelvin Cato."

Cato said his big game was as much luck as anything. "The ball just came to me in the right spots, and I was there for the easy dunks and easy layups. And on the defensive end, I was there for the blocked shots."

His two biggest rejections came in the final two minutes of the game: one on Jaron Boone, the other on NU's Erick Strickland as he drove to the basket with less than a minute to go and ISU clinging to a three-point lead. "I saw him drive around the corner. I just went up and blocked it. Coach told me the last two minutes were going to decide the ball game."

ISU's tournament win over the Huskers was the eighth during the '95-'96 season after it trailed at halftime. Kelvin Cato's 16 points were a career-high. Coach Tim Floyd moved his mark against Nebraska to 5-0.

ROUND TWO: ADIOS, NORM After a tough win over
Nebraska, the Cyclones found themselves in an even more
rugged battle of wills with Missouri, which had to win the
conference tournament to have a shot at the NCAAs.
Stewart's Tigers scored eight more field goals than ISU,
outrebounded them 40-31 and enticed Friday's hero, Cato,
to foul out with more than eight minutes left in the game.

   But like every other statistic and scenario presented
them during the season, the Cyclones turned the
situation on its head and topped the Tigers, 57-53.

   The edge came at the foul line, where ISU converted 24
of 38. Missouri was just 6 of 13. (During the postgame
news conference, Stewart would explode over the free
throw discrepancy. "Look at the box score, man," the
Missouri coach thundered as he abruptly ended his media
session. "Look at the box score. I'm out of here.")

*Norm Stewart
whined about the
officiating, then
walked out during
his own news
conference.*

COMPOSURE The Cyclones hung tough in the game's
waning moments, scoring nine of the final 11 points to
come back and get the win. Willoughby showed the way
with 25, including a 13-foot jumper to tie the game at 51

*Jason Sutherland's
intentional foul on
Dedric Willoughby
ignited the Cyclone
comeback against
Missouri in the
semifinals.*

after he was intentionally clubbed on a layin attempt by the volatile Sutherland. The Cyclones never trailed again.

After Cato fouled out with 8:18 to go, Edwards stepped in and held things down in the middle, grabbing six rebounds. Missouri went 1 of 15 from three-point distance. Through two tournament games ISU was holding foes to 4 for 27 accuracy from beyond the arc.

CHAMPIONSHIP SUNDAY Just as they did one year before, the Cyclone faithful began their pilgrimage to Kemper Arena. It didn't matter that many had no tickets. They wanted to be there — even if they were just in the parking lot — for the dramatic moment. Twice during the season, Big Eight champion Kansas had defeated the runner-up Cyclones. But those games meant nothing now.

Team Unity was to become Team Destiny, thanks to

Kenny Pratt made life miserable for Kansas inside with 20 points and 11 rebounds.

two free throws from Willoughby with 5.5 seconds on the clock. Kansas guard Jacque Vaughn drove the length of the floor and put up a running baseline jumper from the right side, but it clanged off the iron as the buzzer sounded and the jubilant Cyclones streamed onto the Kemper Court wildly celebrating their 56-55 win. The supposed worst was now inarguably first.

PARTY TIME It was the greatest victory in Cyclone basketball lore. In the 89 years of the conference tournament, Iowa State had never sipped from the victor's cup. In their final opportunity, they had overcome.

"It feels like we just won the national championship," screamed tournament MVP Willoughby. His roommate, Cato, walked around the court cradling the tournament championship trophy. "Let me hold that thing," Willoughby pleaded. "No way, this is mine," Cato shot back.

When Willoughby was down on bended knee begging for the prize, Cato finally relented. Willoughby nestled the hardware close to his face and spoke softly.

"We worked so hard for this," he said quietly with his eyes closed. "We worked so hard. I love my team!"

Dedric Willoughby, the tournament MVP, hugged the title hardware and sang the praises of teamwork.

AN INSTANT LEGEND Kansas had led 53-51 with 46 seconds left when Pratt drove the lane, drawing the attention of three Jayhawk defenders with him. Stuffed and cut off from the basket, Pratt dished back out to left wing where Holloway was standing alone outside the three-point arc. The reluctant shooter dialed up with no hesitation as the clock continued to wind down. It showed 43 seconds when the native Kansan drained one of the biggest baskets in Iowa State history.

"All year long last year people in Ames were hollering for Jacy to shoot," said Floyd. "Well, you got your shot today."

"I was open, and I had to take it," said Holloway as he milled around the post-game ecstasy on the floor. "Coach told me it was about time I made one."

Jacy Holloway's dramatic three-pointer is a shot that will live in cardinal and gold lore for all time.

THE FINISHER Still, after two Raef LaFrentz free throws put Kansas back on top 55-54, it was Willoughby who had to step to the line with millions tuning in for the final 5.5 seconds.

"I used to be in my backyard thinking about this, when it comes down to the wire at the free throw line. Will I make my free throws? Today I made them. I'm so happy."

PRAISE FOR THE TEACHER Pratt did a marvelous job of recounting how this team of improbability became probable under the guidance of Floyd.

In just his second season at Iowa State, Coach Tim Floyd got to cut down the nets in Kansas City.

"We didn't know how we were going to connect when we got here at the start of the season," said the forward who stung the Jayhawks for 20 points and 11 rebounds. "But we started listening to Coach Floyd and a lot of guys were saying, 'Man what he says makes a lot of sense. He really knows what he's talking about. We'd better listen to him.'

"As we got into it more and more, and won our first game, we said, 'Man, this thing works. Hands off, no fouling, and get to the line more than your opponents.' It's worked, and we've stuck with it. I think Coach Floyd is the smartest coach in the world."

Tim Floyd was named the Big Eight Coach of the Year in 1995, and just missed being named National Coach of the Year, which went to Purdue's Gene Keady.

WILLIAMS SPEAKS Kansas Coach Roy Williams, who saw his club fumble away a sure No. 1 NCAA Tournament seed with the loss, had nothing but compliments for the seemingly plastic Pratt.

"His ability to spin and score over bigger people ... several years ago I had a guy, Richard Scott, who I thought could score against bigger people better than anyone I'd ever been around. Kenny Pratt has that same ability.

"I think it's his attitude more than anything. He has a relentless attitude. He's just going to keep coming at you."

KEEP THE BUS ROLLING It had become a Cyclone ritual to pull the team bus over to the shoulder of Interstate 35 around 5:30 p.m. on Sunday so the Cyclones could watch the NCAA Tournament selection show.

Although they did it again in 1995, there was no fear and trepidation this time. No bubbles, no fences. Iowa State, the 1996 Big Eight Tournament champions, was in the field of 64. It was just a matter of finding out where and making the appropriate travel plans.

Minutes after pulling over, Tim Floyd's club learned it would be the 5th seed in the Midwest Regional. The site would be Reunion Arena in Dallas, and the opponent would be 12th-seeded California, one of the most talented and yet erratic clubs in the nation.

BEAR-ING DOWN Coach Todd Bozeman's Golden Bears were a Who's Who of prep all-stars. Included in his stable was the National Freshman of the Year, Shareef Abdur-Rahim. Cal was only 17-10 entering the tournament, yet oddsmakers installed the 12th seed as the favorites to upset the Cyclones. All that did was fuel ISU's fire once more.

SPOILING THE PARTY The West Coast media had hyped the game as Abdur-Rahim's coming out party. Now all the nation would know how wonderful this 6-10 freshman actually is, they wrote. The only problem was that no one bothered to consult Cato, the Cyclones' terminator.

The motivated Cato dominated, owned, and schooled Abdur-Rahim to help Iowa State to a 74-64 first-round victory. Cato totaled 11 points, 8 rebounds (4 of them offensive) and recorded 5 blocks in just 23 minutes of action. Abdur-Rahim, who had been averaging better than 21 points a game, finished with a season-low seven points and two rebounds. Cato got help from five other Cyclones against Abdur-Rahim when he wasn't on the floor.

FAST BREAK ISU nearly ran the Golden Bears out of Reunion Arena in the game's opening moments. The Cyclones led it 14-3 before Bozeman could circle the wagons, and ISU upped that margin to 43-29 by halftime. Iowa State shot better than 57 percent in the first half, Cal just under 39 percent.

The Bears put on a run early in the second half to get within a point, but ISU stretched the lead back out again with possession-conscious offense working hand-in-hand with stellar rebounding. ISU won the battle of the boards 40-27, the first time in nine games that Cal had been beaten on the glass. Tremaine Fowlkes scored 26 to lead Cal, but no other player scored in double figures for the Bears. Willoughby paced the Cyclones with 23, followed by Pratt with 18, Cato's 11, and Bankhead with 10.

Dedrick Willoughby was voted Most Valuable Player of the last Big Eight Tournament; Kenny Pratt and Kelvin Cato also were voted to the all-tournament team.

QUIZ

30. Who holds the Cyclone record for most consecutive field goals made in a game with 11?

CYCLONES PREPARE FOR UTES The victory over Cal put 24-8 Iowa State just 40 minutes away from a trip to the Metrodome in Minneapolis for the Sweet 16. The only thing in their path was fourth-seeded Utah, which had routed the Golden Griffins of Canisius in Round One.

A DOUBLE DOSE OF DEFENSE Utah Coach Rick Majerus would be forced to take on Iowa State with his biggest gun, All-American Keith Van Horn, at half-strength due to the flu. It would be up to his teammates to pick up the slack.

The Utes employed defensive pressure akin to ISU's. They shot free throws even better than the Cyclones, and they kept their foes in the lower 60s on average. It was like looking in the mirror.

Kelvin Cato drubbed Utah center Michael Doleac (51) in style points, but Doleac's 23-point night won the game for the Utes.

AN EVEN MATCH ISU held a five-point lead late in the first half, 37-32, but the Utes tied the game by halftime. The game stayed close throughout the second half.

Utah had the ball and the lead, 64-62, with less than 50 seconds left. Mark Rydalch lifted a jumper with the shot clock nearly out, and Cato swatted it away. But fate was cruel to the cardinal and gold. Cato's carom landed in the hands of Utah guard Andre Miller, who calmly hoisted a three-pointer that seared the nets as the shot clock expired. The Utes were suddenly up by five with 43 seconds to go, and the Cyclones were all but finished.

"That took a lot out of us," Willoughby said of Miller's shot. "Miller hadn't hit a jumper all game, but he stepped up and knocked that one down. It hurt."

THE END ARRIVES The final was 73-67. The big difference in the second half, besides Miller's heroics, was Utah's 9 for 9 shooting at the free throw line and ISU's 0 for 5 performance. The Cyclones finished the season with a

Utah's Brandon Jessie played Iowa State-type defense on Kenny Pratt.

school-record 24 wins and 9 losses. But most importantly, all five starters would return the next season.

NO MORE TEARS Emotion was surprisingly absent in the ISU locker room. The team that had taken victory with only a passing interest apparently took defeat the same way.

"I'm going to take a day off and then be back in the gym Monday working out," said Willoughby. "I think the guys need to get back to the gym because now there's going to be expectations next year.

"We left everything we had on that floor. That's why nobody's hanging their heads."

POST-SEASON NEWS Joe Modderman announced that he was leaving school to play his final season of eligibility at Grand Valley State, a Division II school in his hometown of Allendale, Mich. Jason Justus also left school, hoping

DANCE CARD IS FULL

By drawing the fifth seed in the Midwest Regional, Iowa State advanced to the NCAA Tournament for the 10th time in school history, and for the fourth time in five years. Here's a rundown on the Cyclones' performances in the Big Dance:

Year	Seed/Region	Result
1940-41		Lost to Creighton, 57-48, in Kansas City, Mo.
1943-44		Beat Pepperdine, 44-39, in Kansas City, Mo.
		Lost to Utah, 40-31, in Kansas City, Missouri
1984-85	13th/Midwest	Lost to Ohio State, 75-64, in Tulsa, Okla.
1985-86	7th/Midwest	Beat Miami of Ohio, 81-79, in Minneapolis, Minn.
		Beat Michigan, 72-69, in Minneapolis, Minn.
		Lost to North Carolina State, 70-66, in Kansas City, Mo.
1987-88	12th/East	Lost to Georgia Tech, 70-68, In Hartford, Conn.
1988-89	12th/Southeast	Lost to UCLA, 84-74, in Atlanta, Ga.
1991-92	10th/East	Beat UNC-Charlotte, 76-74, in Worcester, Mass.
		Lost to Kentucky, 106-98, in Worcester, Mass.
1992-93	8th/West	Lost to UCLA, 81-70, in Tucson, Ariz.
1994-95	7th/Southeast	Beat Florida, 64-61, in Tallahassee, Fla.
		Lost to North Carolina, 73-51, In Tallahassee, Fla.
1995-96	5th/Midwest	Beat California, 74-64, in Dallas.
		Lost to Utah, 73-67, in Dallas.

to transfer to a Division II school were he would gain more playing time. Brothers Carlo and Shelby Walton also departed. The Cyclones signed three players in April: Stevie Johnson, a 6-5 swingman from Mississippi who is regarded as one of the top 65 players in the nation and finished second to Georgetown's Othella Harrington in all-time Mississippi high school scoring; DeAndre Harris, a 6-0 point guard from Marshalltown (Iowa) Community College and Brad Johnson, a 6-6 off-guard from Indian Hills (Iowa) Community College. Assistant Coach James Green was named the head coach at Southern Mississippi, and he took restricted earnings coach Terry Reed with him. Floyd hired Alcorn State head coach Sam Weaver to fill Green's position, and former ISU assistant Steve Krafcisin to fill Reed's spot.

The 1995-96 Iowa State Cyclones, winners of a school-record 24 games and ISU's first-ever Big Eight Tournament championship.

By the Numbers

The statistics found here are provided by the Iowa State Sports Information department and are updated through the 1995-96 school year.

FOOTBALL SEASON-BY-SEASON SUMMARY

Year	W	L	T	Coach	Captain
1892	1	0	1	I. C. Brownlie	I. C. Brownlie
1893	0	3	0	W. F. Finney	E. A. Mellinger
1894	6	1	0	Bert German	Bert German
1895	3	3	0	Glenn "Pop" Warner	Ed Mellinger
1896	8	2	0	Glenn "Pop" Warner Bert German	Jim Wilson
1897	3	1	0	Glenn "Pop" Warner Bert German	None
1898	3	2	0	Glenn "Pop" Warner	Simon Tarr
1899	5	4	1	Warner/Joe Meyers	C. J. Griffith
1900	2	5	1	C. E. Woodruff	L. M. Chambers
1901	2	6	2	Edgar Clinton	H. C. Scholty
1902	6	3	1	A. W. Ristine	Fred Byl
1903	8	1	0	A. W. Ristine	Preston Daniels
1904	7	2	0	A. W. Ristine	Preston Daniels
1905	6	3	0	A. W. Ristine	Don Stoufer
1906	9	1	0	A. W. Ristine	R. E. Jeanson
1907	7	1	0	Clyde Williams	Ralph McElhinney
1908	6	3	0	Clyde Williams	E. W. Law
1909	4	3	1	Clyde Williams	W. H. Willmarth
1910	4	4	0	Clyde Williams	C. E. Scott
1911	6	1	1	Clyde Williams	E. C. Harte
1912	6	2	0	Clyde Williams	R. L. Hurst
1913	4	4	0	Homer Hubbard	Lyle Cowan
1914	4	3	0	Homer Hubbard	Lew Reeve
1915	6	2	0	Charles Mayser	Edward John
1916	5	2	1	Charles Mayser	Durwood Moss
1917	5	2	0	Charles Mayser	Howard Aldrich
1918	0	3	0	Charles Mayser	V. A. Heater
1919	5	2	1	Charles Mayser	Gil Denfield
1920	4	4	0	Norman Paine	Marshall Boyd
1921	4	4	0	Maury Kent	Polly Wallace
1922	2	6	0	Sam Willaman	Deac Wolters
1923	4	3	1	Sam Willaman	Dick Young
1924	4	3	1	Sam Willaman	Harry Schmidt
1925	4	3	1	Sam Willaman	Johnny Behm
1926	4	3	1	Noel Workman	Roland Coe
1927	4	3	1	Noel Workman	Walt Weiss
1928	2	5	1	Noel Workman	Harry Lindbolm
1929	1	7	0	Noel Workman	Ed Schlenker, Harry Johnson
1930	0	9	0	Noel Workman	Maynard Spear
1931	5	3	0	George Veenker	Rober Bowmen
1932	3	4	1	George Veenker	Dick Grefe
1933	3	5	1	George Veenker	Magnus Lichter
1934	5	3	1	George Veenker	Don Theophilus
1935	2	4	3	George Veenker	Ike Hayes
1936	3	3	2	George Veenker	Clarence Gustine
1937	3	6	0	Jim Yeager	Clarence Dee
1938	7	1	1	Jim Yeager	Ed Bock, Ev Kischer
1939	2	7	0	Jim Yeager	Marvin Boswell
1940	4	5	0	Jim Yeager	Tom Smith
1941	2	6	1	Ray Donels	LaVerne Lewis
1942	1	2	0	Ray Donels	Royal Lohry
	2	4	0	Mike Michalske	
1943	4	4	0	Mike Michalske	None
1944	6	1	1	Mike Michalske	None
1945	4	3	1	Mike Michalske	None
1946	2	6	1	Mike Michalske	None

Year	W	L	T	Coach	Captain
1947	3	6	0	Abe Stuber	Vic Weber, Harley Rollinger
1948	4	6	0	Abe Stuber	Ray Klootwyk
1949	5	3	1	Abe Stuber	Dean Laun
1950	3	6	1	Abe Stuber	Vince Beacom
1951	4	4	1	Abe Stuber	Stan Campbell
1952	3	6	0	Abe Stuber	Bill Byrus, Carl Brettschneider
1953	2	7	0	Abe Stuber	Jim Rawley, Jack Lessin
1954	3	6	0	Vince DiFrancesca	Max Burkett, Weldon Thalacker
1955	1	7	1	Vince DiFrancesca	Jim McCaulley, Mell Wostoupal
1956	2	8	0	Vince DiFrancesca	Oliver Sparks, Chuck Muelhaupt
1957	4	5	1	J. A. Myers	Jack Falter, Marv Walter
1958	4	6	0	Clay Stapleton	Gale Gibson
1959	7	3	0	Clay Stapleton	Dwight Nichols
1960	7	3	0	Clay Stapleton	Arden Esslinger
1961	5	5	0	Clay Stapleton	John Cooper
1962	5	5	0	Clay Stapleton	Jim Clapper
1963	4	5	0	Clay Stapleton	Dave Hoover
1964	1	8	1	Clay Stapleton	Mike Cox
1965	5	4	1	Clay Stapleton	Dick Kasperek, Jim Wipert
1966	2	6	2	Clay Stapleton	Dick Schafroth, Bob Evans
1967	2	8	0	Clay Stapleton	Don Stanley, Dave Mayberry
1968	3	7	0	John Majors	John Warder, George Dimitri
1969	3	7	0	John Majors	Jerry Fiat, Fred Jones
1970	5	6	0	John Majors	Tony Washington, Mark Withrow
1971	8	4	0	John Majors	Dean Carlson, Keith Schroder, Ray Harm
1972	5	6	1	John Majors	George Amundson, Matt Blair
1973	4	7	0	Earle Bruce	Keith Krepfle, Larry Hunt
1974	4	7	0	Earle Bruce	Mike Strachan, Rick Howe
1975	4	7	0	Earle Bruce	Sy Bassett , Bob Bos, Jeff Jones, Ray King
1976	8	3	0	Earle Bruce	Tony Hawkins, Wayne Stanley, Maynard Stensrud, Dave Greenwood
1977	8	4	0	Earle Bruce	Mike Tryon, Kevin Cunningham, Tom Randall, Tom Boskey
1978	8	4	0	Earle Bruce	Tom Boskey, Dexter Green
1979	3	8	0	Donnie Duncan	Dick Cuvelier, Mike Schwartz
1980	7	4	0	Donnie Duncan	Larry Crawford, Cal Jacobs, Kenny Neil, Jack Seabrooke, Tom Stonebrook
1981	5	5	1	Donnie Duncan	Marc Butts, John Quinn
1982	4	6	1	Donnie Duncan	John Arnaud, George Jessen, Karl Nelson, Ron Osborne, James Ransom
1983	4	7	0	Jim Criner	David Archer, Chris Washington
1984	2	7	2	Jim Criner	Alan Hood, Steve Little, Barry Moore, David Smoldt
1985	5	6	0	Jim Criner	Jim Luebbers, Anthony Mayze, Kirk Thomas, Bruce Westemeyer
1986	6	5	0	Jim Criner	Alex Espinoza, Dennis Gibson, Jeff Hansel
1987	3	8	0	Jim Walden	Eddie Bridges, Chris Moore, Randy Richards, Brett Sadek
1988	5	6	0	Jim Walden	Jeff Dole, Joe Henderson, David Heyn, Anthony Hoskins
1989	6	5	0	Jim Walden	Tim Baker, Mike Busch , Mike Shane, Paul Thibodeaux
1990	4	6	1	Jim Walden	Blaise Bryant, Jim Doran, Marcus Robertson, Jeff Shudak
1991	3	7	1	Jim Walden	Chris Pedersen, Larry Ratigan, Matt Rehberg, Paul Schulte
1992	4	7	0	Jim Walden	Malcolm Goodwin, Todd McClish, Chris Spencer, Dan Watkins
1993	3	8	0	Jim Walden	Lamont Hill, Kevin Lazard, Todd Miller, Doug Skartvedt
1994	0	10	1	Jim Walden	Tony Booth, Jim Knott, Marc Lillibridge, Matt Nitchie
1995	3	8	0	Dan McCarney	Byron Heitz, Mike Horacek, Tim Sanders, Matt Straight

COACHING RECORDS

Coach	Tenure	Yrs	Conference				All games			
			W	L	T	Pct.	W	L	T	Pct.
I. C. Brownlie	1892	1					1	0	1	.750
W. F. Finney	1893	1					0	3	0	.000
Bert German	1894	1					6	1	0	.857
Glenn "Pop" Warner	1895-99	5					22	12	1	.643
Joe Meyers	1899	1					4	4	1	.500
C. E. Woodruff	1900	1					2	5	2	.333
Edgar Clinton	1901	1					2	6	2	.300
A. W. Ristine	1902-06	5					36	10	1	.766
Clyde Williams	1907-12	6	8	5	2	.600	33	14	2	.694
Homer C. Hubbard	1913-14	2	4	3	1	.571	8	7	0	.533
Charles Mayser	1915-19	5	10	4	2	.688	21	11	2	.647
Norman C. Paine	1920	1	3	2	0	.600	4	4	0	.500
Maury Kent	1921	1	3	4	0	.429	4	4	0	.500
Sam F. Willaman	1922-25	4	11	10	2	.522	14	15	3	.484
Noel Workman	1926-30	5	8	17	2	.296	11	27	3	.305
George Veenker	1931-36	6	7	18	4	.310	21	22	7	.490

Jim Yeager	1937-40	4	7	12	1	.375	16	19	1	.458
Ray Donels	1941-42	1 1/3	1	4	1	.250	3	8	1	.292
Mike Michalske	1942-46	4 2/3	8	9	2	.474	18	18	3	.500
Abe Stuber	1947-53	7	12	28	1	.305	24	38	3	.393
Vince DiFrancesca	1954-56	3	2	15	1	.139	6	21	1	.232
Jim Myers	1957	1	2	4	0	.333	4	5	1	.450
Clay Stapleton	1958-67	10	22	43	2	.343	42	53	4	.444
John Majors	1968-72	5	9	25	1	.271	24	30	1	.445
Earle Bruce	1973-78	6	18	24	0	.429	36	32	0	.529
Donnie Duncan	1979-82	4	8	18	2	.321	19	23	2	.455
Jim Criner	1983-86	4	9	17	2	.357	17	25	2	.409
Jim Walden	1987-94	8	16	37	3	.313	28	57	3	.335
Dan McCarney	1995-	1	1	6	0	.143	3	8	0	.273

INDIVIDUAL RECORDS

RUSHING ATTEMPTS

Game — 47, Dwayne Crutchfield (168 yards), Colorado, 1981
Season — 345, Troy Davis (2,010 yards), 1995
Career — 738, Dexter Green (3,437 yards), 1975-78

NET RUSHING YARDS

Game — 302, Troy Davis (36 carries), UNLV, 1995
Season — 2,010, Troy Davis (345 carries), 1995
Career — 3,437, Dexter Green (738 carries), 1975-78

HIGHEST RUSHING AVERAGE PER CARRY

Game — 23.8, Max Burkett, South Dakota State, 1954
Season — 7.1, Mickey Fitzgerald, 1954
Career — 6.1, Rocky Gillis, 1978-82

MOST TOUCHDOWNS RUSHING

Game — 5, Troy Davis, UNLV, 1995
Season — 19, Blaise Bryant, 1989
Career — 34, Dexter Green, 1975-78

MOST 100-YARD RUSHING GAMES

Season — 10, Troy Davis, 1995
Career — 19, Dexter Green, 1975-78;

MOST 200-YARD RUSHING GAMES

Season — 4, Troy Davis, 1995
Career — 4, Troy Davis (1994-95)

MOST CONSECUTIVE 100-YARD RUSHING GAMES

6, Troy Davis, 1995

MOST PASSING ATTEMPTS

Game — 48, Bret Oberg, Oklahoma (26 completions), 1989
Season — 403, David Archer (234 completions), 1983
Career — 891, Alex Espinoza (454 completions), 1984-86

MOST PASSING COMPLETIONS

Game — 29, David Archer, Missouri (47 attempts), 1983 and Kansas State (40 attempts), 1983
Season — 234, David Archer (403 attempts), 1983
Career — 454, Alex Espinoza (891 attempts), 1984-86

HIGHEST PASSING COMPLETION PERCENTAGE

Game — .813, Bret Oberg (13-16), Kansas State, 1989
Season — .620, Bret Oberg (152-245), 1989
Career — .592, Bret Oberg (251-424), 1988-89 (Big Eight Record)

MOST PASSING YARDS

Game — 411, Bret Oberg, Oklahoma (48 attempts), 1989
Season — 2,639, David Archer (403 attempts), 1983
Career — 5,307, Alex Espinoza (891 attempts), 1984-85

MOST TOUCHDOWN PASSES

Game — 4, Dick Mann, Nebraska, 1951; Wayne Stanley, Air Force, 1976; Alex Espinoza, Kansas State, 1986; Bret Oberg, Oklahoma, 1989
Season — 18, David Archer, 1983
Career — 33, Alex Espinoza, 1984-86

MOST INTERCEPTIONS

Game — 6, Bret Oberg, Colorado, 1988
Season — 22, George Amundson, 1972
Career — 36, Tim Van Galder, 1964-66

LOWEST INTERCEPTION PERCENTAGE

Season — .029, David Archer, 1983
Career — .035, Alex Espinoza, 1984-86

MOST CONSECUTIVE PASSES ATTEMPTED

Without an Interception
Season — 137, David Archer, 1983

MOST CONSECUTIVE GAMES THROWN TD PASS

10, David Archer, 1983 (games 2-11)

MOST RECEPTIONS

Game — 16, Tracy Henderson, Kansas State (165 yards), 1983
Season — 81, Tracy Henderson (1,051 yards), 1983
Career — 150, Tracy Henderson (2,048 yards), 1982-84

MOST YARDS RECEIVING

Game — 217, Tracy Henderson (11 receptions), Texas A&M, 1984
Season — 1,051, Tracy Henderson (81 receptions), 1983
Career — 2,048, Tracy Henderson (150 receptions), 1982-84

MOST TOUCHDOWN RECEPTIONS

Game — 3, George Gast, Kan. State, 1943; Jim Doran, Missouri, 1950
Season — 8, Tracy Henderson, 1983
Career — 15, Keith Krepfle, 1971-73

HIGHEST AVERAGE RECEIVING YARDS PER CATCH

(Minimum 1.5 per game)
Game — 65.0, James Brooks (2 catches), No. Illinois, 1993
Season — 22.4, Eddie Brown (18 catches, 11 games), 1988
Career — 18.5, Luther Blue (69 catches), 1974-76

MOST 100-YARD RECEIVING GAMES

Season — 5, Jim Doran, 1950; Tracy Henderson, 1983
Career — 8, Tracy Henderson, 1983-84

MOST CONSECUTIVE 100-YARD RECEIVING GAMES

3, Jim Doran, 1950; Tracy Henderson, 1983

TOTAL OFFENSE, MOST PLAYS

Game — 62, Tim Van Galder, Kansas State, 1965; Alex Espinoza, Missouri, 1985
Season — 513, David Archer, 1983
Career — 1,079, Alex Espinoza, 1984-86

TOTAL OFFENSE, MOST YARDS

Game — 449, Bret Oberg, Oklahoma, 1989
Season — 2,698, David Archer, 1983
Career — 5,018, Alex Espinoza, 1984-86

TOTAL OFFENSE, MOST TD RESPONSIBLE (RUSH-PASS)

Game — 6, Bret Oberg, Oklahoma, 1989
Season — 21, George Amundson, 1972
Career — 52, George Amundson, 1970-72

TOTAL OFFENSE, MOST ALL-PURPOSE YARDS

Game — 302, Troy Davis, UNLV, 1995
Season — 2,466, Troy Davis, 1995
Career — 4,065, Dexter Green, 1975-78

MOST PUNTS

Game — 18, George Hess (601 yards), Marquette, 1951
Season — 85, Jim Thompson (3,157 yards), 1984
Career — 268, Rich Miller (10,022 yards), 1978-81

MOST PUNTING YARDS

Game — 601, George Hess (18 punts), Marquette, 1951
Season — 3,422, Rick Frank (81 punts), 1986
Career — 10,022, Rich Miller (268 punts), 1978-81

HIGHEST PUNTING AVERAGE

Game — 58.5, Rick Blabolil (2 punts), Oklahoma State, 1977
Season — 42.9, Judge Johnston (31 punts), 1989
Career — 42.0, Marc Harris (124 punts), 1993-95

MOST PUNT RETURNS

Game — 9, Don Ferguson (112 yards), Kansas State, 1947
Season — 41, Tom Buck (240 yards), 1977
Career — 74, Don Ferguson (811 yards), 1947-49

MOST PUNT RETURN YARDS

Game — 137, James McMillion (5 returns), vs. Tulane, 1992
Season — 435, James McMillion (23 returns), 1992
Career — 843, James McMillion (53 returns), 1991-93

PUNTS RETURNED FOR TOUCHDOWNS

Game — 1 by eight players (done 11 times)
Season — 3, James McMillion, 1992
Career — 3, James McMillion, 1991-93

HIGHEST PUNT RETURN AVERAGE

Game — 27.4, James McMillion (5 returns) vs. Tulane, 1992
Season — 18.9, James McMillion, 1992
Career — 15.9, James McMillion, 1991-93

MOST KICKOFF RETURNS

Game — 7, Richard Hanson (141 yards), Nebraska, 1983
Season — 32, Eddie Bridges (577 yards), 1987
Career — 62, Jeff Allen (1,529 yards), 1968-70

MOST KICKOFF RETURN YARDS

Game — 166, Willie Jones (5 returns), Georgia Tech, 1972
Season — 599, Jeff Allen (23 returns), 1968
Career — 1,529, Jeff Allen (62 returns), 1968-70

HIGHEST KICKOFF RETURN AVERAGE

Season — 32.8, Luther Blue, 1974
Career — 26.5, Luther Blue, 1974-76

MOST TACKLES IN A GAME

Interior Lineman — 23, Chris Boskey, Nebraska, 1978
Linebacker — 27, Chris Moore, Oklahoma, 1986
Defensive Back — 28, Brian Refner, Nebraska, 1985

MOST TACKLES IN A SEASON

Interior Lineman — 131, Chris Boskey, 1978
Linebacker — 168, Chris Washington, 1981
Defensive Back — 135, Jeff Dole, 1988

MOST TACKLES IN A CAREER

Interior Lineman — 352, Larry Hunt (NG-LB), 1971-73; 335, Shamus McDonough (DT), 1979-82
Linebacker — 457, Chris Washington, 1980-83
Defensive Back — 334, Mark DouBrava, 1989-92

MOST INTERCEPTIONS

Game — 4, Barry Hill, Kan., 1974; Everett Kischer, Northwestern, 1937
Season — 9, Barry Hill, 1974
Career — 21, Barry Hill, 1972-74

MOST INTERCEPTIONRETURN YARDS

Game — 123, Larry Carwell, Kansas, 1966
Season — 152, Dick Howard, 1945
Career — 202, Barry Hill, 1972-74

MOST POINTS SCORED (EXCLUDING KICKERS)

Game — 30, Joe Henderson, TB, Kansas, 1988; Troy Davis, TB, UNLV, 1995
Season — 120, Blaise Bryant, TB, 1989
Career — 228, Dexter Green, 1987-90

MOST POINTS SCORED BY KICKERS

Game — 15, Alex Giffords, Colorado State, 1980
Season — 84, Jeff Shudak, 1990
Career — 266, Jeff Shudak, 1987-90

MOST TOUCHDOWNS SCORED

Game — 5, Joe Henderson, TB, Kansas, 1988; Troy Davis, TB, UNLV, 1995
Season — 19, Blaise Bryant, 1989
Career — 38, Dexter Green, 1975-78

MOST CONSECUTIVE GAMES SCORING A TOUCHDOWN

8, Dwayne Crutchfield, final game 1980 through seventh game 1981

MOST FIELD GOALS

Game — 5, Jeff Shudak vs. Missouri, Nov. 10, 1990
Season — 20, Jeff Shudak, 1987
Career — 58, Jeff Shudak, 1987-90

MOST CONSECUTIVE GAMES KICKED FIELD GOALS

11 games, Jeff Shudak, 1987

MOST POINTS AFTER TOUCHDOWNS MADE

Game — 9, Alex Giffords, Colorado State, 1980
Season — 42, Scott Kollman, 1976
Career — 92, Jeff Shudak, 1987-90

MOST CONSECUTIVE EXTRA POINTS
50, Tom Goedjen, 1972-74

TOP 10 SINGLE-GAME RUSHING YARDS
1.	Troy Davis, UNLV, 1995	302
2.	Troy Davis, Ohio, 1995	291
3.	Dave Hoppmann, Kansas St., 1961	271
4.	Harold Brown, Kent State, 1982	242
5.	Joe Henderson, Kansas, 1987	226
6.	Dave Hoppmann, Detroit, 1960	224
7.	Dexter Green, Missouri, 1976	214
8.	Blaise Bryant, Ohio, 1989	213
9.	Blaise Bryant, Oklahoma St., 1989	208
10.	Troy Davis, Colorado, 1995	203
11.	Troy Davis, Oklahoma St., 1995	202

TOP 10 SINGLE-GAME RUSHING ATTEMPTS
1.	Dwayne Crutchfield, Colorado, 1981	47
2.	Dwayne Crutchfield, Oklahoma, 1981	43
3.	Troy Davis, Kansas State, 1995	41
4.	Mike Strachan, Colorado, 1973	40
	Joe Henderson, Kansas State, 1988	40
	Blaise Bryant, Missouri, 1989	40
	Blaise Bryant, Kansas State, 1990	40
	Troy Davis, Ohio, 1995	40
9.	Dexter Green, Missouri, 1976	37
	Dan Goodwin, Colorado, 1979	37
	Dwayne Crutchfield, Missouri, 1980	37
	Harold Brown, Kent State, 1982	37
	Troy Davis, Oklahoma State, 1995	37

TOP 10 SINGLE-GAME PASSING YARDS
1.	Bret Oberg, Oklahoma, 1989	411
2.	David Archer, Nebraska, 1983	346
3.	Tim Van Galder, Arizona, 1966	335
4.	David Archer, Kansas, 1983	300
5.	Brett Sadek, Northern Iowa, 1987	295
6.	Tim Van Galder, Kansas St., 1965	293
7.	David Archer, Kansas, 1983	286
8.	Alex Espinoza, Kansas State, 1986	286
9.	Alex Espinoza, Iowa, 1984	286
10.	John Quinn, San Diego State, 1981	281
	Bill Weeks, Oklahoma, 1949	281
	Alex Espinoza, Drake, 1984	281

TOP 10 SINGLE-GAME PASS COMPLETIONS
1.	David Archer, Kansas State, 1983	29
	David Archer, Missouri, 1983	29
3.	David Archer, Kansas, 1983	28
4.	David Archer, Nebraska, 1983	26
	Bret Oberg, Oklahoma, 1989	26
6.	Tim Van Galder, Arizona, 1966	25
	Alex Espinoza, Kansas, 1986	25
8.	John Quinn, San Diego State, 1981	24
	Alex Espinoza, Drake, 1984	24
	Alex Espinoza, Missouri, 1985	24

TOP 10 SINGLE-GAME PASS ATTEMPTS
1.	Bret Oberg, Oklahoma, 1989	48
2.	David Archer, Kansas, 1983	47
	Alex Espinoza, Drake, 1984	47
	David Archer, Missouri, 1983	47
	Alex Espinoza, Missouri, 1985	47
6.	David Archer, Nebraska, 1983	46
7.	David Archer, New Mexico St., 1983	45
8.	John Quinn, San Diego State, 1981	44
	Tim Van Galder, Kansas State, 1965	44
10.	Alex Espinoza, West Texas State, 1984	41

TOP 10 SINGLE-GAME RECEPTIONS
1.	Tracy Henderson, Kansas St., 1983	16
2.	Tom Busch, Kansas, 1967	13
3.	Steve Lester, Oklahoma, 1989	13
4.	Tracy Henderson, Missouri, 1983	12
5.	Tracy Henderson, Texas A&M, 1984	11
	Jason Jacobs, Nebraska, 1983	11
7.	Tracy Henderson, Kansas, 1983	10
	Tracy Henderson, Nebraska, 1983	10
	Tracy Henderson, Drake, 1984	10
	Steve Lester, Missouri, 1989	10

TOP 10 SINGLE-GAME RECEIVING YARDS
1.	Tracy Henderson, Texas A&M, 1984	217
2.	Jim Doran, Oklahoma, 1949	203
3.	Steve Lester, Oklahoma, 1989	203
4.	Eppie Barney, Arizona, 1966	175
5.	Tracy Henderson, Iowa, 1984	175
6.	Dennis Ross, Northern Iowa, 1987	174
7.	Tracy Henderson, Kansas St., 1983	165
8.	Tracy Henderson, Missouri, 1983	161
9.	Keith Krepfle, San Diego St., 1971	159
10.	Jason Jacobs, Nebraska, 1983	152

TOP 10 SINGLE-GAME TOTAL OFFENSE
1.	Bret Oberg, Oklahoma, 1989	449
2.	David Archer, Nebraska, 1983	377
3.	Tim Van Galder, Arizona, 1966	360
4.	Tim Van Galder, Kansas St., 1965	344
5.	David Archer, Kansas State, 1983	340
6.	David Archer, Kansas, 1983	337
7.	Chris Pedersen, Minnesota, 1990	336
8.	Alex Espinoza, Missouri, 1986	334
9.	Dave Hoppmann, Detroit, 1960	320
10.	Dave Hoppmann, Kansas St., 1960	311

ALL-TIME SEASON RUSHING YARDS
1.	Troy Davis, 1995 (NCAA season leader)	2,010
2.	Blaise Bryant, 1989	1,516
3.	Dwayne Crutchfield, 1980	1,312
4.	George Amundson, 1971	1,260
	Mike Strachan, 1972	1,260
6.	Dexter Green, 1977	1,240
7.	Joe Henderson, 1987	1,232
8.	Dwayne Crutchfield, 1981	1,189
9.	Mike Strachan, 1973	1,103
10.	Dexter Green, 1976	1,074

ALL-TIME SEASON RUSHING ATTEMPTS
1.	Troy Davis, 1995	345
2.	Dwayne Crutchfield, 1981	307
3.	Blaise Bryant, 1989	299
4.	Dwayne Crutchfield, 1980	284
5.	George Amundson, 1972	272
	Mike Strachan, 1973	272
7.	Dexter Green, 1977	271
8.	Mike Strachan, 1972	268
9.	Joe Henderson, 1987	262
10.	Dexter Green, 1978	251

ALL-TIME SEASON PASSING YARDS
1.	David Archer, 1983	2,639
2.	Bret Oberg, 1989	2,242
3.	Alex Espinoza, 1986	2,023
4.	George Amundson, 1972	1,997
5.	Alex Espinoza, 1985	1,704
6.	Tim Van Galder, 1966	1,645
7.	Dean Carlson, 1971	1,637
8.	Chris Pedersen, 1990	1,601
9.	Alex Espinoza, 1984	1,580
10.	John Quinn, 1981	1,576

ALL-TIME SEASON RECEPTIONS

1.	Tracy Henderson, 1983	81
2.	Tracy Henderson, 1984	64
	Jason Jacobs, 1983	64
4.	Otto Stowe, 1970	59
5.	Eppie Barney, 1966	56
6.	Dennis Ross, 1987	53
7.	Ed Williams, 1995	46
	Steve Lester, 1989	46
9.	Jim Doran, 1950	42
10.	Keith Krepfle, 1971	40

ALL-TIME SEASON RECEIVING YARDS

1.	Tracy Henderson, 1983	1,051
2.	Tracy Henderson, 1984	941
3.	Otto Stowe, 1970	822
4.	Eppie Barney, 1966	782
5.	Jim Doran, 1949	689
6.	Dennis Ross, 1987	673
7.	Jim Doran, 1950	652
8.	Luther Blue, 1976	644
9.	Ed Williams, 1995	639
10.	Steve Lester, 1989	612

ALL-TIME SEASON SCORING

1.	Blaise Bryant, 1989	120
2.	Dwayne Crutchfield, 1981	104
3.	Troy Davis, 1995	96
4.	George Amundson, 1971	90
	Dexter Green, 1977	90
6.	Jeff Shudak, 1990	84
7.	Blaise Bryant, 1990	78
8.	Jeff Shudak, 1987	77
9.	Scott Kollman, 1976	75
10.	Tom Goedjen, 1973	70

ALL-TIME SEASON TOTAL OFFENSE

1.	David Archer, 1983	2,698
2.	Bret Oberg, 1989	2,515
3.	George Amundson, 1972	2,387
4.	Chris Pedersen, 1990	2,171
5.	Alex Espinoza, 1986	2,023
6.	Troy Davis, 1995	2,010
7.	Tim Van Galder, 1966	1,749
8.	Bill Weeks, 1950	1,673
9.	John Quinn, 1981	1,658
10.	Dean Carlson, 1971	1,653

ALL-TIME SEASON PUNTING AVERAGE

1.	Judge Johnston, 1989	42.9
2.	Rick Blabolil, 1976	42.8
3.	Doug Myers, 1982	42.7
4.	Marc Harris, 1994	42.4
5.	Rick Frank, 1986	42.2
6.	Rick Blabolil, 1977	41.6
7.	Marc Harris, 1995	41.4
8.	Barney Alleman, 1954	41.3

9.	Jon Schnoor, 1990	41.0
	Jon Schnoor, 1992	41.0

ALL-TIME SEASON PUNT RETURN YARDS

1.	James McMillion, 1992	435
2.	Don Ferguson, 1947 (NCAA season leader)	392
3.	Jeff Dole, 1986	287
4.	John Schweizer, 1971	268
5.	James McMillion, 1991	251
6.	Tony Washington, 1970	246
7.	Tom Buck, 1977	240
8.	George Hess, 1951	236
9.	Billy McCue, 1984	217
10.	Don Ferguson, 1949	209

ALL-TIME SEASON PUNTS RETURNED FOR TOUCHDOWNS

1.	James McMillion, 1992	3
2.	Several	1

ALL-TIME SEASON KICKOFF RETURN YARDS

1.	Jeff Allen, 1968	599
2.	Eddie Bridges, 1987	577
3.	Jeff Allen, 1970	568
4.	Geoff Turner, 1994	546
5.	Tom Busch, 1966	484
6.	Ray Hardee, 1977	483
7.	Ray Hardee, 1975	448
8.	Mike Posey, 1984	446
9.	Kevin Wilson, 1995	444
10.	Paul Thibodeaux, 1989	442

ALL-TIME SEASON TOTAL TACKLES

1.	Chris Washington, 1981, LB	168
2.	Keith Schroeder, 1971, LB	167
3.	Malcolm Goodwin, 1992, LB	162
4.	Keith Schroeder, 1970, LB	161
5.	Brad Storm, 1974, LB	159
6.	Ted Jornov, 1972, LB	151
7.	Ted Jornov, 1973, LB	148
8.	Chris Washington, 1982, LB	147
9.	Chris Moore, 1986, LB	145
10.	Mark Benda, 1975, LB	144

ALL-TIME SEASON INTERCEPTIONS

1.	Barry Hill, 1974	9
2.	Bob Mellgren, 1952	8
3.	Barry Hill, 1973	8
4.	Everett Kischer, 1936	6
	Tony Washington, 1970	6
	John Schweizer, 1971	6
7.	Larry Holton, 1969	5
	Tony Washington, 1969	5
	John Schweizer, 1972	5

CAREER LEADERS RUSHING YARDS

		Att.	Yards	Avg.	TD
1.	Dexter Green (1975-78)	738	3,437	4.7	34
2.	Mike Strachan (1972-74)	728	3,010	4.1	13
3.	Joe Henderson (1985-88)	627	2,715	4.3	18
4.	Dave Hoppmann (1960-62)	588	2,562	4.4	21
5.	Dwayne Crutchfield (1980-81)	591	2,501	4.2	28
6.	Blaise Bryant (1989-90)	486	2,269	4.7	31
7.	Dwight Nichols (1957-59)	638	2,232	3.5	16
8.	Troy Davis (1994-95)	380	2,197	5.8	15
9.	George Amundson (1970-72)	503	2,130	4.3	31
10.	Tom Vaughn (1962-64)	423	1,889	4.5	19

1.	Dexter Green (1975-78)	34
2.	George Amundson (1970-72)	31
3.	Blaise Bryant (1989-90)	31
4.	Dwayne Crutchfield (1980-81)	28
5.	Dave Hoppmann (1960-62)	21
6.	Tom Vaughn (1962-64)	19
7.	Joe Henderson (1985-88)	18
8.	Tom Watkins (1958-60)	17
9.	Dwight Nichols (1957-59)	16
10.	Troy Davis (1994-95)	15

1.	Alex Espinoza (1984-86)	33
2.	Wayne Stanley (1972-76)	25
3.	Dean Carlson (1970-71)	24
4.	David Archer (1982-83)	23
5.	George Amundson (1970-72)	22
6.	Rich Mann (1951-52)	18
7.	Bill Weeks (1948-50)	17
8.	Bret Oberg (1988-89)	15
9.	Tim Van Galder (1964-66)	12
10.	John Warder (1966-68)	10
	Terry Rubley (1977-79)	10
	Bob Utter (1990-93)	10

		Att.	Comp.
1.	Alex Espinoza (1984-86)	891	454
2.	David Archer (1982-83)	647	359
3.	Tim Van Galder (1964-66)	578	259
4.	Bret Oberg (1988-89)	424	251
5.	Dean Carlson (1970-71)	473	228
6.	John Quinn (1977-81)	459	226
7.	Bill Weeks (1948-50)	458	218
8.	George Amundson (1970-72)	436	192
9.	Wayne Stanley (1972-76)	390	180
10.	John Warder (1966-68)	404	171
11.	Bob Utter (1990-93)	283	165

		No.	Yards
1.	Tracy Henderson (1982-84)	150	2,048
2.	Otto Stowe (1968-70)	132	1,751
3.	Dennis Ross (1985-88)	118	1,529
4.	Jim Doran (1948-50)	79	1,410
5.	Keith Krepfle (1971-73)	94	1,368
6.	Eppie Barney (1964-66)	97	1,350
7.	Tom Busch (1965-67)	82	1,295
8.	Willie Jones (1971-73)	72	1,290
9.	Chris Spencer (1988-92)	82	1,278
10.	Robbie Minor (1983-86)	72	1,111

1.	Keith Krepfle (1971-73)	15
2.	Tracy Henderson (1982-84)	14
3.	Willie Jones (1971-73)	12
	Dick Limerick (1961-63)	12
5.	Otto Stowe (1968-70)	10
	Jim Doran (1948-50)	10
7.	Luther Blue (1974-76)	9
8.	Calvin Branch (1992-94)	8
9.	Dennis Ross (1985-88)	7
	Tom Busch (1965-67)	7
	Ed Williams (1994-95)	7

		Plays	Yards
1.	Alex Espinoza (1984-86)	1079	5,018
2.	George Amundson (1970-72)	939	4,798
3.	Dave Hoppmann (1960-62)	808	4,173
4.	David Archer (1982-83)	847	4,170
5.	Dwight Nichols (1957-59)	872	3,949
6.	Bret Oberg (1988-89)	636	3,927
7.	Tim Van Galder (1964-66)	806	3,674
8.	Dexter Green (1975-78)	748	3,500
9.	Wayne Stanley (1972-76)	645	3,326
10.	Dean Carlson (1970-71)	626	3,257

		Att.	Comp.	Pct.	Int.	Yds.	TD
1	Alex Espinoza (1984-86)	891	454	.510	31	5,307	33
2.	David Archer (1982-83)	647	359	.555	25	4,104	23
3.	Bret Oberg (1988-89)	424	251	.592	24	3,602	15
4.	Tim Van Galder (1964-66)	578	259	.448	36	3,417	12
5.	Bill Weeks (1948-50)	458	218	.475	35	3,056	17
6.	Dean Carlson (1970-71)	473	228	.482	33	3,028	24
7.	Wayne Stanley (1972-76)	390	180	.461	28	2,671	25
8.	George Amundson (1970-72)	436	192	.440	28	2,668	22
9.	John Quinn (1977-81)	459	226	.492	24	2,627	7
10.	Bob Utter (1990-93)	283	165	.583	17	2,302	10

		Rec.	Yards	Avg.	TD
1.	Tracy Henderson (1982-84)	150	2,048	13.7	14
2.	Otto Stowe (1968-70)	132	1,751	13.3	10
3.	Dennis Ross (1985-88)	118	1,529	13.0	7
4.	Eppie Barney (1964-66)	97	1,350	13.9	4
5.	Keith Krepfle (1971-73)	94	1,368	14.6	15
6.	Jason Jacobs (1982-83)	83	707	8.4	5
7.	Tom Busch (1965-67)	82	1,295	15.6	7
8.	Chris Spencer (1989-92)	82	1,278	15.6	4
9.	Jim Doran (1948-50)	79	1,410	17.8	10
10.	Mike Busch (1986-89)	78	1,061	13.6	4

CAREER LEADERS ALL-PURPOSE YARDAGE

		Rush	Rec.	Int.	PR	KOR	Total
1.	Dexter Green (1975-78)	3,437	516	0	6	106	4,065
2.	Mike Strachan (1972-74)	3,010	245	0	0	138	3,393
3.	Tom Vaughn (1962-64)	1,889	81	3	415	837	3,225
4.	Dwight Nichols (1957-59)	2,232	0	75	386	397	3,090
	Joe Henderson (1985-88)	2,715	375	0	0	0	3,090
6.	Dave Hoppmann (1960-62)	2,562	43	0	98	354	3,057
7.	Troy Davis (1994-95)	2,197	194	0	0	419	2,810
8.	Dwayne Crutchfield (1980-81)	2,501	253	0	0	0	2,754
9.	Jeff Allen(1968-70)	368	426	104	50	1,529	2,477
10.	Tom Busch (1965-67)	192	1,295	0	29	960	2,476

CAREER LEADERS SCORING

		TD	EP-1	EP-2	FG	TP
1.	Jeff Shudak (1987-90)	0	92	0	58	266
2.	Dexter Green (1975-78)	38	0	0	0	228
3.	Alex Giffords (1979-82)	0	85	0	43	214
4.	Ty Stewart (1991-94)	0	77	0	44	209
5.	Blaise Bryant (1989-90)	32	0	3	0	198
6.	Tom Goedjen (1972-74)	0	76	0	39	193
7.	George Amundson (1970-72)	31	0	0	0	186
8.	Dwayne Crutchfield (1980-81)	28	0	1	0	170
9.	Tom Vaughn (1962-64)	22	7	0	0	139
10.	Joe Henderson (1985-88)	22	0	1	0	134

CAREER LEADERS INTERCEPTIONS

1.	Barry Hill (1972-74)	21
2.	Tony Washington (1968-70)	14
3.	John Schweizer (1970-72)	12
4.	Everett Kischer (1936-38)	11
5.	Don Ferguson (1947-49)	10
6.	Larry Crawford (1977-80)	9
	Jeff Simonds (1966-68)	9
8.	Andrew Buggs (1988-92)	8
9.	Kevin Hart (1976-77)	6
	Marcus Robertson (1987-90)	6

CAREER LEADERS TOTAL TACKLES

1.	Chris Washington (1980-83), LB	457
2.	Keith Schroeder (1969-71), LB	398
3.	Ted Jornov (1971-73), LB	395
4.	Brad Storm (1972-74), LB	354
5.	Larry Hunt (1971-73), NG-LB	352
6.	Shamus McDonough (1979-82), DT	335
7.	Mark DouBrava (1989-92), DB	334
8.	Tom Boskey (1975-78), LB	331
9.	Dan Milner (1990-92), LB	328
10.	Mike Schwartz (1976-79), DB	319

CAREER LEADERS PUNTING AVERAGE

		Avg.
1.	Marc Harris (1993-95)	42.0
2.	Rick Blabolil (1975-77)	41.7
3.	Rick Frank (1985-86)	41.4
4.	Scott Bradley (1973-74)	40.5
5.	Jon Schnoor (1990-92)	40.4
6.	Bob Brouillette (1967-69)	39.3
7.	Judge Johnston (1987-89)	38.8
8.	Steve Balkovec (1963-65)	38.4

CAREER LEADERS KICKOFF RETURN YARDS

		No.	Yds.
1.	Jeff Allen (1968-70)	62	1,529
2.	Ray Hardee (1975-78)	61	1,487
3.	Willie Jones (1971-73)	55	1,240
4.	Luther Blue (1974-76)	38	1,006

CAREER LEADERS PUNT RETURN YARDS

		No.	Yds.
1.	James McMillion (1991-93)	53	843
2.	Don Ferguson (1947-49)	74	811
3.	John Schweizer (1970-72)	45	474
4.	Dwight Nichols (1957-59)	42	386
5.	Tom Buck (1977-78)	61	385
6.	Jeff Dole (1985-87)	48	368

TEAM RECORDS

MOST YARDS RUSHING

Game — 586, UNLV, 1995
Season — 2,970, 1976

MOST RUSHING ATTEMPTS

Game — 79, Kent State, 1982
Season — 636, 1976

MOST RUSHING YARDS PER PLAY

Game — 8.4, UNLV, 1995
Season — 5.0, 1995

MOST TOUCHDOWNS RUSHING

Game — 8, UNLV, 1995
Season — 30, 1989

MOST FIRST DOWNS BY RUSHING

Game — 22, Drake, 1976; Kansas State, 1976; UNLV, 1995
Season — 150, 1976

MOST PASSING ATTEMPTS

Game — 49, Oklahoma (27 completions), 1989
Season — 410, 1983

MOST PASS COMPLETIONS

Game — 29, Missouri, Kansas State, 1983
Season — 236, 1983

MOST PASSING YARDS GAINED

Game — 407, Oklahoma, 1989
(Bret Oberg, 411 yards; Chris Pedersen, -4)
Season — 2,717, 1983

MOST TOUCHDOWN PASSES

Game — 6, Air Force, 1976
Season — 22, 1972

MOST INTERCEPTIONS THROWN

Game — 8, Missouri, 1946
Season — 23, 1970

FEWEST INTERCEPTIONS THROWN

Game — 0, several times
Season — 5, 1958

BEST PASS COMPLETION PERCENTAGE

Game — .824 (14-17), Drake, 1978
(min. 10 att.)
Season — .618 (157-254), 1989

LOWEST PASS INTERCEPTION PCT.

Game — .000, several times
Season — .031, 1986

MOST FIRST DOWNS PASSING

Game — 19, Kansas State, 1983
Season — 130, 1983

TOTAL OFFENSE MOST POINTS SCORED

Game — 87, Simpson, 1904
Season — 369, 1976

MOST CONSECUTIVE GAMES SCORED

49, from Oct. 26, 1991-present

TOTAL OFFENSE MOST PLAYS

Game — 103, Kent State, 1982
Season — 889, 1976

TOTAL OFFENSE MOST YARDS

Game — 668, Dubuque, 1949
Season — 4,836, 1976
Avg. Per Game — 439.6, 1976

TOTAL OFFENSE MOST YARDS PER PLAY

Game — 9.2, Nebraska, 1945
Season — 5.4, 1976

TOTAL OFFENSE MOST TOTAL FIRST DOWNS

Game — 33, Utah, 1976
Season — 261, 1976

TOTAL DEFENSE FEWEST NET YARDS ALLOWED

Game — 62, Nebraska, 1947
Season — 2,095, 1959

TOTAL DEFENSE FEWEST RUSHING NET YARDS ALLOWED

Game — -16, Colorado, 1984
Season — 1,542, 1959

TOTAL DEFENSE FEWEST PASSING YARDS

Game — -3, Nebraska, 1986
Season — 302, 1960

TOTAL DEFENSE FEWEST TD PASSES ALLOWED

Game — 0, several times
Season — 0, 1949 (NCAA record)

TOTAL DEFENSE FEWEST COMPLETIONS ALLOWED

Game — 0, several times
Season — 29, 1943, 1960

TOTAL DEFENSE LOWEST COMPLETION PER. ALLOWED

Game — .000, several times
Season — .312, (29-93), 1960

PUNT RETURN DEFENSE

Lowest Avg. Return Season — 2.5, 1993

KICKOFF RETURN DEFENSE

Lowest Avg. Return Season — 10.5, 1956

FEWEST FIRST DOWNS ALLOWED

Game — 2, Nebraska, 1947
Season — 119, 1949

MOST INTERCEPTIONS

Game — 10, Gustavus Adolphus, 1944
Season — 24, 1971

MOST YARDS RETURNED

Game — 167, Northern Iowa, 1945
Season — 387, 1964

MOST INTERCEPTIONS RETURNED FOR TD

Season — 3, 1972

MOST PUNTS

Game — 18, Marquette, 1951
Season — 100, 1985

FEWEST PUNTS

Game — 0, Oklahoma, 1989
Season — 42, 1993

MOST PUNTING YARDS

Game — 601, Marquette, 1951
Season — 3,796, 1985

HIGHEST PUNTING AVERAGE

Game — 58.5, (2 punts) Oklahoma State, 1977
Season — 42.8, 1976

MOST PUNT RETURNS

Game — 9, Kansas State, 1947
Season — 48, 1947

MOST YARDS RETURNED

Game — 137, Tulane, 1992 (5 returns)
Season — 503, 1947 (48 returns)

HIGHEST AVG. PER RETURN

Game — 27.4, Tulane (5 returns, 137 yards), 1992
Season — 17.8, 1992 (28 returns, 497 yards)

PUNTS RETURNED FOR TD

Game — 1, many times
Season — 3, 1992

MOST KICKOFF RETURNS

Game — 9, Kansas, 1951; Nebraska, 1983
Season — 56, 1995

MOST YARDS RETURNED

Game — 254, Colorado (6 returns), 1968
Season — 1,986 (46 returns), 1970

HIGHEST AVG. PER RETURN

Game — 42.3, Colorado, 1968 (6 returns, 254 yards)
Season — 26.1, 1959 (24 returns, 626 yards)

Season — 2, 1959, 1963

MOST FUMBLES

Game — 12, Northwestern, 1956
Season — 51, 1956

MOST FUMBLES LOST

Game — 7, Drake, 1953
Season — 32, 1956

MOST OPPONENTS' FUMBLES RECOVERED

Game — 7, Arizona, 1968
Season — 30, 1954

FEWEST FUMBLES

Game — 0, many times
Season — 14, 1981

FEWEST FUMBLES LOST

Game — 0, many times
Season — 8, 1963, 1981

MOST PENALTIES

Game — 15, Utah, 1976
Season — 87, 1984

MOST PENALTY YARDS

Game — 156, Utah, 1976
Season — 734, 1986

FEWEST PENALTIES

Game — 0, Drake, 1945; Michigan State, 1947
Season — 26, 1953

FEWEST PENALTY YARDS

Game — 0, Drake, 1945; Michigan State, 1947
Season — 237, 1953

FOOTBALL LETTERMEN

A Brad Abbas, 1982; Chin Achebe, 1995; A. E. Adams, 1916; Jim Affholder, 1964-65; Dean Ahlers, 1988-89; Andy Alcorn, 1992; Howard Aldrich, 1915-16-17; Bruce Alexander, 1953-54-55; Ellis Alexander, 1941; Dennis Alitz, 1963-64; Ken Allbee, 1930; Barney Alleman, 1952-53-54; Bill Allen, 1963-64; Jeff Allen, 1968-69-70; Marcus Allen, 1991-92-93-94; Bill Allender, 1933-34-35; Harry Alley, 1964-65; H. P. Allstrand, 1910; Bill Alsin, 1919-20-21; Leslie Alt, 1924; Ken Ames, 1935; Jason Ambroson, 1993; George Amundson, 1970-71-21; Don Andersen, 1961-62; Bill Anderson, 1923-24; Bob Anderson, 1957-58-59; Dawan Anderson, 1995; Edwin Anderson, 1946; Elmer Anderson, 1922-26; Ernest Anderson, 1926; Jim Anderson, 1977; Joe Anderson, 1923; John Anderson, 1935-36-37; Kent Anderson, 1983-84-85; Norm Anderson, 1945-46-47; Stan Anderson, 1948; Tom Anderson, 1987; Dale Andrews, 1911-12; Derek Andrews, 1979; Tommie Andrews, 1983; Terry Andringa, 1974; Bob Angle, 1947-48-49; Lagrant Anthony, 1974; Terrence Anthony, 1984-85-86; David Archer, 1982-83; Jim Arenston, 1912; Scott Armbrust, 1990-91-92; Bill Armstrong, 1945; Dwayne Armstrong, 1991-92; John Arnaud, 1979-80-81-82; Jahi Arnold, 1994; Rollie Arns, 1950-51-52; Bob Ash, 1941-42; Roger Ashland, 1967; Gary Astleford, 1958-60-61; Patrick Augafa, 1995; Owen Austrheim, 1970-71; Irving Axelson, 1924; Edward Axtheim, 1913-14; Gould Ayres, 1926-27.

B Marc Bachrodt, 1983-84-85; Alvin Baker, 1982-83; Bob Baker, 1968-69; Dennis Baker, 1965-66; Tim Baker, 1986-87-88; Tony Baker, 1964-65; Jim Baldwin, 1922; Jason Bales, 1995; Steve Balkovec, 1963-64-65; R. J. Balthus, 1905; Todd Bandhauer, 1995; Dennis Bandy, 1967; Bob Banger, 1970-71-72; Ralph Baracz, 1969-70; Bill Barger, 1940-41-42; Dick Barker, 1916-17-19; Willie Barker, 1934; Tom Barnes, 1968-69-70; Eppie Barney, 1964-65-66; Jim Barr, 1959; Bob Barrow, 1939; Jerry Bartell, 1955; Neal Barton, 1922; Harold Bassett, 1970-71; Sy Bassett, 1974-75; C. E. Bates, 1921; Jeff Bauer, 1987-88-89-90; Al Bauman, 1931-36-37; George Bazik, 1937-38; Vince Beacom, 1948-49-50; Bruce Beaman, 1974; Clarke Beard, 1909; Jesse Woodrow Beard, 1935; Jim Beasley, 1968-69; Joe Beauchamp, 1964; Adam Beck, 1987-88; Dan Becker, 1972-73; Johnny Behm, 1923-24-25; Norton Behm, 1923-24-25; Dean Beilby, 1977; Frank Belichick, 1962-65; Bob Belluz, 1970-71; Mark Benda, 1975-76; Jim Beneke, 1942; Forrest Bennett, 1928-29-30; Bryce Bennett, 1947; Herschel Bennett, 1920-22-23; Dave Benoit, 1985-87-88-89; Ray Benson, 1919; Scott Benson, 1986-87; Paul Berger, 1932-33-34; Walter Berger, 1922-23; Randy Bern, 1987-88-89; Jerry Berna, 1968-69-70; John Berrington, 1963-64; Bill Berthusen, 1983-84-85-86;

Wayne Beske, 1968-69; J.D. Bewley, 1994; Jack Beyer, 1932-33; *Sammy Beyer, 1904; H. T. Bigelow, 1909; D. H. Biller, 1904-05-06; A. L. Birch, 1920; Bob Bird, 1955-56-57; Harold Birney, 1934; Warren Bissell, 1920; Ken Bixby, 1966-67; Rich Blabolil, 1975-76-77; Matt Blair, 1971-73; Dick Blanch, 1894-95; Brett Blaney, 1980-82-83; Grant Blaney, 1955-56; Joe Blankenship, 1986; Chuck Blaskovich, 1972-73; Bill Bliss, 1938-39; Dick Bliss, 1943; Mike Bliss, 1968-69; Travis Block, 1988-89-90-91; Luther Blue, 1974-75-76; Ed Blumenstein, 1936; Shannon Boals, 1990; Ed Bock, 1936-37-38; Ron Bockhaus, 1978-79; V. C. Bodwell, 1920; Mark Boehm, 1976-77; Eugene Boeke, 1919; Phil Bogdanovitch, 1941; Bob Bognar, 1971; Lloyd Bohannon, 1928; Rob Bolks, 1973-74; Craig Boller, 1967-68-69; Karl Bond, 1924-25; Mort Bonesteel, 1948; Tony Booth, 1991-92-93-94; Bob Bos, 1973-74-75; Chris Boskey, 1978-79-81-82; Tom Boskey, 1975-76-77-78; Lou Bosnyak, 1942-46-48; Marty Boswell, 1937-38-39; Roger Bowen, 1930-31; John Bowers, 1939; Hillford Bowes, 1929-30; Greg Boyd, 1995; Marshall Boyd, 1917-19-20; Randy Bozich, 1972-73; Jerry Boyington, 1968-69-70; Scott Bradley, 1973-74; Calvin Branch, 1993-94; Scott Brandt, 1983-84; Jeff Braswell, 1984-85; Mark Braver, 1977; Lawrence Brazon, 1965; John Breckenridge, 1954-55; Frank Bredahl, 1947; Ron Bredeson, 1955-56; Cyrus Breeden, 1916-17-18; Bill Brennan, 1912-13; Bob Brettman, 1949-50; Carl Brettschneider,' 1950-51-52; Guy Brewer, 1895-96-97; Eddie Bridges, 1986-87; Phil Brinkman, 1948; George Broderson, 1920-21-22; Warren Broms, 1916-19; Bill Brooks, 1965-66; James Brooks, 1992-93; J. B. Brorby, 1920-21-22; Bob Brouillette, 1969-70; Eddie Brown, 1986-88; Harold Brown, 1982; Hunter Brown, 1934; Jason Brown, 1993-94-95; Joe Brown, 1978-79-80-81; Mike Brown, 1986; Norman Brown, 1926; Ralph Brown, 1952-53-54; Stan Brown, 1940; Tim Brown, 1962-63; Ira C. Brownlie, 1892-93-94-95; Howard Brubaker, 1948-49-50; Joe Brubaker, 1947-48-49; F. W. Brugger, 1906-07; Bob Brutsman, 1962-63-64; Blaise Bryant, 1989-90; Howard Buck, 1939; Tom Buck, 1977-78-79; Arthur Buckley, 1902; Andrew Buggs, 1989-90-91-92; Ken Bunte, 1963-64; Rick Burchett, 1965-66-67; J. W. "Joe" Burden, 1960-61; Charlie Burge, 1910-11-12; Max Burkett, 1952-53-54; Dick Burnett, 1949; Steve Burns, 1970-71-72; Warren Burns, 1919; Bob Burrell, 1939-40-41; Jim Burrows, 1907; Bob Burton, 1927-28-29; Mike Busch, 1986-87-88-89; Tom Busch, 1965-67-68; Joe Bush, 1947; James Butler, 1984-85; Marcus Butts, 1979-80-81; Greg Buttz, 1984; F. M. Byl, 1900-01-02; Bill Byers, 1920; Bill Byrus, 1950-51-52.

C Bob Caddock, 1941; Kevin Caldwell, 1991; Dick Callahan, 1954; Bobby Campbell, 1994; George Campbell, 1971-72; Roy Campbell, 1901; Sam Campbell, 1966-67-68; Stan Campbell, 1949-50-51; Brian Cannon, 1970-71-72; Gil Carafiol, 1943; Ken Caratelli, 1970-71-72; Dean Carlson, 1970-71; Lyle Carlson, 1956-57; Mark Carlson, 1979-80-81-82; Tony Carlson, 1980-81; Hugh Carr, 1907; Ray Carreathers, 1987-88; Larry Carwell, 1964-65-66; Harlan Cassin, 1917-18; John Catron, 1933-34-35; J. H. Cave, 1902-05; Dan Celoni, 1959-60-61; Vinny Cerrato, 1977-78-80-81; L. H. Chamberlain, 1894-95; L. M. Chamberlain, 1900-01; Jim Champlin, 1952-53; Terry Chandler, 1962; A. R. Chappell, 1909-10-11; Darrell Chapper, 1976; Martin Chase, 1924; Bill Chauncey, 1946-47-48-49; Dave Cheesebrough, 1978; Dick Cherpinsky, 1951-52; John Chism, 1965; E. W. Church, 1919-20-21; Arlen Ciechanowski, 1974; Jerry Cimburek, 1948-50; John Cinefro, 1986-88; Jon Claborn, 1987; Jim Clapper, 1960-61-62; Ted Clapper, 1979-80-81-82; Bob Clark, 1953; Fred Clausen, 1943; Nick Clausen, 1993-94; Ozzie Clay, 1962-63; Dave Clayberg, 1960-61-62; Sam Clear, 1982-83; Mike Clemons, 1976-77-78; Bob Clendenning, 1950-51-52; B. F. Cockerill, 1909-10; Cliff Cody, 1922-23; Roland "Bud" Coe, 1924-25-26; Chuck Coey, 1952-53; Ray Coffey, 1969; Jeff Cole, 1991-92-93-94; Richard Cole, 1944-45-46; Scott Cole, 1976-77-78; Lon Coleman, 1972-73; Ray Coleman, 1969; Kevin Colon, 1985-86; George Conditt, 1990, 1992; Frank Congiardo, 1950-51-52; Ralph Conner, 1982-83; Frank Copper, 1976-77; John Cooper, 1959-60-61; Michael Cooper, 1994-95; Tim Copeland, 1980; Lincoln Cory, 1925; D. E. Cotter, 1916; William O. Cotter, 1969-70; Theman Couch, 1969-70; Kevin Coughlin, 1980-81; Russ Coundiff, 1934-35; Lynn Cowan, 1912-13; Chris Cox, 1986; Dick Cox, 1951-52-53; Mike Cox, 1962-63-64; Travis Cox, 1993; John Coye, 1900-01; Stan Cozzi, 1951-52; E. F. Cramer, 1914; Alva Crawford, 1910-12; Larry Crawford, 1977-78-79-80; Tim Creasman, 1986-88; Mark Criner, 1986; Hal Crisler, 1943; Steve Cromie, 1986; Carl Crowse, 1918; Dwayne Crutchfield, 1980-81; Cal Cummins, 1976-77; C. W. Cunningham, 1911-13; Jim Cunningham, 1966; Kevin Cunningham, 1975-76-77; Roger Cunningham, 1951-52; Jack Currie, 1919-20-21; Jeff Curry, 1976-77-78; Dick Cuvelier, 1976-77-78-79.

D Robert Dabney, 1986-87; Bill Dailey, 1936; Dan Daly, 1988; Terry Dammann, 1988; P. E. Damon 1895-96-97; Amos Dana, 1932-33; P. H. Daniels, 1901-02-03-04; Phil Danowsky, 1972-73-74; Paul Darling, 1940-41-42; Bob Darrow, 1939; Ole Davidson, 1897; Anthony Davis, 1984; Frank Davis, 1913; Harry Davis, 1908; Sammy Davis, 1968-71; Tommy Davis, 1981-82-83-84; Troy Davis, 1994-95; Tyrone Davis, 1988; Will Davis, 1916-19; W. S. Dawson, 1893; Kelly Day, 1986; M. R. Deakin, 1908; William DeButts, 1914; Francis DeDecker, 1945-46; Clarence Dee, 1936-37; John Dee, 1958; Charles Deering, 1892; Glenn Deffke, 1914-15; Derek DeGennaro, 1985-86-87-88; F. J. Delaney, 1913-14-15; Joe DeLaRosa, 1966; Jack Delbridge, 1949; Gilbert Denfield, 1915-16-19; Bob Dennis, 1946; Brian Dennis, 1956-57; Clifford Dennis, 1944; W. E. Deshler, 1901; Dennis DiBiase, 1994-95; Jim Dickerson, 1948; George Dimitri, 1966-67-68; Jim Dishinger, 1935-36-37; Al Dixon, 1974-75-76; Bill Dixon, 1931-32-33; Pete Doering, 1987; Wendell Dohrman, 1951; Jeff Dole, 1985-86-87-88; Jerry Donohue, 1956-58; Jim Doran, 1949-50; Jim Doran, Jr., 1987-88-89-90; Lant Doran, 1989-90-91; Dan Dostal, 1991-92-93-94; Jesse Doty, 1928; Mark DouBrava, 1989-90-91-92; J. M. Dowell, 1913; Todd Doxzon, 1993-94-95; I. A. Dreher, 1902; R. H. Drennan, 1904-05-06; Marcus Dubel, 1915; Warren Dusenberg, 1929-30-31; Greg Dukstein, 1967-69; Shane Dunlevy, 1990, 1992; Howard Dunn, 1930; Mark Dunn, 1989-90-91; H. E. Dyer, 1895-96-97.

E Terry Earnest, 1977-78-79; Doug Easley, 1995; Bill Easter, 1968; H. N. Ebersole, 1901; Herb Eckles, 1900; Ray Eckles, 1896; Robert Eckles, 1895-96; Dave Eder, 1987-88-89-90; Willis Edson, 1897-98; Bill Edar, 1914; Don Edwards, 1986-87-88-89; Kevin Eggleston, 1983-84-85; Paul Eichling, 1912; Emery Eichorn, 1950-51-52;

Robert Ekins, 1920-21-22; Kern Elerick, 1931; Robert Elkins, 1933; Dave Eller, 1957; Roosevelt Ellerbe, 1963; F. A. Elliott, 1909; Tom Elliott, 1968-69; Gary Ellis, 1960-61-62; W. D. Elwood, 1904; Bob Engebretson, 1964; Dennis Engel, 1976-77; Jon English, 1981-82; Scott English, 1991; Jack Erickson, 1952; Clyde Erskine, 1916; Louie Ervin, 1991-92; Alex Espinoza, 1984-85-86; Dennis Esselmann, ; 1965-66-67; Arden Esslinger, 1958-59-60; Clair Ethington, 1940-41-46; Bob Ettinger, 1942; Sam Etzel, 1931; Bob Evans, 1964-65-66; Harold Evans, 1916; John L. Evans, 1914-15; Seymour Evans, 1916; W. T. Evans, 1914; Elve Everage, 1970; Willie Everett, 1984-85.

F John Falter, 1955-56-57; W. H. Farner, 1914; Ed Farni, 1945-46; Andrew Farrell, 1922; Jack Fathauer, 1943-44-45-46; Ev Faunce, 1945; Ray Fauser, 1958; Oliver Fay, 1898; Burt Fayram, 1925; Don Ferguson, 1947-48-49; Tom Ferrebee, 1958-59; Jerry Fiat, 1967-68-69; Brian Fiekema, 1965-66-67; Jerry Finley, 1954; B. J. "Bugs" Firkins, 1916; Doug Fischer, 1980-81-82-83; Karl Fischer, 1927; Bob Fisher, 1924-25; F. D. Fisher, 1917; Mike Fitzgerald, 1958-59-60; Kevin Fleecs, 1994-95; Bruce Fling, 1973; Vernon Foell, 1917; Bill Fogarty, 1957; Mark Foley, 1987-88; Ron Fontana, 1957; Mike Fontanini, 1969-71; Gerry Forge, 1973-74; Jim Foster, 1961; John Foster, 1915; Howard Foy, 1944; Jim Foy, 1945-48; Rick Frank, 1985-86; W. H. Frakes, 1916; Gary Fraser, 1969; F. C. French, 1894-95-96; George Friedl, 1947-48-49; John Fritsch, 1973-74-75; Henry Fritzel, 1899; Wes Fuchs, 1949; Ed Fuller, 1939; Kevin Fulton, 1991-92-93-94; Robert Fulton, 1909; R. A. Furrow, 1905; Sherman Fyles, 1903-05.

G Larry Gaffin, 1968; Ray Gahone, 1971; Ray Galbraith, 1924-25-27; Mike Gannon, 1978; Danny Gantt, 1983-84-85; Dwight M. Ganer, 1932-33-34; Artis Garris, 1992-93-94; Morrison Garth, 1913; Lou Gartner, 1958-59-60; George Gast, 1941-42-43; Garlon Gaylord, 1921; R. E. Gaylor, 1919; Doran Geise, 1981-82; Pierre Gelinas, 1974-75; Bill George, 1923; Pete Gerdom, 1970; Bert German, 1893-94-95; Damian Gibson, 1995; Dennis Gibson, 1983-84-85-86; Gale Gibson, 1956-57-58; Alex Giffords, 1979-80-81-82; Rocky Gillis, 1978-80-81-82; Willie Gillis, 1972-73; Dwayne Gilyard, 1981-82-83; Duncan Glab, 1938; Greg Gloede, 1987-88-89; John Glotfelty, 1987-88-89-90; Mike Gnade, 1973-74-75; Tom Goedjen, 1972-73-74; Pete Goeser, 1957-58-59; Joe Goldberg, 1938; Melvin "Bud" Goltry, 1946; Kelly Goodburn, 1982; Dan Goodwin, 1979; Malcolm Goodwin, 1990-91-92; Matt Goodwin, 1989-92; Brandon Goodyk, 1994; Jim Graham, 1925; M. L. Graham, 1907-08; Tom Graham, 1959-61; Walter Grant, 1978-79; Bruce Grasser, 1961-62-63; John Graveno, 1933; Don Graves, 1966-67; Doug Graves, 1938-39-40; Roy Gray, 1909; Dexter Green, 1975-76-77-78; Eddy Green, 1948-49-50; King Green, 1982; Bill Greene, 1908; Tony Greene, 1981-82; Reece "Pinkie" Greene, 1922; J. M. Greenfield, 1917; Karl Greenlee, 1923; Dave Greenwood, 1974-75-76; Don Greenwood, 1972-73; J. E. Greer, 1922; Dick Grefe, 1930-31-32; Don Grefe, 1932-35; C. J. Griffith, 1897-98-99; John Griffith, 1947-48; John Griglione, 1968-69-70; Lynn Grimes, 1925-26; Al Grissinger, 1976-77-78; Don Griswold, 1938-39-40; Bill Gross, 1908-09; Greg Grove, 1974-75-76; Matt Grubb, 1989-90-91; Tom Grundman, 1947-48-49; Roger Guge, 1968; Rodney Guggenheim, 1993-94-95; Clarence Gustine, 1935-36; Russell Gute, 1934-35.

H Bobby Hackett, 1985; L. M. Hadley, 1917-19; Webb Halbert, 1947-48; Ron Halda, 1964-65; Scott Hale, 1973-74-75; Daryl Hall, 1993-94; Ted Hall, 1966-68; Vernon Hall, 1925-26-27; Mitch Hallett, 1974; M. J. Hammer, 1896-97-98; Wurdette Hanna, 1936; Larry Hannahs, 1961-62-63; Dan Hanover, 1976; Jeff Hansel, 1986; Jack Hansen, 1955-57; Mike Hansen, 1995; Scott Hansen, 1977; G. D. Hanson, 1917; Richard Hanson, 1983-84; Mel Happe, 1939-40; Ray Hardee, 1975-76-77-78; Buddy Hardeman, 1973-74-75; Bob Harden, 1956-57-58; Weylan Harding, 1991-92-93; Howard Harlan, 1933-34; Ray Harm, 1969-70-71; Ike Harris, 1971-72-73; Marc Harris, 1993-94-95; Mike Harris, 1980; Rodney Harris, 1986-88; Willie Harris, 1969-70; Dan Harrison, 1936;

Maurice Harrison, 1914-16; Kevin Hart, 1976-77; E. C. Harte, 1909-10-11; Ben Harvey, 1991-92-93; Ray Harvey, 1984; George Harville, 1942; John Hauck, 1945; Walter Haugo, 1944; Tony Hawkins, 1974-75-76; Casey Hayes, 1985-86; Claude Hayes, 1941; Ike Hayes, 1933-34-35; A. N. Heggen, 1908-09; John Heggen, 1939-40-41; V. A. "Chick" Heater, 1916-17-18; George Heick, 1951-52; Charles Heidel, 1944; Charles Heileman, 1936-37-38; Howard Heinrich, 1956; Byron Heitz, 1994-95; Darrell Helgens, 1957; H. K. Helseth, 1916; Keith Hemingway, 1951-52; James Henderson, 1995; Joe Henderson, 1985-86-87-88; Tracy Henderson, 1982-83-84; Lance Henkel, 1991; C. E. Henninger, 1904-05-06; Frank Henninger, 1910-11; Pat Henricksen, 1978; Chris Hentges, 1986-87-88; Ray Henteges, 1922; Bob Herman, 1974; Carl Herman, 1917; Bill Herren, 1977-79; George Hess, 1950-51; David Heyn, 1984-86-87-88; Do Hibbs, 1918-19-20; Otis Higgins, 1920-21; Tom Hilden, 1968-70; Barry Hill, 1972-73-74; Charles Hill, 1923-24-25; Lamont Hill, 1990-91-92-93; Phil Hill, 1956-57-58; Sanford Hill, 1927; Arthur Hinderman, 1918-19; Dick Hiserodt, 1945; Gilbert Hitch, 1929; Stan Hixon, 1976-77-78; Daryl Hobbs, 1953-55; Darryl Hobson, 1979-80-81-82; Van Hollaway, 1971-72; Jim Hollingsworth, 1921; Dean Hollrah, 1977; Allen Holman, 1926; Earl A. Holmes, 1913-15; Larry Holton, 1966-67-69; Alan Hood, 1983-84-85; Charles Hood, 1930; Frank Hood, 1933-34; Dave Hoover, 1961-62-63; Dave Hoppmann, 1960-61-62; Mike Horacek, 1993-94-95; Wayne Horras, 1952-53-54; Anthony Hoskins, 1986-87-88; H. S. Hough, 1910; Don Houser, 1952-53; Dick Howard, 1943-44-45-46; Rick Howe, 1972-73-74; Howard Howell, 1983; Larry Howes, 1937; Homer Hubbard, 1905-06-07-08; Kevin Hudson, 1995; Dick Hufman, 1945; Eric Huhndorf, 1984-85-86; Rocky Hughe, 1978; Brandon Hughes, 1990-91-92-93; D. A. Hunt, 1910-11-12; Larry Hunt, 1971-72-73; Kent Hunter, 1986; R. L. "Buck" Hurst, 1910-11-12; Mark Huston, 1972-73-74; Rodney Hutchins, 1980-81-83.

I T. J. Iles, 1913; Ivan Impson, 1930-31-32; Michael Ingram, 1980; Terry Ingram, 1956-57-58; Webster Intermill, 1930; Harold Ireland, 1943; Klarence Isler, 1975; Tim Iversen, 1983-84-85.

J Andrew Jackson, 1985-86; Joe Jackson, 1983-84; Cal Jacobs, 1976-78-80; Jacon Jacobs, 1982-83; Bob Jacobsen, 1949-50-51; Steve Jacobsen, 1969-70-72; Harry Jager, 1917; Ladislus Janda, 1916-19; Jerry Jaksich, 1973-74-75-76; Kenneth James, 1979; Darrell Jansonius, 1970; Vince Jasper, 1984-85-86; Ramsey Jay, 1973-74; Robert "Jobby" Jean, 1904-06-07; Tim Jeffries, 1968-69; Tim Jennings, 1992; Bill Jensen, 1951-55; Bob Jensen, 1945-46-47; Howard Jensen, 1949-50; Mike Jensen, 1980-81; Joel Jenson, 1979-80; George Jessen, 1979-80-81-82; Jim Jessen, 1947-48; Tony Johann, 1983; Ed John, 1913-14-15; Al Johnson, 1976-78-79; Brian Johnson, 1977-78-79; Bruce Johnson, 1945; Dan Johnson, 1980-81; Harry Johnson, 1927-28-29; Harvey "Jock" Johnson, 1968-69-70; J. V. Johnson, 1919; Lyell Johnson, 1916-17; Nick Johnson, 1959; Randono Johnson, 1988; Russell Johnson, 1993-94; Steve Johnson, 1977-78; Ted Johnson, Jr., 1990; Wendell Johnson, 1932; Judge Johnston, 1987-88-89; W. D. Johnston, 1907-09; D. C. Jones, 1914-15-16; Ed Jones, 1914-15-16; Edwin Jones, 1987; Fred Jones, 1967-68-69; Jeff Jones, 1973-74-75; John Jones, 1904-05-06; Marshall Jones, 1920; Ray Jones, 1914; Willie Jones, 1971-72-73; Martin Jordan, 1928; F. F. Jorgenson, 1901-02-03-04; Ted Jornov, 1971-72-73; Dick Joslyn, 1944; Chris Juhl, 1910-11-12.

K Steve Karber, 1968-69-70; Arthur Karr, 1913-14-15; Tom Karr, 1972-73; Dick Kasperek, 1963-65; Lance Keller, 1991; John Kelly, 1969-71; Earnest Kennedy, 1963-64-65; Pat Kennedy, 1976-77-78; Ken Keough, 1944; Doug Keown, 1971-72; Carl Kern, 1928-29; Carl Kessle, 1922; Lynn Kettleson, 1964; James Key, 1981; Randy Kidd, 1961-62-63; Ed Kimbrough, 1964; Jeff Kincart, 1980; Ben King, 1966-67-68; Charles King, 1938; Gary King, 1965-66; Kip King, 1995; Ray King, 1973-74-75; Elmer Kingery, 1925-26; Nile Kinnick, 1913-14; Mike Kirar, 1967-68-69; Bob Kirkpatrick, 1939-

40-41; Everett Kischer, 1936-37-38; Tom Kiska, 1986; Ray Klootwyk, 1946-47-48; Bill Klug, 1926; Dan Kneller, 1971-72-73; Mark Kness, 1977; Werner Knoop, 1924; Carl Knop, 1944-47; Jim Knott, 1991-92-93-94; A. B. Knox, 1905-08; Jim Knuth, 1979-80-82; Randy Koch, 1975-76-78; Jamie Kohl, 1995; Tim Kohn, 1993-94-95; Carter Kokjer, 1943-44-46; Scott Kollman, 1975-76-77; Mark Konopka, 1992-93-95; Paul Konrad, 1973; Harold Kornbaum, 1950; Kip Koski, 1964-66; Brent Kouba, 1991-92; Gene Kowalski, 1952-53; J. H. Kraft, 1909; Merv Krakau, 1970-71-72; Harry Kraus, 1944-46; H. R. Kreger, 1893-94; Ed Krekow, 1927-28; Keith Krepfle, 1971-72-73; Todd Krieger, 1983-84; Wilbur Kroeger, 1934; Milton Kubicek, 1928; Matt Kuhns, 1990; John Kulp, 1928; Ernest Kun, 1963-64; Dennis Kushlak, 1965.

L E. W. Lambert, 1906-07-08; Guy Lambert, 1907-08; Jeff Lambert, 1983-85; Mike Lamberto, 1966-67-68; Prentis Lamont, 1958; Ray Lampman, 1907; Bob Lamson, 1926-27; Chuck Lamson, 1958; Jean Lange, 1939-40-41; Bill Larkin, 1975; Mike Larsen, 1975; C. H. Larson, 1923; Craig Larson, 1958; Elmer Larson, 1928; Eugene Larson, 1923-24; Jim Lary, 1956-57; G. M. LaSourd, 1909; B. J. Lattimer, 1911; Chuck Latting, 1956-57; Clarence Laubenfels, 1917; Louis Laughlin, 1920-21-22; Dean Laun, 1946-47-48-49; Don Laun, 1946-48-50; Perry Laures, 1984-85; F. W. Law, 1907-08; Brett Lawrence, 1983-84-85-86; Kevin Lazard, 1990-91-93; Jeff Leaders, 1986; Mike Leaders, 1977-78-79; Mickey Leafblad, 1976-77-79; Frankie Leaks, 1981-82; Bill Lechtenberg, 1939-40; Bob Lechtenberg, 1949-52; Greg Lempke, 1978; Robert Lendino, 1988; Doug Lenth, 1973-75; Les Leonard, 1975; John Less, 1978-79-80; Jack Lessin, 1951-52-53; Marcus Lester, 1986; Kurt Levetzow, 1995; Curtis Levingston, 1983; Cal Lewis, 1965-66-67; Clarence Lewis, 1893-94-95; Henry Lewis, 1971-72-73; LaVerne "Butch" Lewis, 1939-40-41; Magnus Lichter, 1932-33; Keevin Ligons, 1978; Marc Lillibridge, 1992-93-94; Dick Limerick, 1961-62-63; F. S. Linbach, 1920; Mike Lincavage, 1993-94-95; Harry Lindblom, 1926-27-28; Larry Lindgren, 1945; F. B. Lingenfelter, 1919-20-21; Jeff Lingren, 1978-79; Herb Linn, 1975; Cedric Linwood, 1991,93-94; Greg Liter, 1983-84-85-86; Gary Little, 1972; Steve Little, 1981-82-83-84; Royal Lohry, 1940-41-42; William Lomax, 1927; Steve Loney, 1973; Darren Longshore, 1981-82; Roy Longstreet, 1922-23-24; Donn Lorenzen, 1954-55; Jerry Lorenzen, 1979-80-81-82; Tom Lorenz, 1968-69-70; Ralph Losee, 1956-57-58; Dean Loucks, 1917; Lloyd Lounsbury, 1929; Earl Lowe, 1921; Clint Loy, 1979; Vernon Loyd, 1934; Jim Luebbers, 1982-83-84-85; Wayne Lueders, 1963-64-65; Fred Lutjens, 1927-28; Gary Lutz, 1853-54; Glenn Luymes, 1948; Fred Lyford, 1893-94-95; Wayne Lyles, 1974; R. A. Lyman, 1906; Jim Lyons, 1954-55.

M Ira Mabie, 1905; Victor Mack, 1978-79-80; Norm Madson, 1943; Rick Magill, 1977; Craig Mahoney, 1987-88-89-90; H. A. Maine, 1898-99; Mike Malloy, 1989-91; Dick Mann, 1951-52; Aaron Manning, 1985-86; Duane Marcellus, 1960; Joe Marconi, 1970-71; Craig Manske, 1976; Jim Marks, 1945; Larry Marquardt, 1971-72-73; Leo Marshall, 1958-59; Bill Martin, 1956-58; Bobby Martin, 1972; Charles Martin, 1956-58; Dan Martin, 1981-82-83; Dave Martin, 1986-87; Eric Martin, 1994; George Martin, 1932; Bob Martinson, 1970-71-72; Terry Martinson, 1972-73; Tom Mason, 1974-75; Bob Matey, 1969-70-71; Bob Matheson, 1950-51-52; Horner Mattison, 1913-14; Mark Matuscak, 1984; George Maurer, 1964-65-66; Channon Mawdsley, 1984-85-86; Elmer May, 1953-54; Dave Mayberry, 1965-66-67; Frank Mayer, 1923-24-25; Anthony Mayze, 1984-85; J. M. McAvinchey, 1920-21; Dan McAvoy, 1968; Jon McCarthy, 1974; Jim McCaulley, 1954-55; Larry McCaulley, 1978-79; Todd McClish, 1991-92; Ed McCoy, 1908-09-10; Bill McCue, 1981-82-83-84; Dave McCurry, 1970-71-72; Herb McDermott, 1949-50-54; Dennis McDonald, 1969-70-71; Roy McDonald, 1910-11-12; Everett McDonnell, 1914; Shamus McDonough, 1979-80-81-82; Ralph McEilhinney, 1904-05-06-07; Dick McFarland, 1917; Ron McFarland, 1973-74-75-77; Jerry McGlynn, 1948-49-50; John

McGonegie, 1962; LaVerne McGraw, 1940-41-42; M .W. McGuire, 1918; Azel McIlrath, 1919; E. G. McKibbon, 1920; John McKillop, 1971-72-73; Harold McKinley, 1913-14-15; E. M. McLaughlin, 1894; James McMillion, 1989-91-92-93; Gilbert McQuern, 1932; Cliff McTaggert, 1920; Randy Means, 1969-70; Greg Meckstroth, 1978; Ralph Meckstroth, 1978; Howard Medin, 1939; Royal Meeker, 1895-96-97; John Meis, 1977-78; Bill Melham, 1920; Bob Meling, 1956; Mel Meling, 1949-50-51; Bob Mellgren, 1951-52; A. E. Mellinger, 1892-93-94-95; Don Metcalf, 1956-57; Jim Meyer, 1979-80-81-82; Robert Meyer, 1955; Chuck Meyers, 1980-81-82-83; Joe Meyers, 1893-94-95; Ivory Mhoon, 1993-94; B. O. Mickelson, 1939-40; Harold Miller, 1933-34-35; John Miller, 1926-27; Merritt Miller, 1940; Rich Miller, 1978-79-80-81; Sherman Miller, 1972-73-74; Todd Miller, 1990-92-93; Tom Miller, 1976; M. A. Mills, 1905; Dan Milner, 1990-91-92; Robbie Minor, 1983-84-86; Ben Mitchell, 1986-87-88; Les Mitchell, 1970-72; Dick Mitchell, 1935; Byron Moad, 1911-12-13; Jim Moeller, 1960; John Moen, 1930; Larry Montre, 1960-61-62; Bob Moody, 1938-39; Barry Moore, 1981-82-83-84; Chris Moore, 1985-86-87; Kelvin Moore, 1995; Moses Moore, 1971-72-73; Rich Moore, 1987-88; Troy Moore, 1988-89-90; Erhard Moosman, 1952-53; Paul Morin, 1937-38; Jim Morrison, 1920-21; Bernard Mortensen, 1943; John A Mortimer, 1952; John R. Mortimer, 1961-62-63; Ed Morton, 1974; Jerry Moses, 1972-73; Durwood Moss, 1914-15-16; Al Moton, 1977-78; Jim Mraz, 1971; Ernest Muehler, 1938; Chuck Muelhaupt, 1954-55-56; Willie Muldrew, 1966-67-68; Greg Mulhall, 1970-71-72; R. G. Mullen, 1914; Dick Muller, 1969; Dave Munger, 1956-57-58; Geary Murdock, 1970-71-72; J. L. Murphy, 1907-08; John Murphy, 1954-55-56; Benn Musgrave, 1980-81-82-83; Chris Mussman, 1987-88-89-90; Tendai Muyengwa, 1994; Bill Myers, 1947-48-49; Doug Myers, 1982-83; Jim Myers, 1948.

N Clarence Nagel, 1912-14; Gordon Nagel, 1929-30-31; Sheldon Napastuk, 1993-94-95; Eric Nasstrom, 1990-91; W. L. "Spike" Nave, 1923-24; Adam "Jud" Neal, 1917-19; Brian Neal, 1977-78-80-81; Tom Neal, 1934-35-36; Kenny Neil, 1977-78-80-81; Arthur Nelson, 1917; Bervin, Nelson, 1954; Jay Nelson, 1983; Jim Nelson, 1977; Karl Nelson, 1979-80-81-82; L. A. "Bat" Nelson, 1906-06-08; Mort Nelson, 1950; Scott Nelson, 1981-82-83; Truman Nelson, 1929-30; Harry Neyenesch, 1922-23; Dwight Nichols, 1952; Dwight Nichols, 1957-58-59; Floyd Nichols, 1930; T. E. Nichols, 1902; Sylvester Nickerson, 1986-87-88; Dick Niemann, 1982; Tim Niggeling, 1984; Jim Nissen, 1978-79-80; Matt Nitchie, 1990-91-93-94; Joe Noble, 1943-44; Frank Nolte, 1929-30-31; Dean Norman, 1948-49; Ron Norman, 1942-46-47; Graston Norris, 1993-94-95; Harold Nowlin, 1920-21.

O Bret Oberg, 1988-89; Marv Oberg, 1934; Duane Ohrt, 1974; Herb Ohrt, 1932; Brent Olsen, 1992; Bob Olson, 1950-51; Dana Omer, 1947-48-49; Ron Onopa, 1963; R. E. Orr, 1919; Dell Osborn, 1971-72-73; Merle Osborne, 1938-39-40; Ron Osborne, 1979-80-81-82; Carl Ours, 1928; Rob Overton, 1973-74; Fred Owen, 1898-99; Larry Owens, 1940; Todd Oxley, 1985.

P Roscoe Packer, 1914-15-16; Tom Padjen, 1973; Carl Paetz, 1944-45-46; Will Paige, 1916-19; Cyril Palm, 1921-22-24; Cloyce Palmer, 1952-53; Denny Palmer, 1954; Mike Palmer, 1969-70; Joe Palmisano, 1973-74-75; Foster Parker, 1895-96-97; Joe Parmentier, 1995; Tom Parrish, 1962; Will Parsons, 1895-96; Win Parsons, 1895-96; Alan Patten, 1986-87-88; Sundiata Patterson, 1990-91-92; Dick Paukert, 1964-65; Lawrence Paulson, 1947-48-49; Michael Payne, 1979-80; Bob Pearson, 1943; Terry Pearson, 1957; Chris Pedersen, 1989-90-91; Gary Pedersen, 1988-90; Scott Pederson, 1977; Chuck Penn, 1973; Alex Perez, 1959; A. C. Perrin, 1904-05; Lenzy Perrine, 1974-75-76; Wayne Perr, 1967; Tom Perticone, 1976-77-78; Carl Peterson, 1928; Stan Peterson, 1943; Troy Petersen, 1991-92-93-94; Rich Petrovich, 1993; Gerry Petsch, 1974-76; F. H. Pfautz, 1912; Hans Pfund, 1911-12; John Pflum, 1945; Gene Phelps, 1944-45; Henry Philmon, 1953-54-55; Bob Pierson, 1943; Ken Pigott, 1964; F. A. Pielsticker, 1903; M. A. Piper, 1917;

Dave Pittman, 1970-71-72; Greg Pittman, 1975; Milon Pitts, 1985-86; L. W. Plager, 1906; Bill Plantan, 1952-53; Ron Pohl, 1956-57-58; Andrius Poncius, 1956-57; Fred Poole, 1934-35-36; Don Poprilo, 1984-85; Mike Posey, 1983-84; John Pottebaum, 1948; Jimmy Potter, 1974; Tom Potter, 1968-69-71; Harold Potts, 1954-55; Frank Powell, 1956-57; Lester Powell, 1913; Steve Powers, 1968-69; Tom Powers, 1972-73-74; Carroll Preston, 1944; Guy Preston, 1974-75-77-78; Carl Proto, 1960-61-62; Angelo Provenza, 1994-95; Ron Puettman, 1992; Ed Pundt, 1966-67; Jim Pusch, 1945; Jason Putz, 1993-94-95.

Q Brian Quarrie, 1970; John Quinn, 1977-79-80-81.

R Tom Radke, 1995; Doug Ragaller, 1992-93-94; Matt Rahfaldt, 1994-95; Sam Ramensofsky, 1963-64-65; Howard Ramsey, 1919; Tom Randall, 1974-75-76-77; Jimm Randolph, 1975; James Ransom, 1979-80-81-82; John Rasmess, 1923-24-25; Ned Rasmussen, 1980-81-82; Larry Ratigan, 1988-89-90-91; Jim Rawley, 1951-52-53; Charles Rawn, 1942; Ralph Reese, 1944; J. J. Reeve, 1910; Lew Reeve, 1912-13-14; Lowell Reeve, 1915; Brian Reffner, 1985-86; Matt Rehberg, 1987-89-90-91; Ted Reimer, 1967-68; Bruce Reimers, 1979-81-82-83; Steve Renfrow, 1987; Greg Rensink, 1977; Phil Reppert, 1906-07-08; Gordon Reupke, 1936-37-38; Preston Rhamy, 1994-95; Dan Rice, 1952-53; S. O. Rice, 1894-95; Tom Rice, 1893-94-95; Randy Richards, 1983-84-85-87; Steve Richards, 1968; Bob Richardson, 1970-71; Clif Rick, 1958-59-60; A. L. Rickert, 1957; Paul Ridder, 1972-73; Jim Riding, 1944-45-46; Lester Ridley, 1991-92; I. S. "Zeke" Riggs, 1920-21-22; Horace Ringheim, 1909-10-11; Fred Rippel, 1955-56; Tom Roach, 1978-79-80-81; Guy Roberts, 1897-98-99; Guy M. Roberts, 1922-23-24; H. L. Roberts, 1910; Hugh Roberts, 1936; Lawrence Roberts, 1991; Mike Roberts, 1983-84-85; Marcus Robertson, 1987-88-89-90; Shane Robertson, 1991-92; Dan Robinson, 1967-68; Doug Robinson, 1965-66-67; Willie Robinson, 1965-66; Bill Robitaille, 1959; Otis Rodgers, 1975-76; Terron Rodgers, 1980-81; Hiram Roe, 1932-33; Orrie Roe, 1927-29; Clarence "Buck" Rogers, 1934; Glover Rogers, 1974-75-76; Bob Rohwedder, 1951-52-53; Harley Rollinger, 1945-46-47; Tom Roloson, 1976; David Rom, 1977; V. H. Rompel, 1920; Dennis Ross, 1985-86-87-88; Mark Rothacker, 1948-49-50; Andre Roundtree, 1973-74; Matt Rouse, 1989-90-91-92; Gene Rowell, 1976; Dale Rowley, 1992-93-94-95; Terry Rubley, 1977-78-79; Carl Rudi, 1927-28; Randy Ruffolo, 1995; Jim Ruprecht, 1979-80; Rowland Rushmore, 1935-36-37; Rod Rust, 1947-48-49; I. C. Rutledge, 1907-08; R. L. Rutledge, 1909-10-11; Maurice Ryan, 1941-42; Matt Rysavy, 1995.

S Craig Sabatini, 1972; Erwin Sadanowic, 1959; Cecil Saddoris, 1931; Brett Sadek, 1986-87; Evan Sage, 1923; Lee Sage, 1974; Mike Sakalas, 1994; Tom Salerno, 1968-69-70; Ted Sandberg, 1950; Lyman Sanders, 1922-23; Tim Sanders, 1993-94-95; Clive Sands, 1975; C. G. Saurberg, 1908; Ken Sandbloom, 1986; Dick Scesniak, 1959-60-61; Dick Schafroth, 1965-66; Ed Schafroth, 1931-32-33; Harold Schafroth, 1934-35-36; Charles "Bud" Schalk, 1941-42; K. W. Schalk, 1913; Louis Schalk, 1916-17-18; John Scheldrup, 1956; Ed Schillmoeller, 1950-51-52; Ed Schlenker, 1927-28-29; Harry Schmidt, 1922-23-24; Mal Schmidt, 1949-50-51; Maury Schmidt, 1949-50-51; Fred Schneider, 1946; Walt Schneiter, 1980-81; Jon Schnoor, 1990-91-92; George Schoel, 1942-46; Gerald Schoendfelder, 1957-59; William Scholty, 1898-99-01; Floyd Schooley, 1919-20-21; Greg Schoon, 1995; Carl Scholz, 1919-20; Keith Schrage, 1985-86; Larry Schreiber, 1961-62; Keith Schroeder, 1969-70-71; Ben Schuler, 1901; Paul Schulte, 1988-89-90-91; Tom Schulting, 1986-87; Don Schulze, 1954; Scott Schulz, 1991-92; Mike Schwartz, 1976-77-78-79; Ron Schwartz, 1956; John Schweickert, 1956; John Schweizer, 1970-71-72; Harold Schweppe, 1928; A. B. Scott, 1901; A. Floyd Scott, 1911-12; Anthony Scott, 1991-92-93-94; Cliff Scott, 1908-09-10; Jack Seabrooke, 1977-78-79-80; Bob Seabury, 1939-40-41; Scott Seeliger, 1971; Don Seibold, 1942-43-46; Wayne Seibold, 1947-48; Marv Seiler, 1990-91-92; Bob Sennewald, 1951; Mark Settle, 1975-76-77; Mel Shanda,

1943; Mike Shane, 1987-88-89; Willis Shaner, 1950; E. P. Sharp, 1909; Ralph Shawhan, 1926; Norville Shearer, 1932; Terry Sheffey, 1985-86; Bill Shellabarger, 1972; Bill Sherman, 1927; Bob Shibley, 1952; Clarence Shiflet, 1944; Mike Shindelar, 1982-83; Harold Shoemaker, 1917; Reggie Shoemake, 1970-71; Burt Shoen, 1942; Jeff Shudak, 1987-88-89-90; Clyde Shugart, 1937-38; Harold Shugart, 1947; Paul Shupe, 1951-52-56; Jeff Simonds, 1966-67-68; Keith Sims, 1985-86-88-89; Herb Sindt, 1921-22-23; Vernon Singleton, 1984; Doug Skartvedt, 1990-91-92-93; Paul Skartvedt, 1994-95; Vern Skripsky, 1968-69; A. C. Sloss, 1911; John Sloss, 1915-16; Tom Smit, 1938-39-40; Bob Smith, 1929-30-31; Dick Smith, 1933; Donnie Smith, 1992; Forry Smith, 1974-75; Gerald Smith, 1931-32-33; Greg Smith, 1978-79; H. M. Smith, 1904-05; Harold Smith, 1922-23; Holloway Smith, 1926-27; Jim Smith, 1950; John Smith, 1983-85-86-87; W. A. Smith, 1908-09-10; Dave Smoldt, 1981-83-84; Elwin Snell, 1935; Roy Snell, 1968-69; Lon Snook, 1967; Jim Snyder, 1922-23; Tony Sobers, 1978; John Sokol, 1940; John Solomon, 1975-76-77; Jim Solus, 1978; Jon Soucek, 1966; Tom Southard, 1947-48; Mike Sparks, 1991-92-93-94; Oliver Sparks, 1955-56; Roger Spaulding, 1957; Maynard Spear, 1928-29-30; Ralph Spears, 1940; Jon Spelman, 1959-61; Lee Spence, 1952; Chris Spencer, 1990-91-92; Al Spindler, 1945; B.J. Spyksma, 1993-94-95; Jeff St. Clair, 1994-95; Al Staidl, 1968; Jeff Stallworth, 1979-80-81; Don Stanley, 1966-67; Wayne Stanley, 1973-74-76; Otto Starzinger, 1900-01-02; Tom Stawniak, 1984-85-86-87; Bradd Steckmesser, 1971; G. L. Steelsmith, 1895-96; Ray Steffy, 1961-62; Jim Stehbens, 1959; Charles Steimle, 1962-63; Maynard Stensrud, 1974-75-76; Mike Stensrud, 1974-76-77-78; Shawn Stevens, 1977; S. W. Stevens, 1899-1900; Bob Stevenson, 1928; Glen "Bus" Steward, 1949-50; Lincoln Stewart, 1939-40-41; Ty Stewart, 1991-92-93-94; Al Stoecker, 1937; Rob Stoffel, 1974-75-76; Tim Stonerook, 1978-79-80; Tom Stonerook, 1976-77-78; Dennis Storey, 1965-66-67; Brad Storm, 1972-73-74; Don Stoufer, 1904-05-07; P. L. Stow, 1914; Otto Stowe, 1968-69-70; Mike Strachan, 1972-73-74; Lee Straight, 1931; Matt Straight, 1993-94-95; Max Strain, 1970; Eli Strand, 1963-64; Bill Strickler, 1908; Paul Štrohman, 1950-54; Dick Stuber, 1953; Lloyd Studniarz, 1977-78-79-80; Jim Stuelke, 1954-55-57; Steve Sturek, 1959-61; Hughes Suffren, 1985-87; Paul Sullivan, 1959-61; Lamar Summers, 1979-81; Jim Sutherland, 1948; Terry Sutton, 1970-71; Mike Swale, 1952; John Swan, 1915; Ron Swanton, 1951; Jim Sweeney, 1977-78-79; Homer Sweet, 1922; Larry Switzer, 1962, 63; Franz Swoboda, 1929-30-31.

T Simon Tarr, 1897-08; Bill Taylor, 1939; Grady Taylor, 1939; Michael Taylor, 1984-85; Norm Taylor, 1962-63-64; Wilford Taylor, 1911; George Tellier, 1908; H. O. Tellier, 1901-02-03; R. W. Tedrick, 1904; Rudolph Tegland, 1928-29-30; Harold Templeton, 1931-32; Wilfrid Tener, 1902-03-04; Ed TeHeltrup, 1910; John Tenges, 1945; Ray Tenhoff, 1941; Mike Terrizzi, 1970-71; Weldon Thalacker, 1952-53-54; Home Thayer, 1916; Starr Thayer, 1905-06-07; Don Theophilus, 1932-33-34; Paul Thibodeaux, 1985-87-88-89; Bob Thomas, 1968; Clint Thomas, 1993-94; Dean Thomas, 1942; Ernie Thomas, 1982; Jack Thomas, 1973-74; Kirk Thomas, 1983-84-85; Leonard Thomas, 1940; Norm Thomas, 1925-26; Steve Thomas, 1982-83; A. J. Thompson, 1904; E. J. Thompson, 1911; F. E. Thompson, 1916; Jim Thompson, 1984; Jim Thompson, 1992-93-94; Ron Thompson, 1952-53; Al Thornburg, 1923-24-25; Kim Tidd, 1952-53-54; Joe Tiernan, 1913; Jack Tilles, 1957; John Tillo, 1948-49-50; Howard Tippee, 1941-43; Obert Tisdale, 1968-69-70; Clyde Titus, 1951; Lowell Titus, 1949-50; Gabe Toft, 1994; Lawrence Tollenaere, 1943; Harry Toom, 1926; Paul Trauger, 1928-29-30; Merlin Trausch, 1965; John Travis, 1926; J. G. Treloar, 1921; Russ Trenary, 1939; Jack Trice, 1923; Darrin Trieb, 1986; Paul C. Troeger, 1909; Ron Troyan, 1980; Ken Trommler, 1943; Mike Tryon, 1975-76-77; George Tsiotsias, 1989-90; Frank Tucker, 1916-19; Tony Tucker, 1984-85; Ted Tuinstra, 1965-66; Charles Turner, 1920;

Geoff Turner, 1994; Paul Turner, 1982; Ray Tweeten, 1954-55; John Tyson, 1958; Mike Tyson, 1973.

U Mike Uhl, 1913-14-15; Chris Ulrich, 1992-93; Bill Unsderfer, 1933; John Usmial, 1970; Bob Utter, 1990-92-93.

V John Valasa, 1975; Dick Valentine, 1930; Tim VandeMerkt, 1979; Larry Van Der Heyden, 1958-59-60; V. B. Vanderloo, 1917-19-20; Tim Van Galder, 1964-65-66; Trent Van Hoosen, 1985-87-88-89; Kevin Van Meter, 1977; John VanSicklen, 1962-63-64; Doug Van Sloten, 1983-84-85; Tom Vaughn, 1962-63-64; Hugh Vickerstaff, 1937-38; Lou Vieceli, 1978-79-80; Ralph Vincent, 1910-11-12; Lindsay Vinsel, 1938-39; Howard Voelker, 1944-45; Bob Voetberg, 1950-51; Henry Vogelman, 1959; Craig Volkens, 1974-76-77; Charles Vondra, 1986-87-88-89; Greg Vondrak, 1972; Ron Vorwald, 1973; Terry Voy, 1966-68.

W Michael Wade, 1980-81-82-83; Rex Wagner, 1943-44; Ron Wagner, 1980; Al Waite, 1935-36-37; George Walker, 1980-82-83-84; Shawn Walker, 1989-90-91-92; Walter "Bo" Walker, 1952; Joe Wall, 1910-11; Leigh "Polly" Wallace, 1917-20-21; Andy Waller, 1968-69; Marv Walter, 1955-56-57; Ray Walter, 1955; Ron Walter, 1959-60; Charles Walton, 1961-62; Dave Ward, 1990; Marv Warden, 1902-03-04-05; John Warder, 1967-68; Steve Wardlaw, 1970-71; Hussein Warmack, 1989-90-93; Roger Warne, 1979-81; Meredith Warner, 1943-44; Curtis Warren, 1986-88; Chris Washington, 1980-81-82-83; Jerry Washington, 1977-78; Tony Washington, 1968-69-70; Glenn Waterhouse, 1993; Dan Watkins, 1989-90-91-92; Thaddeus Watkins, 1980; Tom Watkins, 1958-59-60; Al Watson, 1983-84-85; Cleal Watts, 1923; Tom Watts, 1904; Don Webb, 1958-59-60; John Webb, 1919-20; Ralph Weber, 1929; Vic Weber, 1946-47; Les Webster, 1965-66-67; Bill Weeks, 1948-49-50; Mark Weidemann, 1980; Steve Weidemann, 1977-78; Walter Weiss, 1926-27; Chad Welding, 1986-87-88; Bob Wellendorf, 1954; Ken Wells, 1929-30-31; Rick Wells, 1986-87; W. W. Wentch, 1894-95-96; Edwin Wernentin, 1925; Steve Weron, 1989-90-91; Jack West, 1937-38-39; Bruce Westemeyer, 1983-84-85; Roger Westman, 1957-58; Ed Weyraich, 1911-12; Russ Whalen, 1947-48; Charles Wheeler, 1923; Robert Whitaker, 1920; Dean White, 1988; E. L. White, 1920; Rick White, 1976-77-78; Stewart White, 1919-20; Ed Wiemer, 1925; Dick Wilcoz, 1928-29-30; Harley Wilcox, 1929; Tom Wilcox, 1971; Henry Wilder, 1938-40; Sy Wilhelmi, 1948-50; Doug Wilke, 1972-73; Bill Wilkinson, 1991; Brian Wilkinson, 1993-94; Charles Wilkinson, 1968-69-70; Ron Wilkinson, 1988; Wendell "Bud" Willer, 1946; Tom Willett, 1905-06-07; Bob Williams, 1968-69-70; Ed Williams, 1994-95; Gene Williams, 1987-88-89-90; Kevin Williams, 1983-84; L. A. Williams, 1909; Lester Williams, 1982-83-84-85; Lopey Williams, 1987; Mark Williams, 1973-76; Marlowe Williams, 1932-33-34; Mike Williams, 1974-75-76; Otis Williams, 1902-03; Otis Williams, 1962-63-64; Roe Williams, 1942; Scott Williams, 1982-83-84; Sherman Williams, 1989-90-91-92; Tracy Williams, 1995; W. H. Williams, 1902-03; R. H. Wilmarth, 1908-09; Ben Wilson, 1904-05-06; Bill Wilson, 1952-53; Dave Wilson, 1912; James W. Wilson, 1894-95-96; Jim Wilson, 1977-78; Kevin Wilson, 1995; Merle Wilson, 1920; Ray Wilson, 1913-14; Lee Wiltsie, 1943-46; Vern Winfrey, 1949; Jim Wingender, 1974-75; Claire Wingert, 1922-23; Jim Winstead, 1958; Wes Winnekins, 1984; Wilbur Winter, 1933-34; Jimmy Wipert, 1964-65; Mark Withrow, 1968-69-70; Jeff Wodka, 1982-83-84-85; Bill Wolfe, 1956; A. E. "Deac" Wolters, 1921-22; O. P. Woodburn, 1894-95; Tom Woolwine, 1971; Henry Wormhoudt, 1913; David Worsham, 1980; Mel Wostoupal, 1953-54-55; Charles Wright, 1943-44-46.

Y Mike Ybarra, 1972; Henry "Lafe" Young, 1918-19-20; Ira Young, 1921-22-23; Randy Young, 1973-74-75; Wes Young, 1919; Roger Youngblut, 1983-84; Jeff Yurchak, 1978.

Z Leland Zink, 1919-21; Charles Zlomke, 1945-46.

BASKETBALL SEASON-BY-SEASON RESULTS

Year	Coach	W	L	Captains
1908	S. Clyde Williams	1	1	H. S. Luberger
1909	S. Clyde Williams	4	10	Joe D. Brown
1910	S. Clyde Williams	9	7	H. M. Herbert
1911	S. Clyde Williams	6	11	Clark D. Mosher
1912	Homer Hubbard	8	7	A. R. Chappele
1913	Homer Hubbard	3	13	Hans Pfund
1914	Homer Hubbard	4	14	Harry Hansel
1915	Homer Hubbard	6	7	J. D. Swiney
1916	H. H. Walters	4	12	Earl A. Holmes
1917	H. H. Walters	12	6	W. H. Boynton
1918	H. H. Walters	6	9	Howard Aldrich
1919	H. H. Walters	5	11	
1920	R. N. Berryman	6	12	Stewart N. White
1921	Maury Kent	10	8	Harry L. Shepard
1922	Bill Chandler	10	8	Jack M. Currie
1923	Bill Chandler	9	9	Reese H. Greene
1924	Bill Chandler	2	16	Guy Roberts
1925	Bill Chandler	2	15	Leonard T. Ruff
1926	Bill Chandler	4	14	Ernest J. Anderson
1927	Bill Chandler	8	10	Aaron Miller
1928	Bill Chandler	3	15	Max Strayer
1929	Louis Menze	8	7	Lester Lande
1930	Louis Menze	9	8	Glenn Woods
1931	Louis Menze	8	8	Al Heitman, Dick Hawk
1932	Louis Menze	9	6	Jack Roadcap
1933	Louis Menze	6	10	Ralph Thompsen
1934	Louis Menze	6	11	Waldo Wegner
1935	Louis Menze	*13	3	Frank Hood
1936	Louis Menze	8	8	Torvald Holmes
1937	Louis Menze	3	15	Jack Flemming
1938	Louis Menze	6	9	Bob Blahnik
1939	Louis Menze	8	9	Bob Menze
1940	Louis Menze	9	9	Bob Menze, Gordon Nicholas
1941	Louis Menze	#*15	4	Gordon Nicholas, Al Budolfson
1942	Louis Menze	11	6	Al Budolfson
1943	Louis Menze	7	9	No captain
1944	Louis Menze	#*14	4	No captain
1945	Louis Menze	*11	5	Bill Block
1946	Louis Menze	8	8	Ron Norman
1947	Louis Menze	7	14	Ray Wehde
1948	Clay Sutherland	14	9	Ron Norman
1949	Clay Sutherland	8	14	Bob Petersen
1950	Clay Sutherland	6	17	Don Paulsen
1951	Clay Sutherland	9	12	Sy Wilhelmi
1952	Clay Sutherland	10	11	Jim Stange
1953	Clay Sutherland	10	11	Delmar Diercks, Sam Long
1954	Clay Sutherland	6	15	Jerry Davis, Carl VanCleave
1955	Bill Strannigan	11	10	Chuck Duncan, Larry Wetter
1956	Bill Strannigan	18	5	Jerry Sandbulte, Arnie Gaarde
1957	Bill Strannigan	16	7	Gary Thompson, Chuck Vogt
1958	Bill Strannigan	16	7	John Crawford, Lyle Frahm, Don Medsker
1959	Bill Strannigan	9	16	Ron Baukol
1960	Glen Anderson	15	9	Larry Fie
1961	Glen Anderson	14	11	Henry Whitney
1962	Glen Anderson	13	12	Bob Stoy, Gary Wheeler, John Ptacek
1963	Glen Anderson	14	11	Dave Groth
1964	Glen Anderson	10	16	Rich Froistad, Tim Lowe, Tom Peterson
1965	Glen Anderson	9	16	Bob Vander Wilt
1966	Glen Anderson	11	14	Al Koch, Bob Ziegler
1967	Glen Anderson	13	12	Dave Fleming
1968	Glen Anderson	12	13	Don Smith
1969	Glen Anderson	14	11	Tom Kreamer, Tom Pyle, Tom Goodman
1970	Glen Anderson	12	14	Jim Abrahamson, Bill Cain
1971	Glen Anderson	5	21	Jack DeVilder
1972	Maury John	12	14	(rotated captains)
1973	Maury John	16	10	(rotated captains)
1974	Maury John	15	11	Eric Heft, Wes Harris, John John

Year	Coach	W	L	Captains
1975	Ken Trickey	10	16	Larry Loots, Craig DeLoss
1976	Ken Trickey	3	24	Hercle Ivy
1977	Lynn Nance	8	19	Steve Burgason
1978	Lynn Nance	14	13	Steve Burgason, Ricky Byrdsong
1979	Lynn Nance	11	16	Andrew Parker, Carlton Evans
1980	Lynn Nance	11	16	None .
1981	Johnny Orr	9	18	Lefty Moore
1982	Johnny Orr	10	17	John Kunnert, Malvin Warrick, Ron Harris
1983	Johnny Orr	13	15	Ron Harris
1984	Johnny Orr	^16	13	Ron Harris, Terrence Allen
1985	Johnny Orr	#21	13	Barry Stevens, Jeff Hornacek
1986	Johnny Orr	#22	11	Jeff Hornacek, Ron Virgil
1987	Johnny Orr	13	15	Sam Hill, Jeff Grayer
1988	Johnny Orr	#20	12	Jeff Grayer, Gary Thompkins
1989	Johnny Orr	#17	12	Mike Born, Marc Urquhart
1990	Johnny Orr	10	18	Victor Alexander, Terry Woods
1991	Johnny Orr	12	19	Victor Alexander, Doug Collins
1992	Johnny Orr	#21	13	Brian Pearson, Justus Thigpen
1993	Johnny Orr	#20	11	Justus Thigpen, Morgan Wheat
1994	Johnny Orr	14	13	Fred Hoiberg
1995	Tim Floyd	#23	11	Fred Hoiberg
1996	Tim Floyd	#24	9	

#NCAA Tournament appearance
^NIT appearance
*won conference championship

COACHING RECORDS

Years	Coach	Seasons	W	L	Pct.
1908-11	S. Clyde Williams	4	20	29	.408
1912-15	Homer Hubbard	4	21	41	.339
1916-19	H. H. Walters	4	27	38	.415
1920	R. N. Berryman	1	6	12	.333
1921	Maury Kent	1	10	8	.555
1922-28	Bill Chandler	7	38	87	.304
1929-47	Louis Menze	19	166	153	.520
1948-54	Clay Sutherland	7	63	89	.414
1955-59	Bill Strannigan	5	70	45	.609
1960-71	Glen Anderson	12	142	160	.470
1972-74	Maury John	3	43	35	.551
1975-76	Ken Trickey	2	13	40	.245
1977-80	Lynn Nance	4	44	64	.407
1981-94	Johnny Orr	14	218	200	.522
1995-96	Tim Floyd	2	47	20	.701

TEAM RECORDS

MOST GAMES PLAYED
Season — 34, 1984-85; 1991-92; 1994-95

MOST WINS
Season — 24, 1995-96

MOST LOSSES
Season — 24, 1975-76

BEST WIN-LOSS PERCENTAGE
.813, 1934-35 (13-3)

MOST CONSECUTIVE WINS
9, 1994-95

MOST CONSECUTIVE LOSSES
13, Dec. 18, 1936-Dec. 3, 1937

LONGEST WINNING STREAK AT HOME
22, Feb. 16, 1985-Dec. 22, 1986
22, March 4, 1992-Dec. 21, 1993
(Over three different seasons)

LONGEST WINNING STREAK ON THE ROAD
5, Feb. 5, 1944-Mar. 24, 1944

LONGEST LOSING STREAK AT HOME
7, Feb. 28, 1925-Feb. 1, 1926
(Over two different seasons)

LONGEST LOSING STREAK ON THE ROAD
19, Dec. 15, 1923-Dec. 28, 1925
(Over three different seasons)

BEST BIG EIGHT RECORD
9-1, 1943-44

MOST CONFERENCE GAMES WON
9, three times

MOST POINTS
Half-76 vs. Nebraska-Omaha, Dec. 31, 1991
Game — 129 vs. Northeastern Illinois, Nov. 24, 1978
Season — 2,886, 1987-88
Season Avg.-90.2, 1987-88

MOST CONSECUTIVE 70 OR MORE POINT GAMES
41-Feb. 27, 1988-Dec. 23, 1989

MOST CONSECUTIVE 80 OR MORE POINT GAMES
10-Dec. 29, 1987-Jan. 30, 1988

MOST CONSECUTIVE 90 OR MORE POINT GAMES
5-Jan. 16, 1990-Jan. 31, 1990

MOST POINTS SCORED IN A LOSING GAME
102-vs. Stanford (103), at Kansas City,
Dec. 28, 1951

LEAST POINTS SCORED (SINCE 1939-40)
Game — 16 vs. Missouri, at Ames, Jan. 15, 1940
Game Prior to 1939-40-1 vs. Grinnell, at Grinnell,
Feb. 7, 1913

FEWEST POINTS SCORED IN A WINNING GAME
11-vs. Drake, at Des Moines, Jan. 18, 1913

MOST FIELD GOALS SCORED
Game — 52 vs. Northeastern Illinois, Nov. 24, 1978
(98 attempted)
Season — 1,110, 1987-88 (2,886 attempted)

MOST FIELD GOALS ATTEMPTED
Game — 101 vs. Morgan State, Jan. 3, 1985 (50
made)
Season — 2,886, 1987-88 (1,100 made)

MOST THREE-POINT SHOTS SCORED
Game — 13 vs. Butler, Dec. 28, 1987 (26 attempted)
Season — 175, 1994-95 (453 attempted)

MOST THREE-POINT SHOTS ATTEMPTED
Game — 27 vs. Nebraska, Feb. 22, 1992 (8 made)
Season — 464, 1991-92 (162 made)

HIGHEST FIELD GOAL PERCENTAGE
Game — .691 at Chaminade, Nov. 23, 1990
Season — .512, 1984-85 (1,031-2,012)

MOST FREE THROWS SCORED
Game — 43 vs. Illinois-Chicago, Jan. 9, 1989 (52
attempted)
Season — 546, 1988-89 (745 attempted)

MOST FREE THROWS ATTEMPTED
Game — 54 vs. Drake, Dec. 14, 1967
Season — 806, 1994-95 (610 made)

FEWEST FREE THROWS ATTEMPTED
Game — 0 vs. Kansas State, Feb. 25, 1981

MOST ASSISTS
Game — 35 vs. Texas Southern, Dec. 22, 1992;
North Florida, Dec. 22, 1994
Season — 694, 1987-88

HIGHEST FREE THROW PERCENTAGE
Game — 1.000, several times
Season — .759, 1992-93 (465-613)

MOST STEALS
Game — 27 vs. Bethune Cookman, Dec. 31, 1992
Season — 381, 1991-92

MOST BLOCKED SHOTS
Game — 13 vs. Drake, Jan. 2, 1991
Season — 134, 1990-91

MOST TURNOVERS
Game — 31 vs. Oklahoma, Feb. 6, 1989; Colorado,
Jan. 7, 1995
Season — 583, 1990-91

MOST PERSONAL FOULS
Game — 35 vs. Drake, Dec. 22, 1951;
vs. Missouri, Jan. 29, 1977
Season — 687, 1991-92

DISQUALIFICATIONS
Game — 4 vs. USC, Dec. 20, 1971; vs. Oklahoma,
Mar. 6, 1987
Season — 38, 1951-52

MOST REBOUNDS
Game — 68 vs. St. Cloud State, Nov. 30, 1979
Season — 1,364, 1974-75
Season Avg.-44.4, 1974-75

INDIVIDUAL RECORDS

MOST GAMES PLAYED

Season — 34, Fred Hoiberg, Loren Meyer, Julius Michalik, Hurl Beechum, James Hamilton, Derrick Hayes, Jacy Holloway, Jason Kimbrough; 1994-95; Justus Thigpen, Ron Bayless, Julius Michalik, Fred Hoiberg, Howard Eaton, Loren Meyer, Brad Pippett, 1991-92; Barry Stevens, Sam Hill, Jeff Hornacek, Gary Thompkins; 1984-85
Career — 126, Fred Hoiberg,1992-95; Julius Michalik, 1992-95

MOST GAMES STARTED

Season — 34, Fred Hoiberg, Loren Meyer, 1994-95; Howard Eaton, 1991-92; Barry Stevens, Jeff Hornacek, 1984-85
Career — 124, Jeff Grayer, 1985-88
Consecutive-111, Ron Harris, 1981-84

MOST MINUTES PLAYED

Season — 1,252 Fred Hoiberg, 1994-95
Career — 4,398, Jeff Grayer, 1985-88

MOST POINTS SCORED

Game — 54, Lafester Rhodes vs. Iowa, Dec. 19, 1987
Season — 811, Jeff Grayer, 1987-88
Career — 2,502, Jeff Grayer, 1987-88

HIGHEST SCORING AVERAGE

Season — 28.3, Hercle Ivy, 1974-75 (26 games)
Career — 22.2, Hercle Ivy, 1973-76 (79 games); 22.3, Don Smith, 1966-68 (75 games)

MOST POINTS SCORED BY CLASS

Senior-811, Jeff Grayer, 1987-88 (32 games)
Junior-737, Hercle Ivy, 1974-75 (26 games)
Sophomore-684, Jeff Grayer, 1985-86 (33 games)
Freshman-427, Julius Michalik, 1991-92 (34 games)

MOST FIELD-GOALS SCORED

Game — 20, Lafester Rhodes vs. Iowa, Dec. 19, 1987 (31 attempted)
Season — 315, Hercle Ivy, 1974-75 (692 attempted)
Career — 974, Jeff Grayer, 1985-88 (125 games, 1,852 attempted)

MOST FIELD-GOALS ATTEMPTED

Game — 38, Hercle Ivy vs. Oklahoma, Feb. 5, 1975 (15 made)
Season — 692, Hercle Ivy, 1974-75 (315 made)
Career — 1,852, Jeff Grayer, 1985-88 (974 made)

HIGHEST FIELD-GOAL PERCENTAGE

Game — 1.000, (11-11), Mark Baugh vs. Western Illinois, Jan. 25, 1989
Season — (min. 100 made), .659, (294-446) Victor Alexander, 1990-91
Career — (min. 200 made), .611, (778-1,274), Victor Alexander, 1988-91

CONSECUTIVE FIELD-GOALS MADE

Game — 11, Mark Baugh vs. Western Illinois, Jan. 25, 1989

MOST FREE-THROWS SCORED

Game — 19, Gary Thompson vs. Houston, Dec. 3, 1956 (22 attempted)
Season — 210, Don Smith, 1967-68 (298 attempted)
Career — 527, Jeff Grayer, 1985-88 (768 attempted)

MOST FREE-THROWS ATTEMPTED

Game — 24, Don Smith vs. Drake, Dec. 14, 1967 (17 made); Don Smith vs. Kansas State, Jan. 14, 1967 (17 made); Gary Thompson vs. Vanderbilt, Dec. 23, 1956 (18 made)
Season — 298, Don Smith, 1967-68 (210 made)
Career — 778, Don Smith, 1966-68 (502 made)

MOST CONSECUTIVE FREE THROWS

34, Fred Hoiberg, Jan. 13, 1990-Feb. 15, 1992 (Over 14 games)

HIGHEST FREE-THROW PERCENTAGE

Game — 1.000 (15-15), Sam Mack vs. Oklahoma State, Feb. 18, 1989; (15-15), John Crawford vs. Nebraska, Dec. 29, 1956
Season — (min. 50 made), .879, (87-99), Mike Born, 1988-89
Career — (min. 150 made), .861 (179-208) Ron Bayless, 1991-93

THREE-POINT SHOTS SCORED

Game — 8, Fred Hoiberg vs. Missouri, Jan. 30, 1995 (14 attempts)
Season — 89, Fred Hoiberg, 1994-95 (216 attempted)
Career — 183, Fred Hoiberg, 1992-95 (457 attempted)

THREE-POINT SHOTS ATTEMPTED

Game — 14, Fred Hoiberg vs. Missouri, Jan. 30, 1995 (8 made)
Season — 216, Fred Hoiberg, 1994-95 (89 made)
Career — 457, Fred Hoiberg, 1992-95 (183 made)

MOST ASSISTS

Game — 16, Eric Heft vs. Nebraska, Feb. 5, 1974
Season — 219, Jeff Hornacek, 1985-86
Career — 665, Jeff Hornacek, 1983-86

MOST REBOUNDS

Game — 26, Bill Cain vs. Minnesota, Dec. 9, 1969
Season — 396, Bill Cain, 1969-70
Career — 1,233, Dean Uthoff, 1977-80

HIGHEST REBOUNDING AVERAGE

Season — 15.2, Bill Cain, 1969-70 (26 games)
Career — 13.7, Don Smith, 1966-68 (75 games)

REBOUNDS BY CLASS

Senior-396, Bill Cain, 1969-70 (26 games)
Junior-337, Bill Cain, 1968-69 (25 games)
Sophomore-378, Dean Uthoff, 1977-78 (27 games)
Freshman-306, Dean Uthoff, 1976-77 (27 games)

MOST PERSONAL FOULS

Season — 125, Sam Hill, 1984-85
Career — 389, Sam Hill, 1984-87

MOST DISQUALIFICATIONS

Season — 13, Chuck Duncan, 1953-54
Career — 28, Sam Hill, 1984-87

MOST STEALS

Game — 7, Justus Thigpen vs. Kansas, Jan. 9, 1993; Fred Hoiberg vs. American University, Nov. 30, 1991
Season — 72, Justus Thigpen, 1992-93
Career — 210, Justus Thigpen, 1990-93

MOST BLOCKED SHOTS

Game — 6, Loren Meyer vs. Drake, Dec. 6, 1994
Season — 71, Kelvin Cato, 1995-96
Career — 134, Loren Meyer, 1992-95

MOST TURNOVERS

Game — 11, Terry Woods vs. Illinois Chicago, Jan. 3, 1990
Season — 121, Doug Collins, 1990-91
Career — 319, Terry Woods, 1986-1990

SINGLE-SEASON SCORING

1.	811	Jeff Grayer	1987-88
2.	739	Barry Stevens	1984-85
3.	737	Hercle Ivy	1974-75
4.	724	Victor Alexander	1990-91
5.	720	Lafester Rhodes	1987-88
6.	684	Jeff Grayer	1985-86
7.	677	Fred Hoiberg	1994-95
8.	644	Barry Stevens	1983-84
9.	619	Don Smith	1966-67
10.	605	Jeff Grayer	1986-87
		Andrew Parker	1977-78

SEASON REBOUNDING

1.	396	Bill Cain	1969-70
2.	378	Dean Uthoff	1977-78
3.	365	Don Smith	1967-68
4.	337	Bill Cain	1968-69
5.	334	Don Smith	1966-67
6.	326	Don Smith	1965-66
7.	307	Dean Uthoff	1978-79
8.	306	Dean Uthoff	1976-77
9.	304	Loren Meyer	1994-95
10.	302	Henry Whitney	1960-61

SEASON ASSISTS

1.	219	Jeff Hornacek	1985-86
2.	198	Jeff Hornacek	1983-84
3.	180	Doug Collins	1990-91
4.	173	Terry Woods	1989-90
5.	169	Terry Woods	1987-88
6.	167	Jacy Holloway	1994-95
7.	166	Gary Thompkins	1986-87
		Jeff Hornacek	1984-85
9.	159	Ron Bayless	1992-93
10.	158	Terry Woods	1988-89

SEASON MINUTES PLAYED

1.	1252	Fred Hoiberg	1994-95
2.	1229	Jeff Hornacek	1985-86
3.	1224	Jeff Hornacek	1984-85
4.	1211	Barry Stevens	1984-85
5.	1165	Jeff Grayer	1987-88
6.	1159	Jeff Grayer	1985-86
7.	1119	Jeff Grayer	1984-85
8.	1100	Lafester Rhodes	1987-88
9.	1065	Jeff Hornacek	1983-84
10.	1059	Barry Stevens	1983-84

SEASON FIELD-GOALS MADE

1.	315	Hercle Ivy	1974-75
2.	312	Jeff Grayer	1987-88
3.	301	Barry Stevens	1984-85
4.	294	Victor Alexander	1990-91
5.	287	Lafester Rhodes	1987-88
6.	281	Jeff Grayer	1985-86
7.	257	Barry Stevens	1983-84
8.	242	Hercle Ivy	1975-76
9.	240	Victor Alexander	1988-89
10.	236	Andrew Parker	1977-78

SEASON FIELD-GOALS ATTEMPTED

1.	692	Hercle Ivy	1974-75
2.	607	Barry Stevens	1984-85
3.	597	Jeff Grayer	1987-88
4.	564	Lafester Rhodes	1987-88
5.	557	Hercle Ivy	1975-76
6.	544	Barry Stevens	1983-84
7.	514	Jeff Grayer	1985-86
8.	502	Art Johnson	1975-76
9.	477	Justus Thigpen	1991-92
10.	475	Justus Thigpen	1992-93

SEASON FREE-THROWS MADE

1.	210	Don Smith	1967-68
2.	194	Bill Cain	1968-69
3.	177	Bill Cain	1969-70
4.	175	Don Smith	1966-67
5.	174	Fred Hoiberg	1994-95
6.	167	Jeff Grayer	1987-88
7.	155	Gary Thompson	1955-56
8.	147	Bill Cain	1967-68
9.	146	Andrew Parker	1978-79
10.	142	Jeff Grayer	1986-87

SEASON FREE-THROWS ATTEMPTED

1.	298	Don Smith	1967-68
2.	272	Bill Cain	1968-69
3.	264	Don Smith	1966-67
4.	242	Bill Cain	1969-70
5.	235	Jeff Grayer	1987-88
6.	215	Don Smith	1965-66
7.	202	Fred Hoiberg	1994-95
		Gary Thompson	1955-56
9.	201	Victor Alexander	1990-91
10.	197	Bill Cain	1967-68
		John Crawford	1956-57

SEASON THREE-POINT GOALS MADE

1.	89	Fred Hoiberg	1994-95
2.	65	Hurl Beechum	1994-95
3.	59	Fred Hoiberg	1993-94
4.	50	Ron Bayless	1992-93
5.	42	Justus Thigpen	1992-93
		Justus Thigpen	1991-92
7.	39	Hurl Beechum	1993-94
		Terry Woods	1989-90
		Mike Born	1988-89
10.	38	Ron Bayless	1991-92

SEASON THREE-POINT GOALS ATTEMPTED

1.	216	Fred Hoiberg	1994-95
2.	162	Hurl Beechum	1994-95
3.	131	Fred Hoiberg	1993-94
4.	124	Ron Bayless	1992-93
5.	113	Justus Thigpen	1992-93
		Justus Thigpen	1991-92
7.	101	Hurl Beechum	1993-94
	101	Ron Bayless	1991-92
9.	96	Elmer Robinson	1987-88
10.	95	Terry Woods	1989-90

STEALS

1.	72	Justus Thigpen	1992-93
2.	65	Fred Hoiberg	1991-92
		Jeff Hornacek	1984-85
4.	64	Ron Bayless	1992-93
		Jeff Hornacek	1985-86
6.	62	Jeff Grayer	1985-86
7.	61	Justus Thigpen	1991-92
		Jeff Hornacek	1983-84
9.	59	Ron Bayless	1991-92
10.	58	Jeff Grayer	1987-88

BLOCKED SHOTS

1.	71	Kelvin Cato	1995-96
2.	51	Victor Alexander	1990-91
3.	50	Loren Meyer	1994-95
4.	46	Lafester Rhodes	1987-88
5.	42	Sam Hill	1984-85
6.	37	Julius Michalik	1991-92
7.	34	Victor Alexander	1989-90
		Sam Hill	1985-86
9.	32	Ron Falenschek	1982-83
10.	31	Loren Meyer	1993-94
		Phil Kunz	1989-90

CAREER SCORING

1.	2,502	Jeff Grayer	1985-88
2.	2,190	Barry Stevens	1982-85
3.	1,993	Fred Hoiberg	1992-95
4.	1,892	Victor Alexander	1988-91
5.	1,825	Julius Michalik	1992-95
6.	1,752	Hercle Ivy	1973-76
7.	1,724	Justus Thigpen	1990-93
8.	1,672	Don Smith	1966-68
9.	1,531	Andrew Parker	1976-79
10.	1,498	Bill Cain	1968-70

CAREER REBOUNDING

1.	1,233	Dean Uthoff	1977-80
2.	1,025	Don Smith	1966-68
3.	957	Bill Cain	1968-70
4.	910	Jeff Grayer	1985-88
5.	810	Victor Alexander	1987-91
6.	748	Fred Hoiberg	1992-95
7.	705	Sam Hill	1985-88
8.	677	Loren Meyer	1992-95
9.	674	Vince Brewer	1960-63
10.	672	Henry Whitney	1959-61

CAREER ASSISTS

1.	665	Jeff Hornacek	1983-86
2.	600	Gary Thompkins	1985-88
3.	564	Terry Woods	1986-90
4.	374	Justus Thigpen	1990-93
5.	350	Fred Hoiberg	1992-95
6.	308	Julius Michalik	1992-95
7.	296	Ron Bayless	1991-93
8.	289	Doug Collins	1989-91
9.	262	Hercle Ivy	1973-76
10.	261	Terrence Allen	1981-84

CAREER STEALS (SINCE 1979)

1.	211	Jeff Hornacek	1983-86
2.	210	Justus Thigpen	1990-93
3.	207	Fred Hoiberg	1992-95
4.	199	Jeff Grayer	1985-88
5.	169	Ron Harris	1981-84
6.	146	Terry Woods	1986-90
7.	134	Julius Michalik	1992-95
8.	133	Terrence Allen	1981-84
9.	132	Barry Stevens	1982-85
10.	123	Ron Bayless	1991-93

CAREER BLOCKS (SINCE 1979)

1.	134	Loren Meyer	1992-95
2.	120	Victor Alexander	1988-91
3.	115	Sam Hill	1984-87
4.	82	Julius Michalik	1992-95
5.	71	Ron Falenschek	1980-83
6.	71	Kelvin Cato	1995-96
7.	62	Elmer Robinson	1986-89
8.	61	Jeff Grayer	1985-88
9.	57	Phil Kunz	1990-91
		David Moss	1983-86

CAREER TURNOVERS (SINCE 1979)

1.	319	Terry Woods	1987-90
2.	316	Gary Thompkins	1985-88
3.	312	Justus Thigpen	1990-93
4.	281	Jeff Hornacek	1983-86
5.	277	Julius Michalik	1992-95
6.	242	Jeff Grayer	1985-88
7.	231	Fred Hoiberg	1992-95
8.	220	Barry Stevens	1982-85
9.	208	Victor Alexander	1988-91
10.	198	Ron Bayless	1992-93

CAREER FIELD-GOALS MADE

1.	974	Jeff Grayer	1985-88
2.	880	Barry Stevens	1982-85
3.	778	Victor Alexander	1988-91
4.	742	Hercle Ivy	1974-76
5.	731	Julius Michalik	1992-95
6.	693	Justus Thigpen	1990-93
7.	672	Fred Hoiberg	1992-95
8.	592	Ron Harris	1981-84
9.	585	Don Smith	1966-68
10.	570	Andrew Parker	1976-79

CAREER FIELD-GOALS ATTEMPTED

1.	1,852	Jeff Grayer	1985-88
2.	1,847	Barry Stevens	1982-85
3.	1,648	Hercle Ivy	1974-76
4.	1,552	Justus Thigpen	1990-93
5.	1,370	Julius Michalik	1992-95
6.	1,341	Ron Harris	1981-84
7.	1,316	Fred Hoiberg	1992-95
8.	1,274	Victor Alexander	1988-91
9.	1,245	Don Smith	1966-68
10.	1,170	Robert Estes	1979-82

CAREER THREE-POINT GOALS MADE

1.	183	Fred Hoiberg	1992-95
2.	128	Hurl Beechum	1992-95
3.	125	Justus Thigpen	1989-93
4.	88	Ron Bayless	1991-93
5.	80	Terry Woods	1987-90
6.	75	Brian Pearson	1989-92
		Mike Born	1988-89
8.	71	Julius Michalik	1992-95
9.	52	Elmer Robinson	1986-89
10.	48	Doug Collins	1990-91

CAREER THREE-POINT FIELD GOALS ATTEMPTED

1.	457	Fred Hoiberg	1992-95
2.	345	Justus Thigpen	1989-93
3.	339	Hurl Beechum	1992-95
4.	225	Ron Bayless	1991-93
5.	218	Terry Woods	1987-90
6.	213	Julius Michalik	1992-95
7.	207	Brian Pearson	1989-92
8.	181	Mike Born	1988-89
9.	151	Elmer Robinson	1986-89
10.	112	Doug Collins	1990-91

CAREER FREE-THROWS MADE

1.	527	Jeff Grayer	1985-88
2.	502	Don Smith	1966-68
3.	466	Fred Hoiberg	1992-95
4.	430	Barry Stevens	1982-85
5.	409	Gary Thompson	1955-57
6.	394	John Crawford	1956-58
7.	391	Andrew Parker	1976-79
8.	336	Victor Alexander	1988-91
9.	323	Dean Uthoff	1977-80
10.	311	Loren Meyer	1992-95

LETTERMEN

A Ha-Keem Abdel-Khaliq, 1994-95; James Abrahamson, 1968-69-70; Wendell Allan, 1938-39; Robert L. Alleman, 1953-54; Leonard Allen, 1977; Terrence Allen, 1981-82-83-84; Victor Alexander, 1988-89-90-91; Chester W. Anderson, 1933-34; Eddie Anderson, 1947; Gaylord Anderson, 1948-49-50-51; Joe Ashley, 1980.

B Gregg Barcus, 1973; Samuel C. Barnard, 1961; Mark Baugh, 1988-89; Ronald O. Baukol, 1957-58-59; Ron Bayless, 1992-93; Hurl Beechum, 1992-93-94-95; Paul Beene, 1982-83; Mike Benjamin, 1974-76; Bill Benson, 1973-74; Don R. Beresford, 1938-39-40; Norman J. Bergman, 1958-59; Mike Bergman, 1991-92; Donnell Bivens, 1991-92-93-94; Robert L. Blahnik, 1937-38; Laurel K. Bland, 1935; William R. Bliss, 1938-39; William S. Block, 1944-45-47-48; Michael J. Born, 1988-89; Jeff Branstetter, 1974-75; Dick Breitbach, 1988; Vincent Brewer, 1960-62-63; Price Brookfield, 1941; Fred Brown, 1993-94; Norman Brown, 1988-90-91-92; Sam Brown, 1971-72; Robert D. Bruns, 1966-67; Bill Buchanan, 1980-81; James Buck, 1946; Albert C. Budolfson, 1940-41-42; Ted Burbach, 1983; Steve Burgason, 1974-75-77-78; Lodell Burnett, 1974-75; Roman Butkus, 1976; Julian Butler, 1976; Virgil Byerly, 1951-52-53; Ricky Byrdsong, 1977-78.

C Eddie Calhoun, 1947; William Cain, 1968-69-70; Mike Capobianco, 1972-73-74; Marc Carlson, 1993-94; Theodore Chamberlain, 1945; Eldon T. Clement, 1949-50-51; Gerald R. Closter, 1965-66; David Collins, 1968-69-70; Doug Collins, 1990-91; Ronald E. Concavage, 1966; Steve Cooper, 1968; Jack H. Cowen, 1934-35-36; John A. Cowen, 1934-35; John Crawford, 1956-57-58; John Culbertson, 1984; Jerry Culshall, 1972.

D Harle H. Damon, 1942; Eric Davis, 1979; Gary C. Davis, 1957-58-59; Jerry Davis, 1952-53-54; Sam Deal, 1945-46; Mike DeCello, 1982; Dale DeKoster, 1940-41; Don DeKoster, 1954-55; Craig Deloss, 1973-74; Martinez Denmon, 1972-73; Jack DeVilder, 1969-70-71; Delmar Diercks, 1951-52-53; Clyde Dills, 1933; Al Dixon, 1976; Paul Doerrfeld, 1987-88-90-91; Darrell D. Don Carlos, 1940; Edward C. Doty, 1934; Paul M. Duarte, 1966-67; Brad Dudek, 1984-85; Charles Duncan, 1953-54-55.

E Howard Eaton, 1992-93; Theodore J. Ecker, 1959; Rick Engel, 1970-71-72; Robert Estes, 1979-80-81-82; Carlton Evans, 1977-78-79.

F Ron Falenschek, 1980-81-82-83; Richard Farwell, 1957-58; Everett Faunce, 1946; Donald Ferguson, 1948-49-50; Orlyn G. Feuerbach, 1943-45; Larry E. Fie, 1958-59; David C. Fleming, 1965-66-67; Jack G. Flemming, 1935-36-37; Bob Fowler, 1978-79; Lyle Frahm, 1956-57-58; Stanley Frahm, 1954-55; Howard P.

Franks, 1954; Calvin Freeman, 1976-77; Charles Fritz, 1974-75; Melvin R. Froistad, 1963-64; Richard Froistad, 1962.

G Arnold Gaarde, 1956; Dick Garth, 1947; George O. Gibson, 1936; Larry Gibson, 1971; Joe Gideon, 1978; Jay Goodman, 1989; Thomas Goodman, 1967-68-69; Fred Gordon, 1939-40-41; Charles B. Gradoville, 1943; Jeff Grayer, 1985-86-87-88; David A. Groth, 1961-62-63; Ivan Gruhl, 1979.

H Roy Hackbarth, 1947; James Hamberlin, 1967-68; James Hamilton, 1994-95; Chuck Harmison, 1977-78-79-80; Steven A. Harmon, 1963-64; Charles Harris, 1978-79-80-81; Clinton Harris, 1972-73; Raynal Harris, 1982-83-84-85; Robert B. Harris, 1939-40-42; Ron Harris, 1981-82-83-84; David Hartman, 1967-68; David G. Harvey, 1967; George L. Harville, 1942; Richard Hawk, 1930-31-32; Derrick Hayes, 1994-95; Robert H. Hayes, 1943; Joe Hebert, 1995; Jim Heck, 1972; Eric Heft, 1972-73-74; Bryan Heger, 1987-88-89-90; Charles D. Heileman, 1937; Al Heitman, 1930-31-32; Charles Herbert, 1949; George Hess, 1951-52; Greg Hester, 1991-92-93; David Hickman, 1995; Joe Hicks, 1946; Clarence Hill, 1994; Sam Hill, 1984-85-86-87; Gilbert Hitch, 1929; Fred Hoiberg, 1992-93-94-95; Jack Holloway, 1994-95; Herman Holmes, 1932; Torvald J. Holmes, 1934-35-36; Jeff Hornacek, 1983-84-85-86; Frank Hood, 1933-34-35; Scott Howard, 1980-81; Joseph R. Hurst, 1964.

I Hercle Ivy, 1974-75-76.

J Saun Jackson, 1991-92-94-95; Aaron Jenkins, 1969-70; Cole Johansen, 1967-68; John John, 1973-74-75; Art Johnson, 1974-75-76; Dan Johnson, 1972; Garth Johnson, 1971; Howard Johnson, 1954; Maurice C. Johnson, 1936-37; Robert Johnson, 1988; Doug Jones, 1980-81-82-83; Edwin Jones, 1939; Gary Jones, 1965-66.

K Ron Kaufman, 1968-70; Lloyd Kester, 1944-47-48-49; Jim Kilgariff, 1946; Mike Kilmartin, 1971; Jason Kimbrough, 1994-95; Gary L. Kleven, 1961-62-63; Rollie Knight, 1947; Allan J. Koch, 1964-65-66; Paul Koch, 1952; Thomas Kreamer, 1967-68-69; John W. Krocheski, 1957-58-59; Rollin M. Kuebler, 1942; John Kunnert, 1979-80-81-82; Phil Kunz, 1990-91.

L Ronald P. Lammers, 1967; Lester Lande, 1929; Paul Landsberger, 1977; Jamie Lilly, 1978; Sam Long, 1951-52-53; Larry Loots, 1973-74-75; Timothy J. Lowe, 1963-64; Adolph Ludwig, 1932; Fred Ludwig, 1929; Jack Luhring, 1952.

M Gene Mack, 1970-71-72; Sam Mack, 1989; Matt Margenthaler, 1987; Alex Mazeika, 1974-75; Skip

McCoy, 1991-92; John E. McGonigle, 1966-67-68; Donald M. McKale, 1965; Robert McLuen, 1947-49-50; Ronald Medsker, 1956-57-58; Glen Mente, 1961; Robert E. Menze, 1938-39-40; Loren Meyer, 1992-93-94-95; Julius Michalik, 1992-93-94-95; Reuben S. Mickelson, 1942; Jim Miller, 1972; Larry W. Miller, 1965; Ronald L. Millik, 1965; Guy Minnifield, 1980; Joe Modderman, 1994-95; Adrian Moore, 1987-88-89; Keith Moore, 1980-81; Richard O. Moorehouse, 1937; Bob Moser, 1971; David Moss, 1983-84-85-86; Robert E. Mott, 1945; Jake Muehlenthaler, 1954; Jim Murphy, 1976-77; Mike Murray, 1968-69-70; Jay M. Murrell, 1960-61; Edward M. Myers, 1966; James L. Myers, 1944-45-47.

N Lyle Naylor, 1944; Jon Ness, 1978-79-80; Gordon Nicholas, 1939-40-41; Dean Nims, 1954; Dean Norman, 1947; Ronald Norman, 1943-46-47-48; Tom Norman, 1974-75.

O Tom O'Connor, 1972-73; Gene H. Oulman, 1943-44.

P Gene W. Paetz, 1951; Andrew Parker, 1976-77-78-79; Eli Parker, 1985-86; Donald Paulsen, 1947-48-49-50; Brian Pearson, 1989-90-91-92; Bob Petersen, 1945-46-48-49; Doyle T. Peterson, 1963-64; Therol Peterson, 1949; Tom Peterson, 1962-63-64-65; Tom Peterson, 1982-83-84-85; Brad Pippett, 1991-92; Harlan Platte, 1947; Frederick T. Poole, 1936-37; Maurice Poole, 1986-87; Dick Powell, 1947; John J. Ptacek, 1960-61-62; Thomas Pyle, 1967-68-69.

R Tony Rasheed, 1981; Dave Rauker, 1981-82-83-84; Jim Reinebach, 1971-73; Lafester Rhodes, 1985-86-87-88; Max Rieke, 1930-31-32; Jack Roadcap, 1930-31-32; Terry D. Roberts, 1959-60-61; Elmer Robinson, 1986-87-88-89; Walter Robinson, 1973; Harry E. Roschlau, 1937; Carl Rudi, 1929; Dudley Ruisch, 1949-50; Clare Russie, 1952-53; Hilary K. Ryan, 1938.

S Gerald Sandbulte, 1955-56; Wilbur G. Sandbulte, 1965; Robert Sauer, 1944; Tom Schafer, 1986-87; Carol F. Schneider, 1940-41-42; Leo Schneider, 1947-48-49; David W. Schworm, 1966; John Sheperd, 1947-48-49; Lonzell Simmons, 1982; Dale Smith, 1974-75-76; Don Smith, 1966-67-68; Norman Smith, 1947; Bill Snell, 1971; James Stange, 1949-50-51-52; James Stark, 1946; Barry Stevens, 1982-83-84-85; Robert L. Stoy, 1960-61-62; Marvin L. Straw, 1961-62-63; Hughes Suffren, 1989; Jim Sutherland, 1947.

T M. Harrison Taylor, 1929; Kenneth Teske, 1969; Justus Thigpen, 1990-91-92-93; Derrick Thomas, 1981; Gary Thompkins, 1985-86-87-88; Gary Thompson, 1955-56-57; Berton C. Thompson, 1937; Ralph Thomson, 1932; Jim Thorup, 1974-75; John Tillo, 1977-78-79-80; Wayne Tjernagel, 1967-68; Allan R. Tubbs, 1965-66.

U Leon L. Uknes, 1941-42; Marc Urquhart, 1986-87-88-89; Dean Uthoff, 1977-78-79-80.

V Carl VanCleave, 1052-53-54; Jim Vanderwilt, 1964-65; Jim Van Deusen, 1947; Evan Varley, 1976; Ron Virgil, 1983-84-85-86; Charles Vogt, 1955-56-57.

W Robert F. Walker, 1942; William L. Wantiez, 1965-66; Wes Wallace, 1982-83-84-85; Malvin Warrick, 1981-82; David Washington, 1990; Waldo Wegner, 1933-34; Ray C. Wehde, 1943-44-47-48; Roy Wehde, 1943-44-47-48; Dennis Wells, 1972; Mark West, 1978; Larry Wetter, 1953-54; Morgan Wheat, 1993; Gary L. Wheeler, 1960-61-62; Henry L. Whitney, 1959-60-61; Richard Wilcox, 1930-31; Sylvester L. Wilhelmi, 1949-50-51; Wayne Williams, 1972; Don Wilson, 1929; Robert Wilson, 1974; Clyde Winters, 1973; Glenn Woods, 1929-30; Terry Woods, 1987-88-89-90; John Wroan, 1947.

Y Dan Youngblade, 1951-52.

Z Donald R. Ziegler, 1965-66-67; Robert Ziegler, 1964-65-66.

MANAGERS

John Adams, 1993-94-95; Ross Anthony, 1975; Jerry Bannerman, 1982-83; Kenneth Bawek, 1954; Jim Bell, 1951-52; Dan Bianchi, 1985-86-87; Bob Bruns, 1968; Eric Carlson, 1984-85-86; Kirt Carstens, 1986-87-88-89; Pete Cecil, 1990-91; Keith Champman, 1955; Richard C. Dennier, 1934; Noel DreDahl, 1956; Jason Egli, 1993-94-95; Jennings Falcon, 1932; David Foster, 1989; Thomas G. Goodale, 1959-60-61; William H. Haugan, 1947; James Haverman, 1991; Donald D. Jensen, 1945; Dan Johnson, 1973-74; Ralph L. Kitchell, 1943; John Krogman, 1987-88; William K. Lambert, 1944; Ronald P. Lammers, 1965; Warren Lundsgaard, 1946; Scott McKinnie, 1973; Robert Mumma, 1953; Edward M. Myers, III, 1964-65; Paul Newgaard, 1989-90; Troy O'Banion, 1992; Roy Olson, 1929; Kris Olson, 1991-92-93-94-95; Kerry Osgerby, 1995; Kim Palmer, 1979; Mark Pearson, 1994-95; Jim Peterson, 1971; William Peterson, 1949; Edwin Pierce, 1957; Richard L. Potter, 1938; Darrell Robinson, 1981-82-83-86; Wilbur M. Toth, 1963; Theo Rubyor, 1931; William Russell, 1933; May Ryerson, 1941; David O. Scheiding, 1962; Dick Schulze, 1975; Jeff Sesker, 1986-87; Donald Smucker, 1930; Henry C. Spencer, 1936; Tim Stiles, 1979-80; Doug Tjelmeland, 1982-83-84; Fred Walker, 1978-79; Robert F. Walker, 1942; John Walz, 1988; Scott Wand, 1992-93; James W. White, 1940; Richard Wyglé, 1951;

TRIVIA ANSWERS

1. I.C. Brownlie apparently thought a great deal of himself, for he was also the team captain in addition to the coach in 1892.

2. Glen Mason led Kansas to a top 10 finish in 1995. He was an Iowa State assistant from 1975-1976.

3. Tight end Keith Krepfle is Iowa State's all-time leader in touchdown catches with 15.

4. Kischer was also adept at playing defense. From 1936-1938 Kischer picked off 11 enemy passes, ranking him fourth on the ISU all-time list in interceptions.

5. Davis passed George Amundson (2,130), Tom Vaughn (1,889) and Tommy Davis (1,661) to move into eighth place with 2,145 yards.

6. Meredith Warner ran from his own one-yard-line to the other one-yard-line against Iowa Pre-Flight in 1943.

7. Lawrence ``Big Daddy" Hunt is the career leader in interior line tackles, having pillaged opponents from 1971-1973.

8. Brigham Young was the victim, by a 28-20 score.

9. Five Cyclone pass catchers have become All-Americans: Jim Doran in 1950, Eppie Barney in 1966, Luther Blue in 1976, Tracy Henderson on two occasions, 1984 and 1984, and Mike Busch, who earned the honor in 1989.

10. Nebraska quarterback Tommie Frazier, Northwestern running back Darnell Autry, Florida quarterback Danny Wuerffel and Ohio State running back Eddie George were the other four Heisman finalists.

11. Clay Stapleton is ISU's all-time winningest coach with 42 triumphs from 1958-1967.

12. Vince DiFrancesca is ISU's all-time losingest coach with a winning percentage of just .232. He went 6-21-1 from 1954-1956.

13. The Cyclones pounded UCLA by the score of
20-0.

14. From September 13, 1980 to October 11, 1980, Iowa State went 5-0 under coach Donnie Duncan.

15. The last Iowa State shutout came in a 69-0 smashing of Colorado State in 1980.

16. Robert Estes.

17. Joe Brown in 1911; Hans Pfund in 1913.

18. The Cyclones put up a school-record 101 field goal attempts.

19. Mike Born, during the 1988-89 season.

20. Sam Hill.

21. Lew Alcindor of UCLA, later known as Kareem Abdul-Jabbar.

22. 70 points, over SUNY-Buffalo in a 106-36 rout on December 1, 1992.

23. Indiana handed the Cyclones a 115-66 humiliation at Assembly Hall on December 23, 1989.

24. Morgan Wheat, Fred Hoiberg, Loren Meyer and Klay Edwards.

25. Guy Minnifield last wore No. 15 during the 1980 season.

26. Colorado played the Cyclones to a five-overtime game in 1960. The Cyclones won the game, 93-80.

27. Ken Trickey won just 13 of 53 games over his two-year stint as Iowa State coach in 1975 and 1976.

28. Bill Cain grabbed 26 rebounds against the Gophers in 1969.

29. Hercle Ivy cracked the 30-point barrier repeatedly for the Cyclones from 1973-1976.

30. Mark Baugh hit all 11 of his shots in a game against Western Illinois on January 25, 1989.

COLLEGE SPORTS HANDBOOKS

Stories, Stats & Stuff About America's Favorite Teams

U. of Arizona	Basketball	Arizona Wildcats Handbook
U. of Arkansas	Basketball	Razorbacks Handbook
Baylor	Football	Bears Handbook
Clemson	Football	Clemson Handbook
U. of Colorado	Football	Buffaloes Handbook
U. of Florida	Football	Gator Tales
Georgia Tech	Basketball	Yellow Jackets Handbook
Indiana U.	Basketball	Hoosier Handbook
U. of Kansas	Basketball	Crimson & Blue Handbook
Kansas State	Sports	Kansas St Wildcat Handbook
LSU	Football	Fighting Tigers Handbook
U. of Louisville	Basketball	Cardinals Handbook
U. of Miami	Football	Hurricane Handbook
U. of Michigan	Football	Wolverines Handbook
U. of Missouri	Basketball	Tiger Handbook
U. of Nebraska	Football	Husker Handbook
U. of N. Carolina	Basketball	Tar Heels Handbook
N.C. State	Basketball	Wolfpack Handbook
U. of Oklahoma	Football	Sooners Handbook
Penn State	Football	Nittany Lions Handbook
U. of S. Carolina	Football	Gamecocks Handbook
Stanford	Football	Stanford Handbook
Syracuse	Sports	Orange Handbook
U. of Tennessee	Football	Volunteers Handbook
U. of Texas	Football	Longhorns Handbook
Texas A&M	Football	Aggies Handbook
Texas Tech	Sports	Red Raiders Handbook
Virginia Tech	Football	Hokies Handbook
Wichita State	Sports	Shockers Handbook
U. of Wisconsin	Football	Badgers Handbook

Also:

Big 12 Handbook: Stories, Stats and Stuff About The Nation's Best Football Conference

The Top Fuel Handbook: Stories, Stats and Stuff About Drag Racing's Most Powerful Class

For ordering information call Midwest Sports Publications at:

1-800-492-4043